His kisses are dreamy . . .
But those HAIRBALLS down
my CLEAVAGE . . . !

Books by Berkeley Breathed

Loose Tails

'Toons for Our Times

Penguin Dreams and Stranger Things

Bloom County Babylon: Five Years of Basic Naughtiness

Billy and the Boingers Bootleg

Tales Too Ticklish to Tell

The Night of the Mary Kay Commandos

Happy Trails

Classics of Western Literature: *Bloom County* 1986–1989

A Wish for Wings That Work

The Last Basselope

Politically, Fashionably, Aerodynamically Incorrect: The First *Outland* Collection

Goodnight Opus

His Kisses Are Dreamy . . . But Those Hairballs Down My Cleavage . . . ! Another Tender *Outland* Collection

Berkeley Breathed

His kisses are dreamy . . . But those HAIRBALLS down my CLEAVAGE . . . !

Another Tender *Outland* Collection

Little, Brown and Company

Boston New York Toronto London

First Edition

Outland is syndicated by the Washington Post Writers Group.

Library of Congress Cataloging-in-Publication Data
Breathed, Berke.
    His kisses are dreamy . . . but those hairballs down my
  cleavage . . . ! : another tender outland collection / Berkeley Breathed.
      p.   cm.
    ISBN 0-316-10867-7
    I. Title.
  PN6728.092B74   1994
  741.5'973 — dc20   93-47592

10 9 8 7 6 5 4 3 2 1

RRD-OH

Designed by Barbara Werden

Published simultaneously in Canada by Little, Brown & Company
(Canada) Limited

Printed in the United States of America

His kisses are dreamy . . .
But those HAIRBALLS down
my CLEAVAGE . . . !

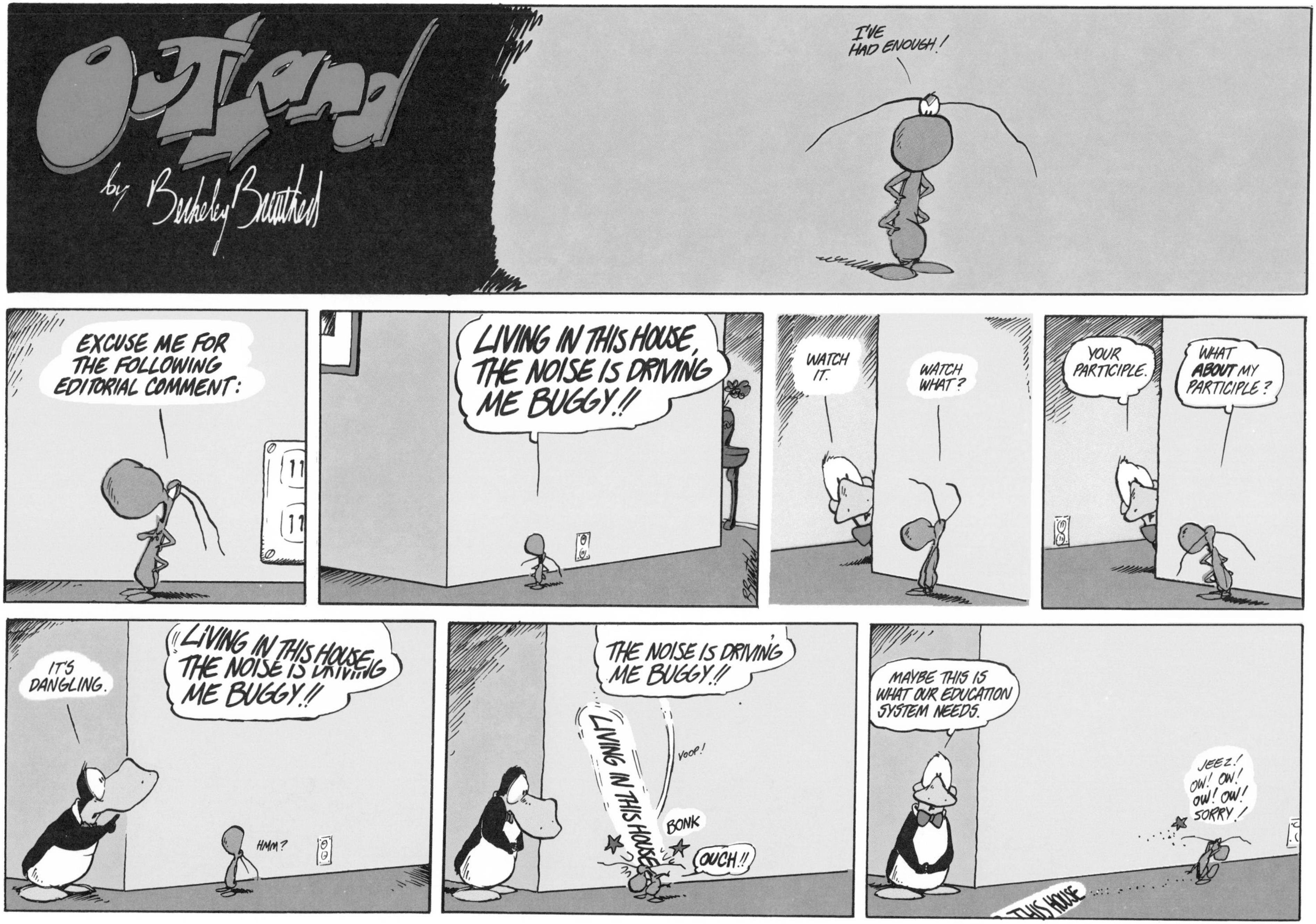
Outland
by Berkeley Breathed
I'VE HAD ENOUGH!
EXCUSE ME FOR THE FOLLOWING EDITORIAL COMMENT:
LIVING IN THIS HOUSE, THE NOISE IS DRIVING ME BUGGY!!
WATCH IT.
WATCH WHAT?
YOUR PARTICIPLE.
WHAT ABOUT MY PARTICIPLE?
IT'S DANGLING.
LIVING IN THIS HOUSE THE NOISE IS DRIVING ME BUGGY!!
HMM?
THE NOISE IS DRIVING ME BUGGY!!
LIVING IN THIS HOUSE
VOOP!
BONK
OUCH!!
MAYBE THIS IS WHAT OUR EDUCATION SYSTEM NEEDS.
JEEZ! OW! OW! OW! OW! SORRY!
THIS HOUSE

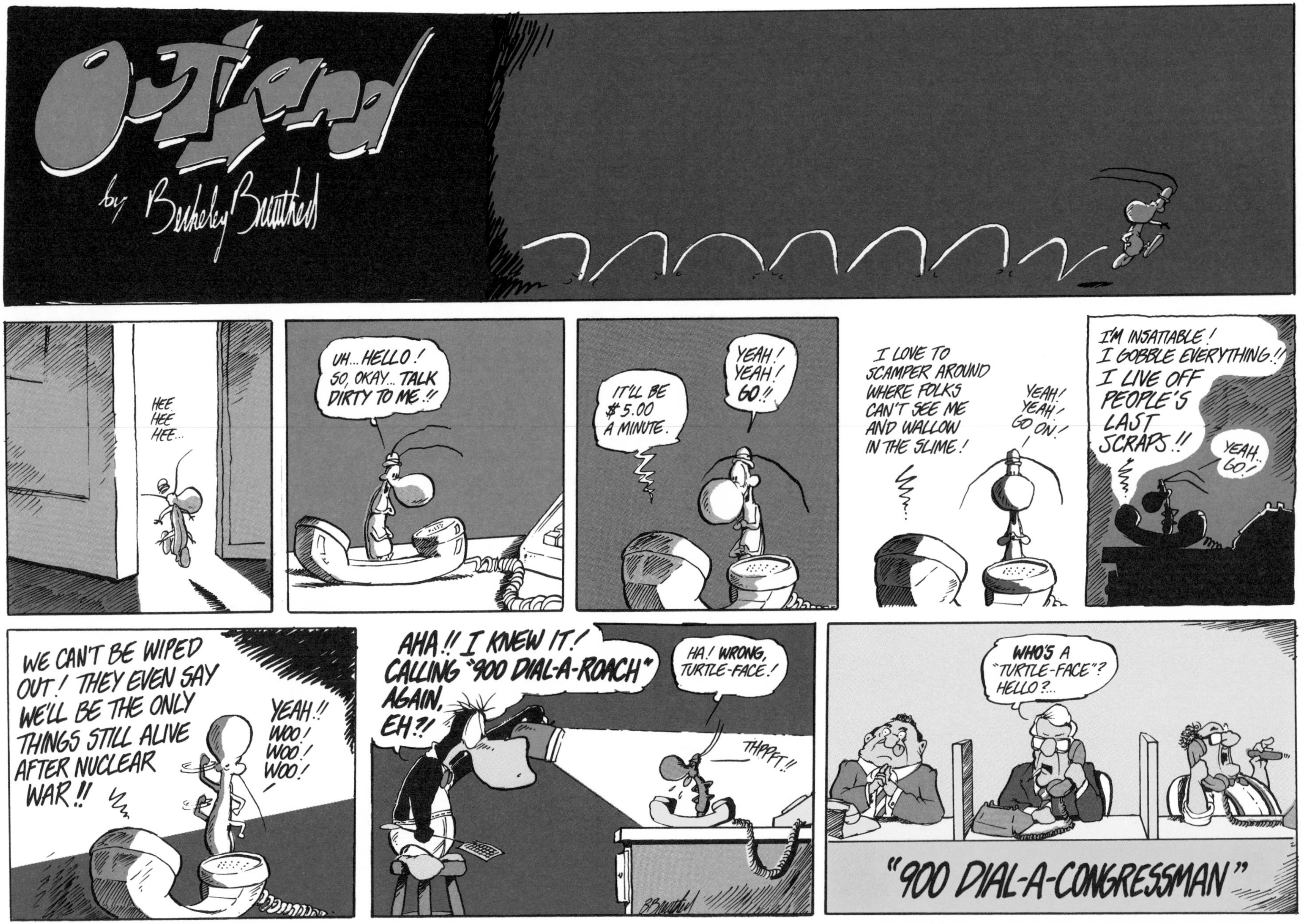
Outland
by Berkeley Breathed
HEE HEE HEE...
UH... HELLO! SO, OKAY... TALK DIRTY TO ME.!!
IT'LL BE $5.00 A MINUTE.
YEAH! YEAH! GO!!
I LOVE TO SCAMPER AROUND WHERE FOLKS CAN'T SEE ME AND WALLOW IN THE SLIME!
YEAH! YEAH! GO ON!
I'M INSATIABLE! I GOBBLE EVERYTHING!! I LIVE OFF PEOPLE'S LAST SCRAPS!!
YEAH.. GO!
WE CAN'T BE WIPED OUT! THEY EVEN SAY WE'LL BE THE ONLY THINGS STILL ALIVE AFTER NUCLEAR WAR!!
YEAH!! WOO! WOO! WOO!
AHA!! I KNEW IT! CALLING "900 DIAL-A-ROACH" AGAIN, EH?!
HA! WRONG, TURTLE-FACE!
THPPFT!!
WHO'S A "TURTLE-FACE"? HELLO?...
"900 DIAL-A-CONGRESSMAN"

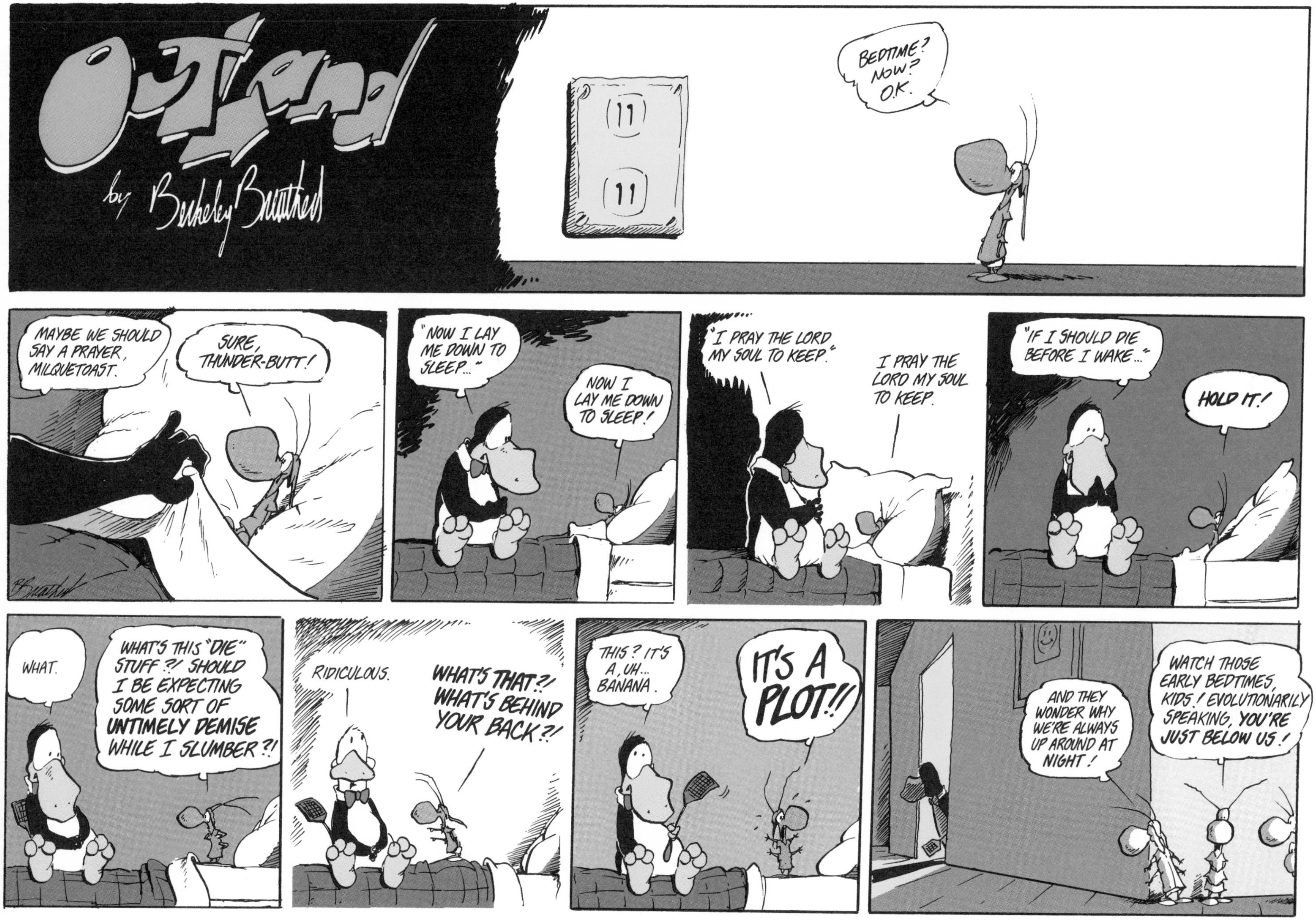
Outland
by Berkeley Breathed
BEDTIME? NOW? O.K.
MAYBE WE SHOULD SAY A PRAYER, MILQUETOAST.
SURE, THUNDER-BUTT!
"NOW I LAY ME DOWN TO SLEEP..."
NOW I LAY ME DOWN TO SLEEP!
"I PRAY THE LORD MY SOUL TO KEEP."
I PRAY THE LORD MY SOUL TO KEEP.
"IF I SHOULD DIE BEFORE I WAKE..."
HOLD IT!
WHAT.
WHAT'S THIS "DIE" STUFF?!' SHOULD I BE EXPECTING SOME SORT OF UNTIMELY DEMISE WHILE I SLUMBER?!
RIDICULOUS.
WHAT'S THAT?!' WHAT'S BEHIND YOUR BACK?!
THIS? IT'S A, UH... BANANA.
IT'S A PLOT!!
AND THEY WONDER WHY WE'RE ALWAYS UP AROUND AT NIGHT!
WATCH THOSE EARLY BEDTIMES, KIDS! EVOLUTIONARILY SPEAKING, YOU'RE JUST BELOW US!

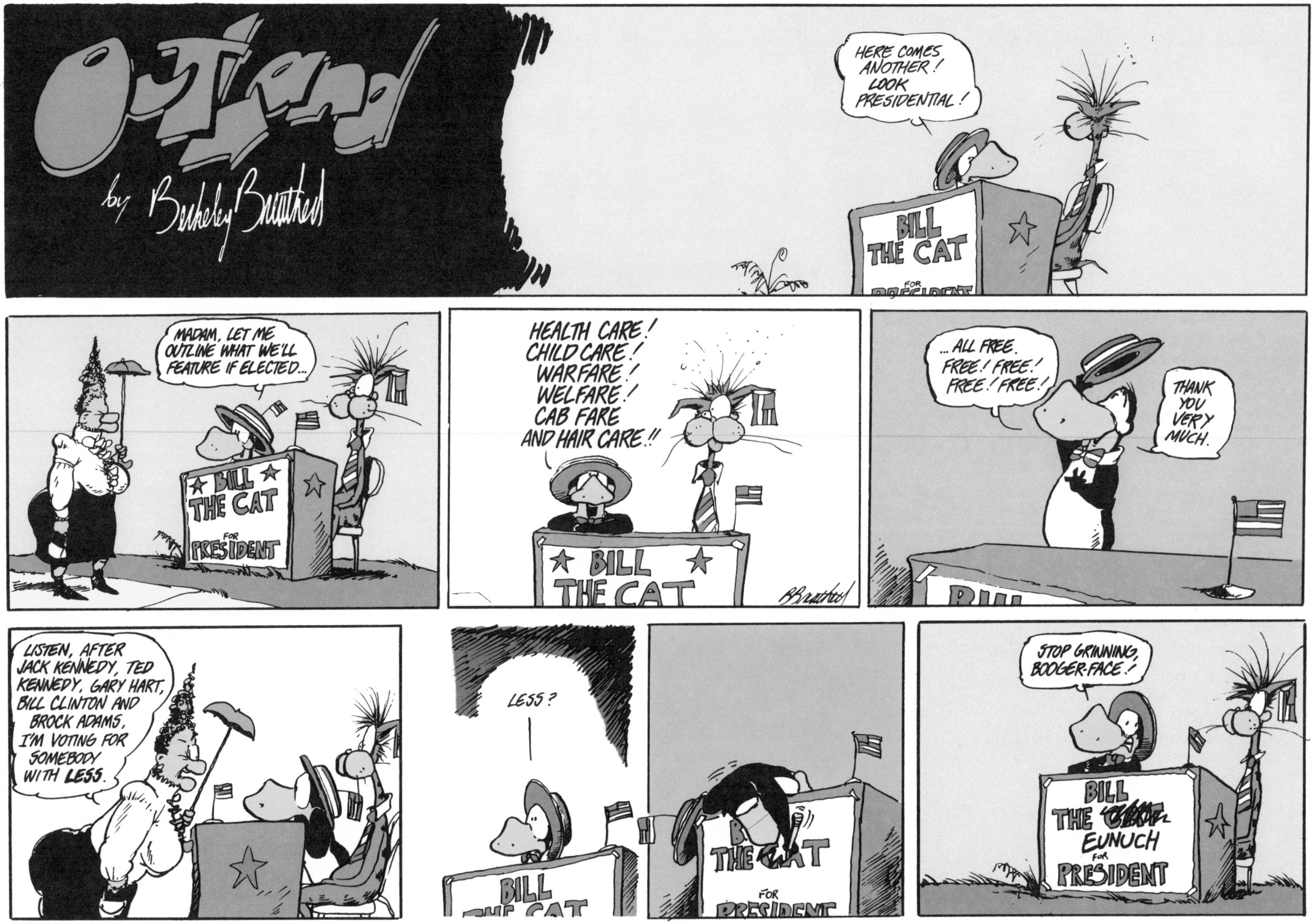
Outland
by Berkeley Breathed
HERE COMES ANOTHER! LOOK PRESIDENTIAL!
BILL THE CAT FOR PRESIDENT
MADAM, LET ME OUTLINE WHAT WE'LL FEATURE IF ELECTED...
BILL THE CAT FOR PRESIDENT
HEALTH CARE! CHILD CARE! WARFARE! WELFARE! CAB FARE AND HAIR CARE!!
BILL THE CAT
B Breathed
...ALL FREE. FREE! FREE! FREE! FREE!
THANK YOU VERY MUCH.
LISTEN, AFTER JACK KENNEDY, TED KENNEDY, GARY HART, BILL CLINTON AND BROCK ADAMS, I'M VOTING FOR SOMEBODY WITH LESS.
LESS?
BILL THE CAT
THE CAT FOR PRESIDENT
STOP GRINNING, BOOGER-FACE!
BILL THE ~~CAT~~ EUNUCH FOR PRESIDENT

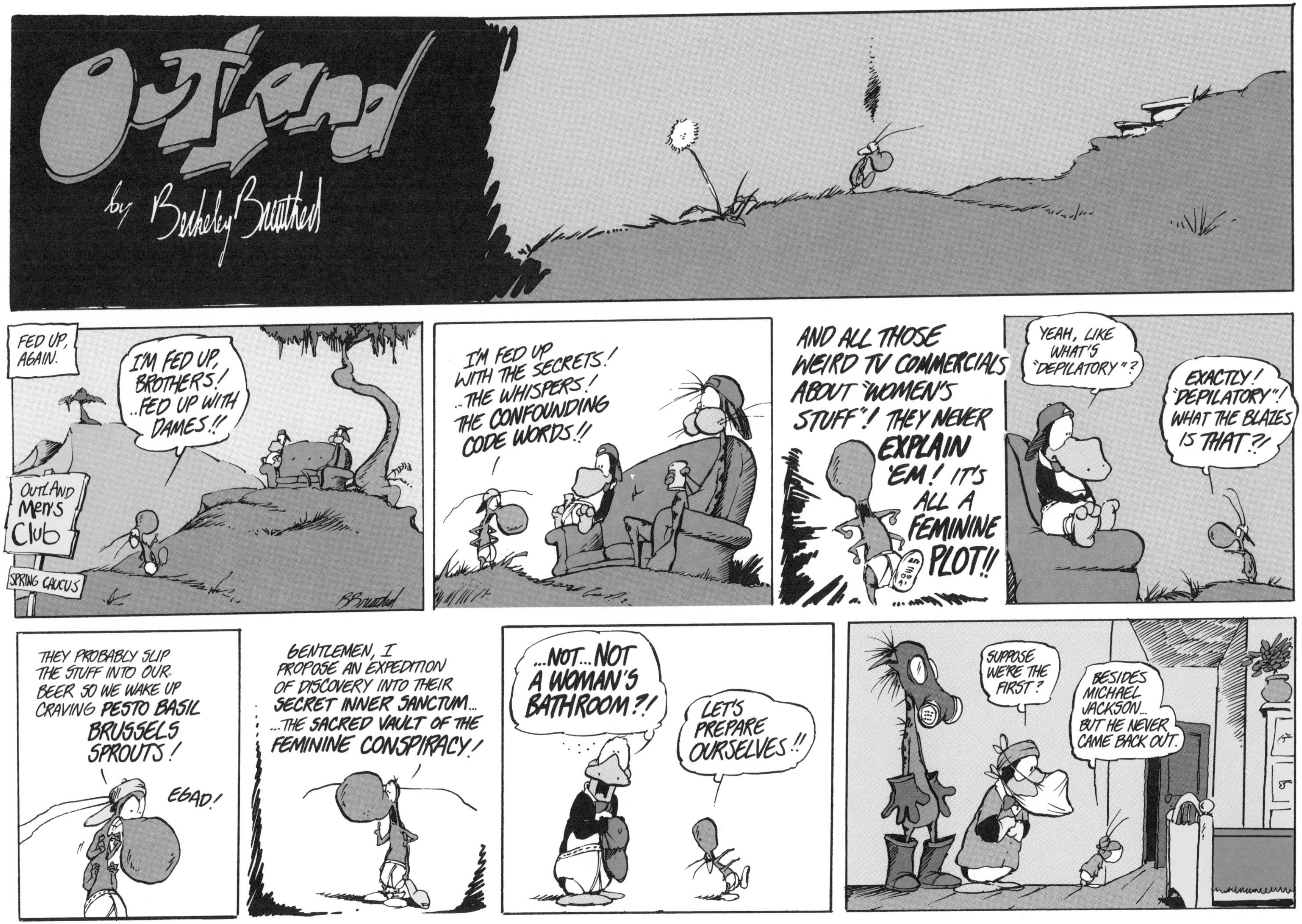
Outland
by Berkeley Breathed
FED UP, AGAIN.
I'M FED UP, BROTHERS! ..FED UP WITH DAMES!!
OUTLAND MEN'S CLUB
SPRING CAUCUS
I'M FED UP WITH THE SECRETS! ...THE WHISPERS! THE CONFOUNDING CODE WORDS!!
AND ALL THOSE WEIRD TV COMMERCIALS ABOUT "WOMEN'S STUFF"! THEY NEVER EXPLAIN 'EM! IT'S ALL A FEMININE PLOT!!
YEAH, LIKE WHAT'S "DEPILATORY"?
EXACTLY! "DEPILATORY"! WHAT THE BLAZES IS THAT?!
THEY PROBABLY SLIP THE STUFF INTO OUR BEER SO WE WAKE UP CRAVING PESTO BASIL BRUSSELS SPROUTS!
EGAD!
GENTLEMEN, I PROPOSE AN EXPEDITION OF DISCOVERY INTO THEIR SECRET INNER SANCTUM... ...THE SACRED VAULT OF THE FEMININE CONSPIRACY!
...NOT...NOT A WOMAN'S BATHROOM?!
LET'S PREPARE OURSELVES!!
SUPPOSE WE'RE THE FIRST?
BESIDES MICHAEL JACKSON... BUT HE NEVER CAME BACK OUT.

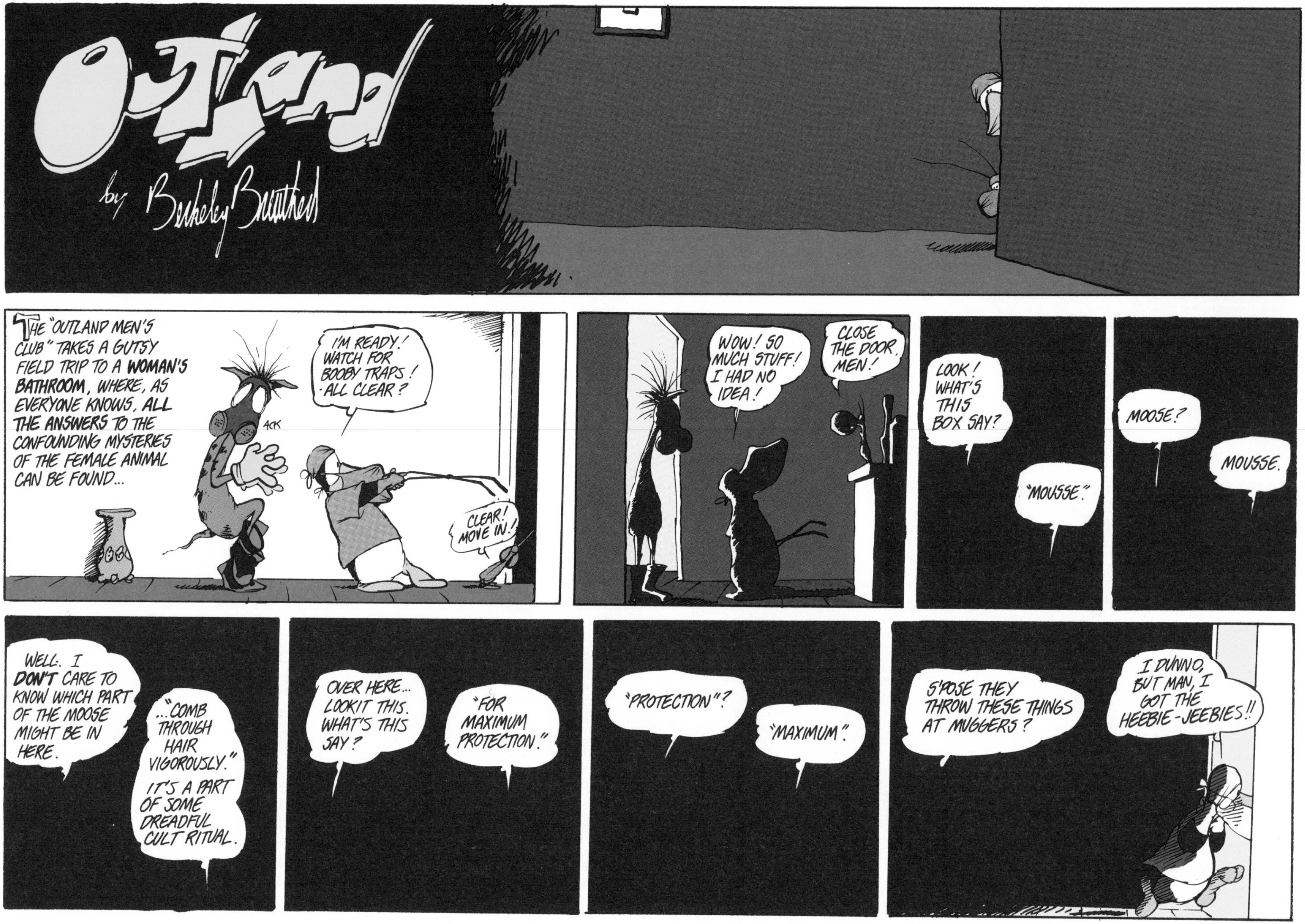

Outland
by Berkeley Breathed
THE "OUTLAND MEN'S CLUB" TAKES A GUTSY FIELD TRIP TO A WOMAN'S BATHROOM, WHERE, AS EVERYONE KNOWS, ALL THE ANSWERS TO THE CONFOUNDING MYSTERIES OF THE FEMALE ANIMAL CAN BE FOUND...
ACK
I'M READY! WATCH FOR BOOBY TRAPS! ·ALL CLEAR?
CLEAR! MOVE IN!
WOW! SO MUCH STUFF! I HAD NO IDEA!
CLOSE THE DOOR, MEN!
LOOK! WHAT'S THIS BOX SAY?
"MOUSSE."
MOOSE?
MOUSSE.
WELL.. I DON'T CARE TO KNOW WHICH PART OF THE MOOSE MIGHT BE IN HERE.
..."COMB THROUGH HAIR VIGOROUSLY." IT'S A PART OF SOME DREADFUL CULT RITUAL.
OVER HERE... LOOKIT THIS. WHAT'S THIS SAY?
"FOR MAXIMUM PROTECTION."
"PROTECTION"?
"MAXIMUM."
S'POSE THEY THROW THESE THINGS AT MUGGERS?
I DUNNO, BUT MAN, I GOT THE HEEBIE-JEEBIES!!

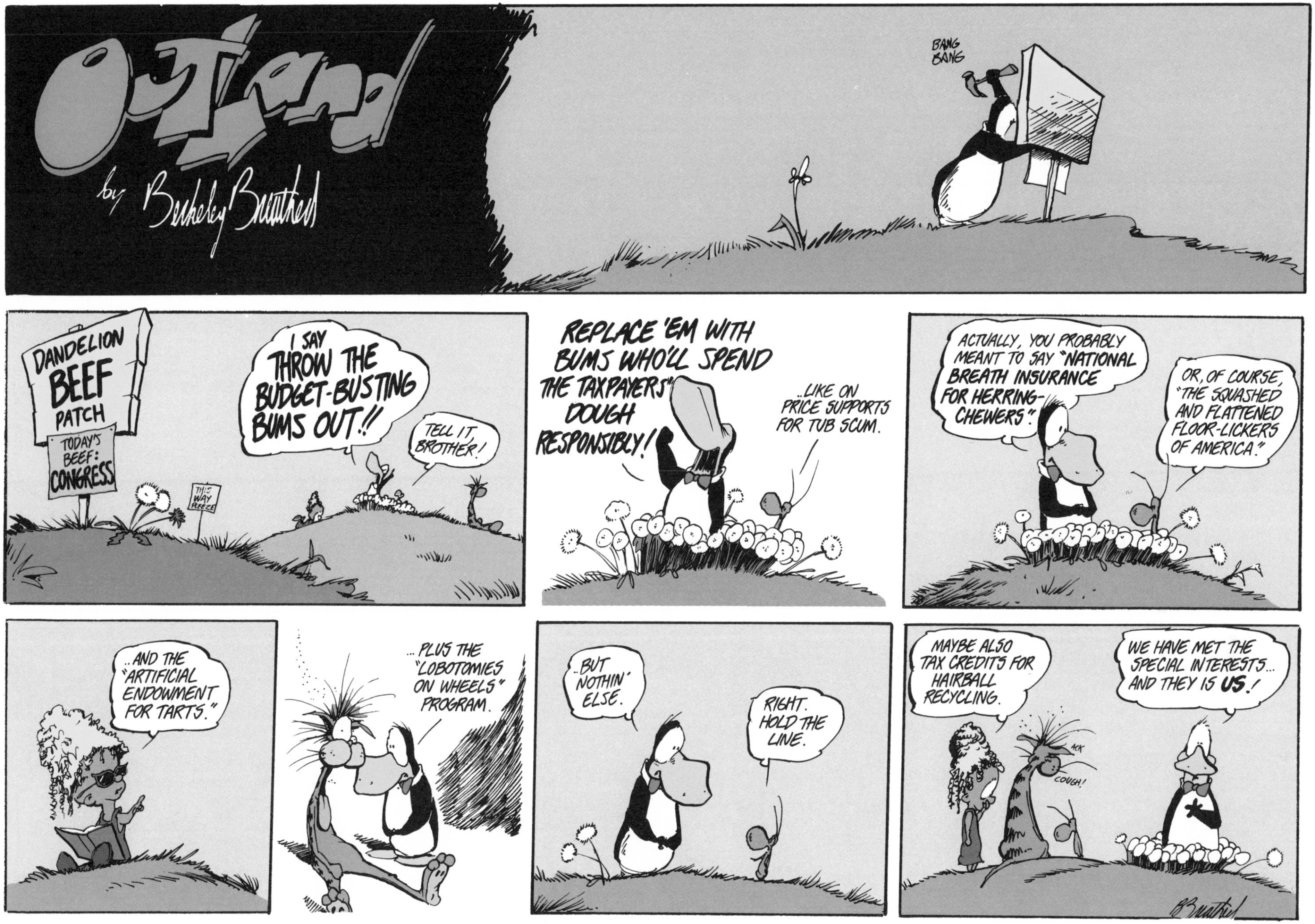
Outland
by Berkeley Breathed
BANG BANG
DANDELION BEEF PATCH
TODAY'S BEEF: CONGRESS
THIS WAY PLEEZE
I SAY THROW THE BUDGET-BUSTING BUMS OUT!!
TELL IT, BROTHER!
REPLACE 'EM WITH BUMS WHO'LL SPEND THE TAXPAYERS' DOUGH RESPONSIBLY!
..LIKE ON PRICE SUPPORTS FOR TUB SCUM.
ACTUALLY, YOU PROBABLY MEANT TO SAY "NATIONAL BREATH INSURANCE FOR HERRING-CHEWERS".
OR, OF COURSE, "THE SQUASHED AND FLATTENED FLOOR-LICKERS OF AMERICA."
..AND THE "ARTIFICIAL ENDOWMENT FOR TARTS."
... PLUS THE "LOBOTOMIES ON WHEELS" PROGRAM.
..BUT NOTHIN' ELSE.
RIGHT. HOLD THE LINE.
MAYBE ALSO TAX CREDITS FOR HAIRBALL RECYCLING.
ACK
COUGH!
WE HAVE MET THE SPECIAL INTERESTS... AND THEY IS US!
B Breathed

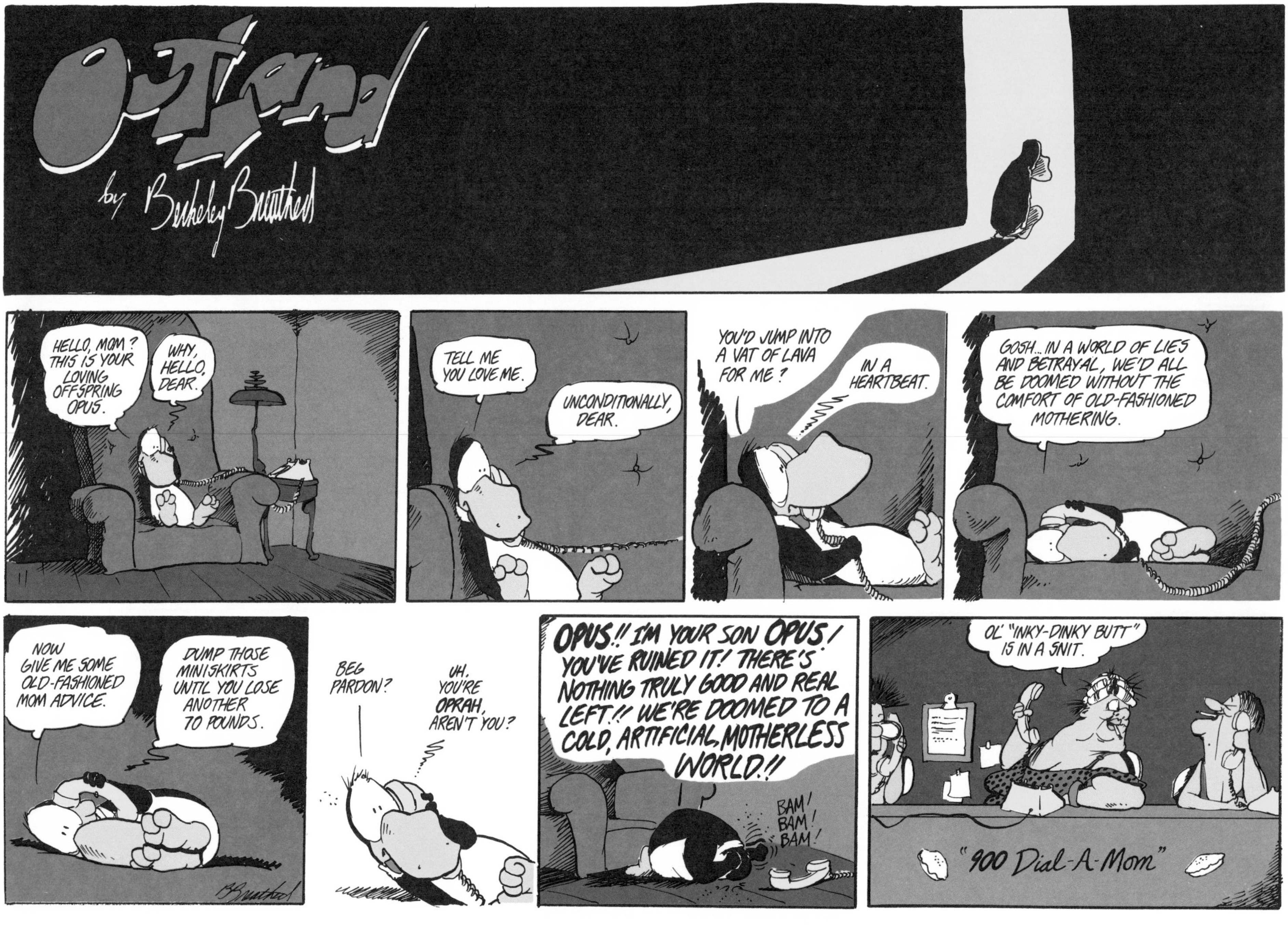
Outland
by Berkeley Breathed
HELLO, MOM? THIS IS YOUR LOVING OFFSPRING OPUS.
WHY, HELLO, DEAR.
TELL ME YOU LOVE ME.
UNCONDITIONALLY, DEAR.
YOU'D JUMP INTO A VAT OF LAVA FOR ME?
IN A HEARTBEAT.
GOSH... IN A WORLD OF LIES AND BETRAYAL, WE'D ALL BE DOOMED WITHOUT THE COMFORT OF OLD-FASHIONED MOTHERING.
NOW GIVE ME SOME OLD-FASHIONED MOM ADVICE.
DUMP THOSE MINISKIRTS UNTIL YOU LOSE ANOTHER 70 POUNDS.
BEG PARDON?
UH. YOU'RE OPRAH, AREN'T YOU?
OPUS!! I'M YOUR SON OPUS! YOU'VE RUINED IT! THERE'S NOTHING TRULY GOOD AND REAL LEFT!! WE'RE DOOMED TO A COLD, ARTIFICIAL, MOTHERLESS WORLD!!
BAM! BAM! BAM!
OL' "INKY-DINKY BUTT" IS IN A SNIT.
"900 Dial-A-Mom"

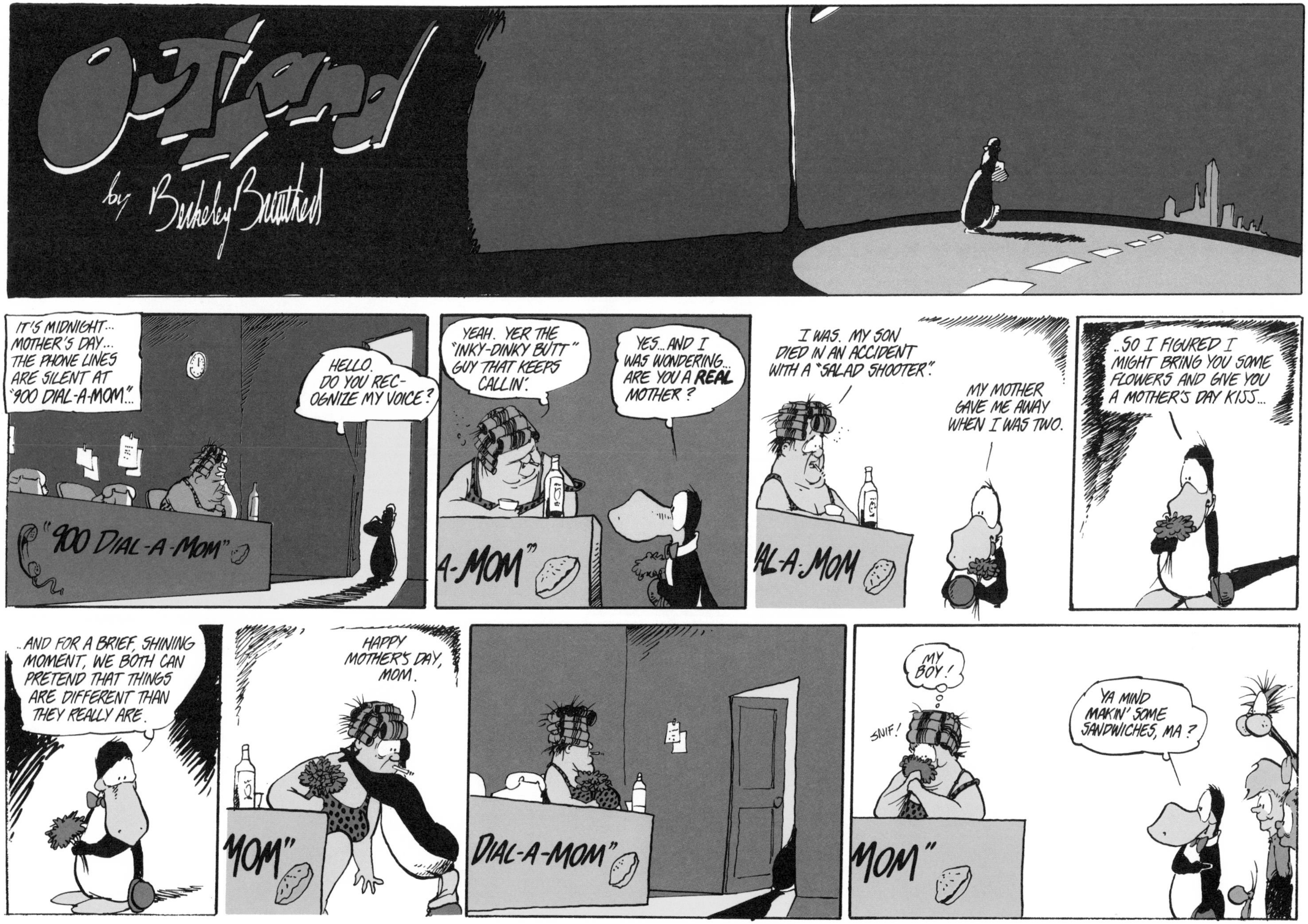
Outland
by Berkeley Breathed
IT'S MIDNIGHT... MOTHER'S DAY... THE PHONE LINES ARE SILENT AT "900 DIAL-A-MOM"...
HELLO. DO YOU REC-OGNIZE MY VOICE?
"900 DIAL-A-MOM"
YEAH. YER THE "INKY-DINKY BUTT" GUY THAT KEEPS CALLIN'.
YES... AND I WAS WONDERING... ARE YOU A **REAL** MOTHER?
A-MOM"
I WAS. MY SON DIED IN AN ACCIDENT WITH A "SALAD SHOOTER".
MY MOTHER GAVE ME AWAY WHEN I WAS TWO.
AL-A-MOM
..SO I FIGURED I MIGHT BRING YOU SOME FLOWERS AND GIVE YOU A MOTHER'S DAY KISS...
..AND FOR A BRIEF, SHINING MOMENT, WE BOTH CAN PRETEND THAT THINGS ARE DIFFERENT THAN THEY REALLY ARE.
HAPPY MOTHER'S DAY, MOM.
MOM"
DIAL-A-MOM"
MY BOY!
SNIF!
YA MIND MAKIN' SOME SANDWICHES, MA?
MOM"

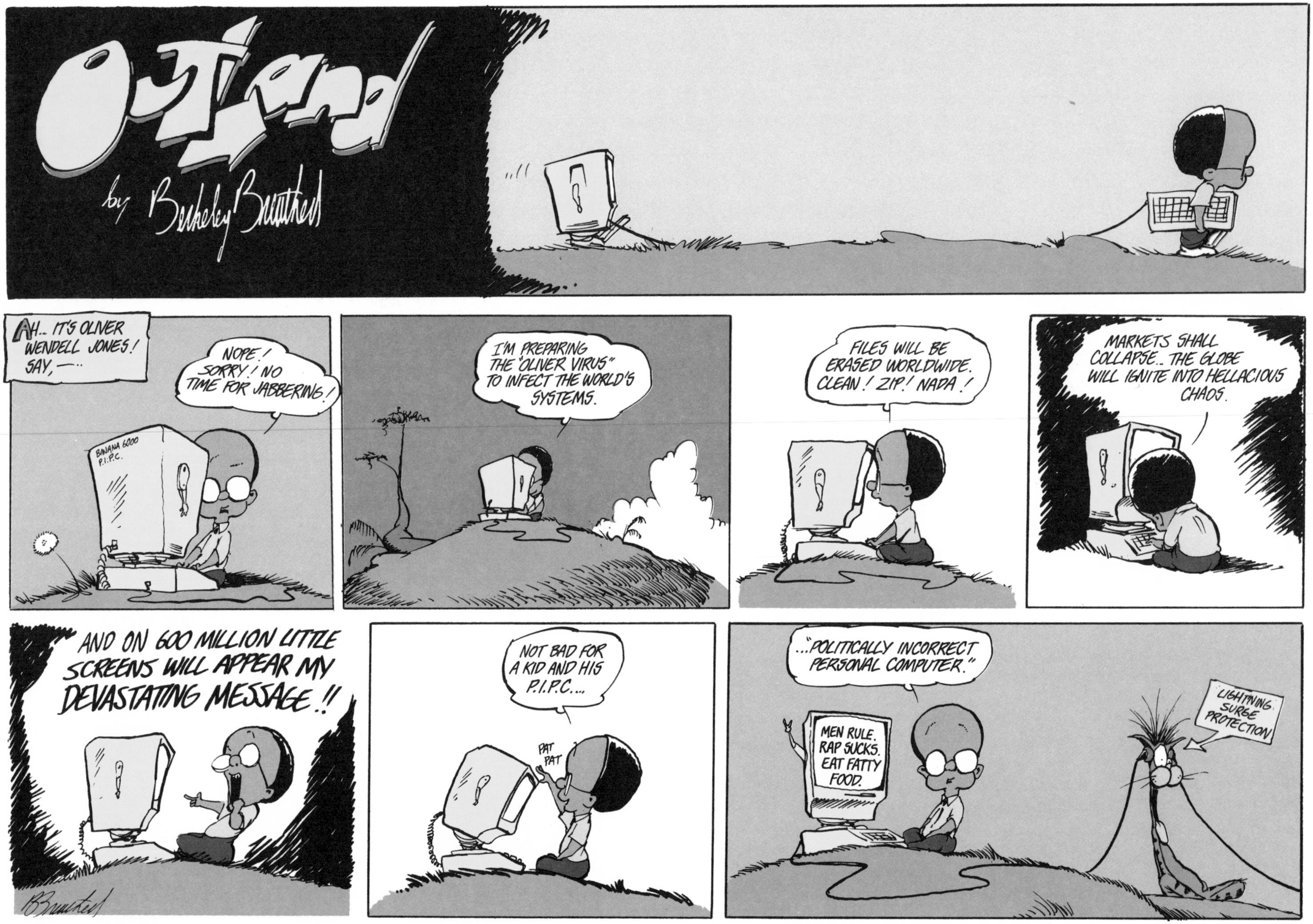

Outland
by Berkeley Breathed
AH... IT'S OLIVER WENDELL JONES! SAY, —...
NOPE! SORRY! NO TIME FOR JABBERING!
BANANA 6000 P.I.P.C.
I'M PREPARING THE "OLIVER VIRUS" TO INFECT THE WORLD'S SYSTEMS.
FILES WILL BE ERASED WORLDWIDE. CLEAN! ZIP! NADA!
MARKETS SHALL COLLAPSE.. THE GLOBE WILL IGNITE INTO HELLACIOUS CHAOS.
AND ON 600 MILLION LITTLE SCREENS WILL APPEAR MY DEVASTATING MESSAGE!!
NOT BAD FOR A KID AND HIS P.I.P.C....
PAT PAT
..."POLITICALLY INCORRECT PERSONAL COMPUTER."
MEN RULE. RAP SUCKS. EAT FATTY FOOD.
LIGHTNING SURGE PROTECTION
B Breathed

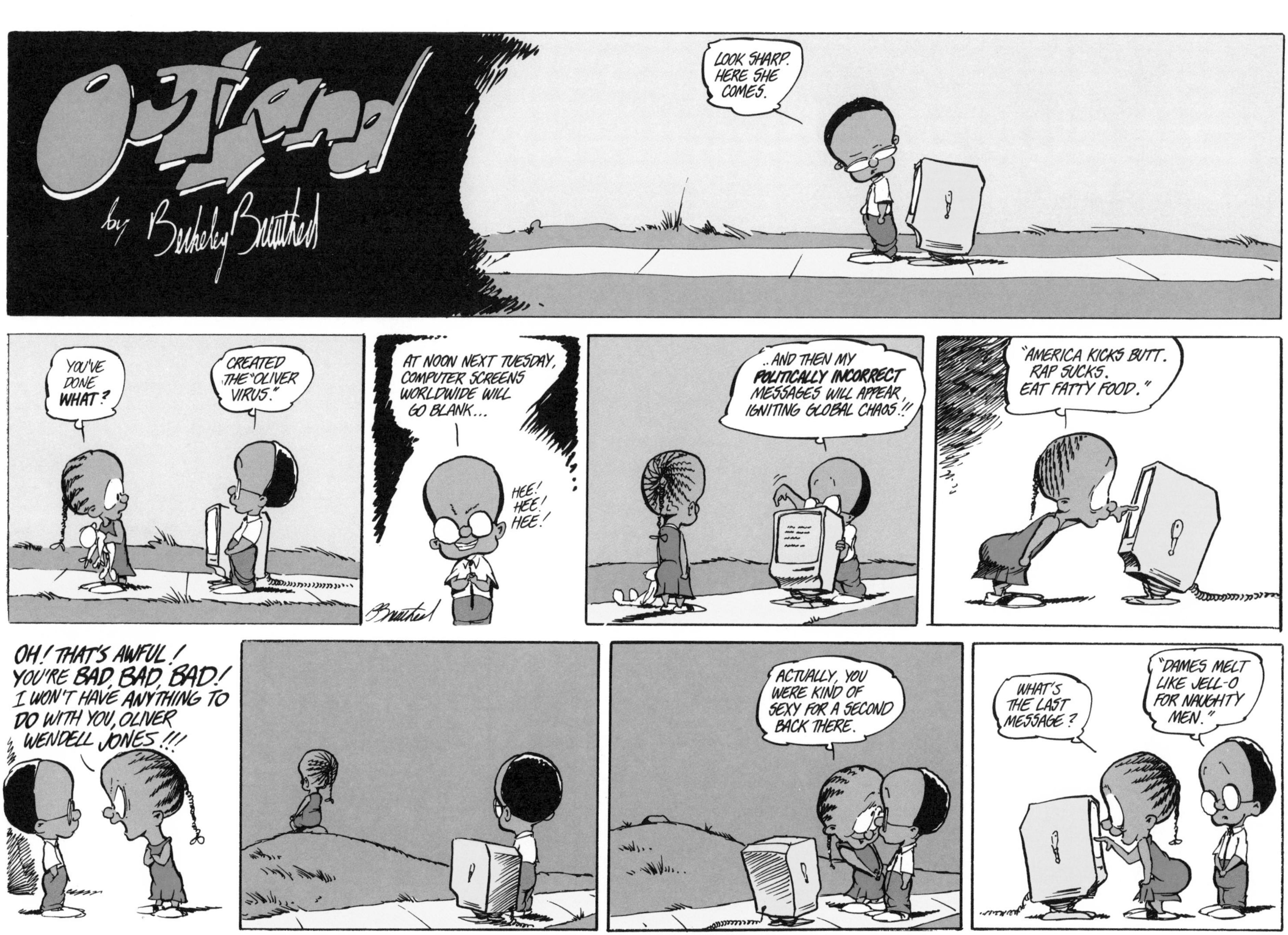
Outland
by Berkeley Breathed
LOOK SHARP. HERE SHE COMES.
YOU'VE DONE WHAT?
CREATED THE "OLIVER VIRUS."
AT NOON NEXT TUESDAY, COMPUTER SCREENS WORLDWIDE WILL GO BLANK...
HEE! HEE! HEE!
Breathed
..AND THEN MY POLITICALLY INCORRECT MESSAGES WILL APPEAR, IGNITING GLOBAL CHAOS!!
"AMERICA KICKS BUTT. RAP SUCKS. EAT FATTY FOOD."
OH! THAT'S AWFUL! YOU'RE BAD, BAD, BAD! I WON'T HAVE ANYTHING TO DO WITH YOU, OLIVER WENDELL JONES!!!
ACTUALLY, YOU WERE KIND OF SEXY FOR A SECOND BACK THERE.
WHAT'S THE LAST MESSAGE?
"DAMES MELT LIKE JELL-O FOR NAUGHTY MEN."

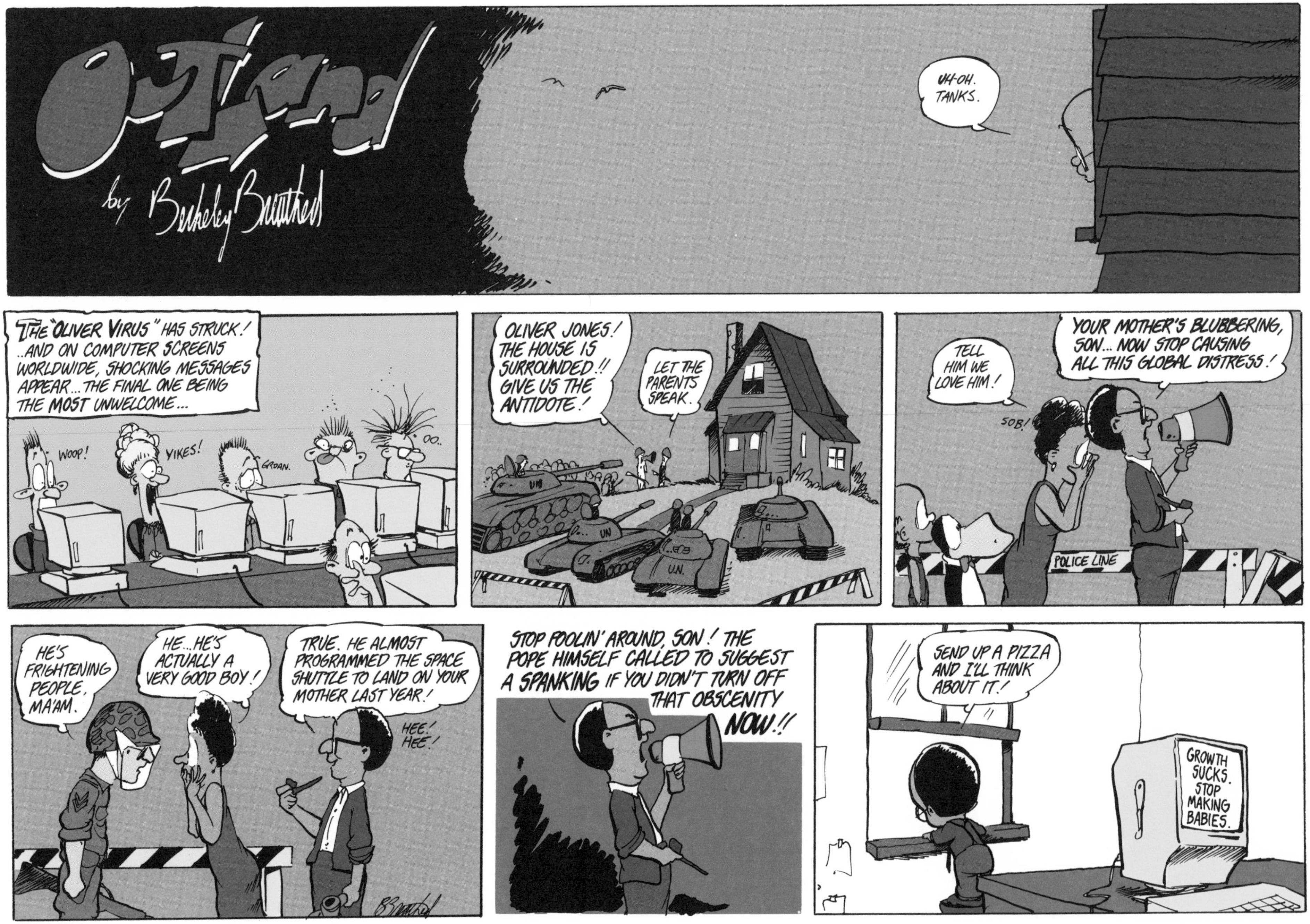
Outland
by Berkeley Breathed
UH-OH. TANKS.
THE "OLIVER VIRUS" HAS STRUCK! ..AND ON COMPUTER SCREENS WORLDWIDE, SHOCKING MESSAGES APPEAR... THE FINAL ONE BEING THE MOST UNWELCOME...
WOOP!
YIKES!
GROAN.
OO..
OLIVER JONES! THE HOUSE IS SURROUNDED!! GIVE US THE ANTIDOTE!
LET THE PARENTS SPEAK.
UN
U.N.
TELL HIM WE LOVE HIM!
SOB!
YOUR MOTHER'S BLUBBERING, SON... NOW STOP CAUSING ALL THIS GLOBAL DISTRESS!
POLICE LINE
HE'S FRIGHTENING PEOPLE, MA'AM.
HE...HE'S ACTUALLY A VERY GOOD BOY!
TRUE. HE ALMOST PROGRAMMED THE SPACE SHUTTLE TO LAND ON YOUR MOTHER LAST YEAR!
HEE! HEE!
STOP FOOLIN' AROUND, SON! THE POPE HIMSELF CALLED TO SUGGEST A SPANKING IF YOU DIDN'T TURN OFF THAT OBSCENITY NOW!!
SEND UP A PIZZA AND I'LL THINK ABOUT IT!
GROWTH SUCKS. STOP MAKING BABIES.

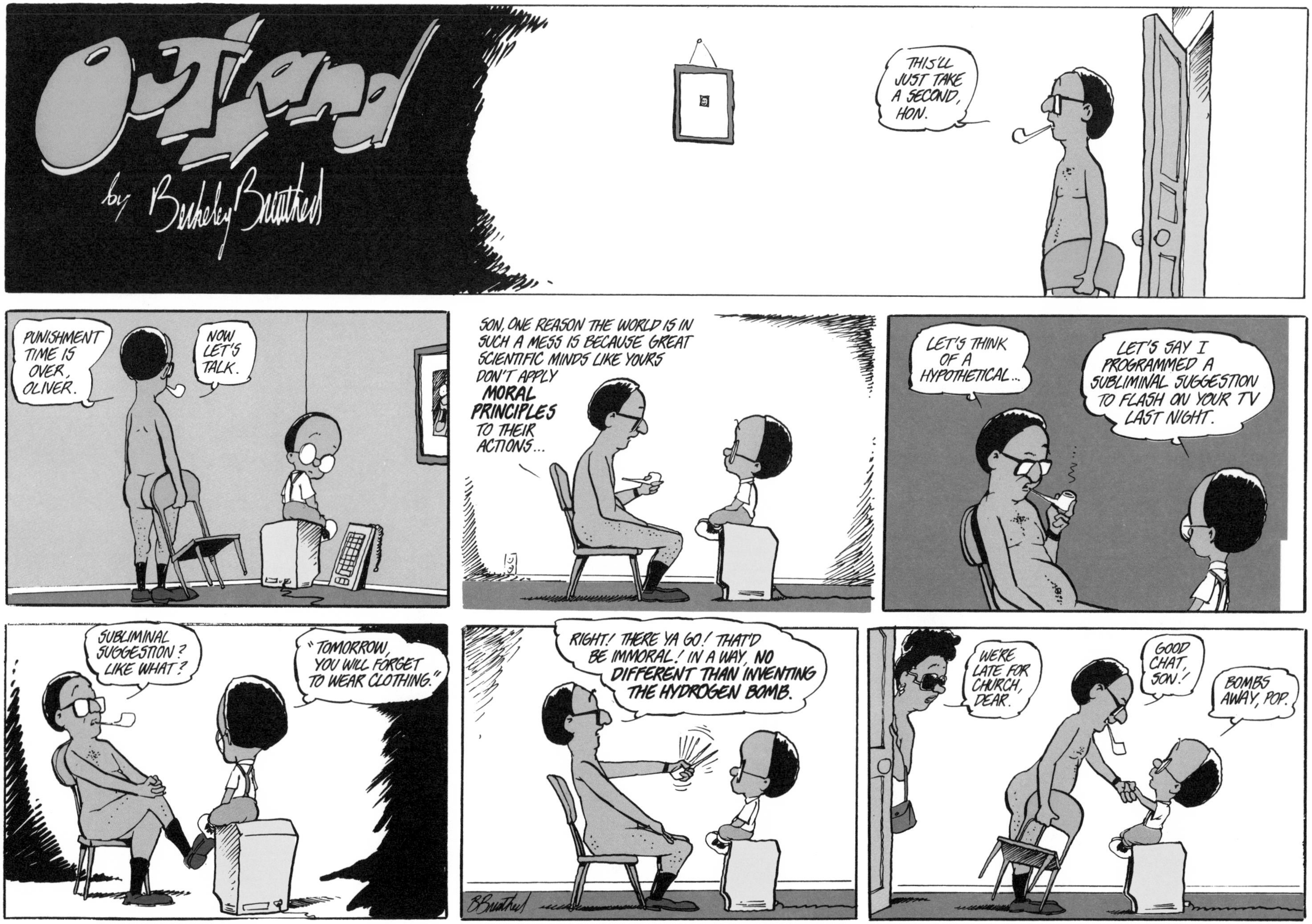

Outland
by Berkeley Breathed
THIS'LL JUST TAKE A SECOND, HON.
PUNISHMENT TIME IS OVER, OLIVER.
NOW LET'S TALK.
SON, ONE REASON THE WORLD IS IN SUCH A MESS IS BECAUSE GREAT SCIENTIFIC MINDS LIKE YOURS DON'T APPLY MORAL PRINCIPLES TO THEIR ACTIONS...
LET'S THINK OF A HYPOTHETICAL...
LET'S SAY I PROGRAMMED A SUBLIMINAL SUGGESTION TO FLASH ON YOUR TV LAST NIGHT.
SUBLIMINAL SUGGESTION? LIKE WHAT?
"TOMORROW, YOU WILL FORGET TO WEAR CLOTHING."
RIGHT! THERE YA GO! THAT'D BE IMMORAL! IN A WAY, NO DIFFERENT THAN INVENTING THE HYDROGEN BOMB.
B Breathed
WE'RE LATE FOR CHURCH, DEAR.
GOOD CHAT, SON!
BOMBS AWAY, POP.

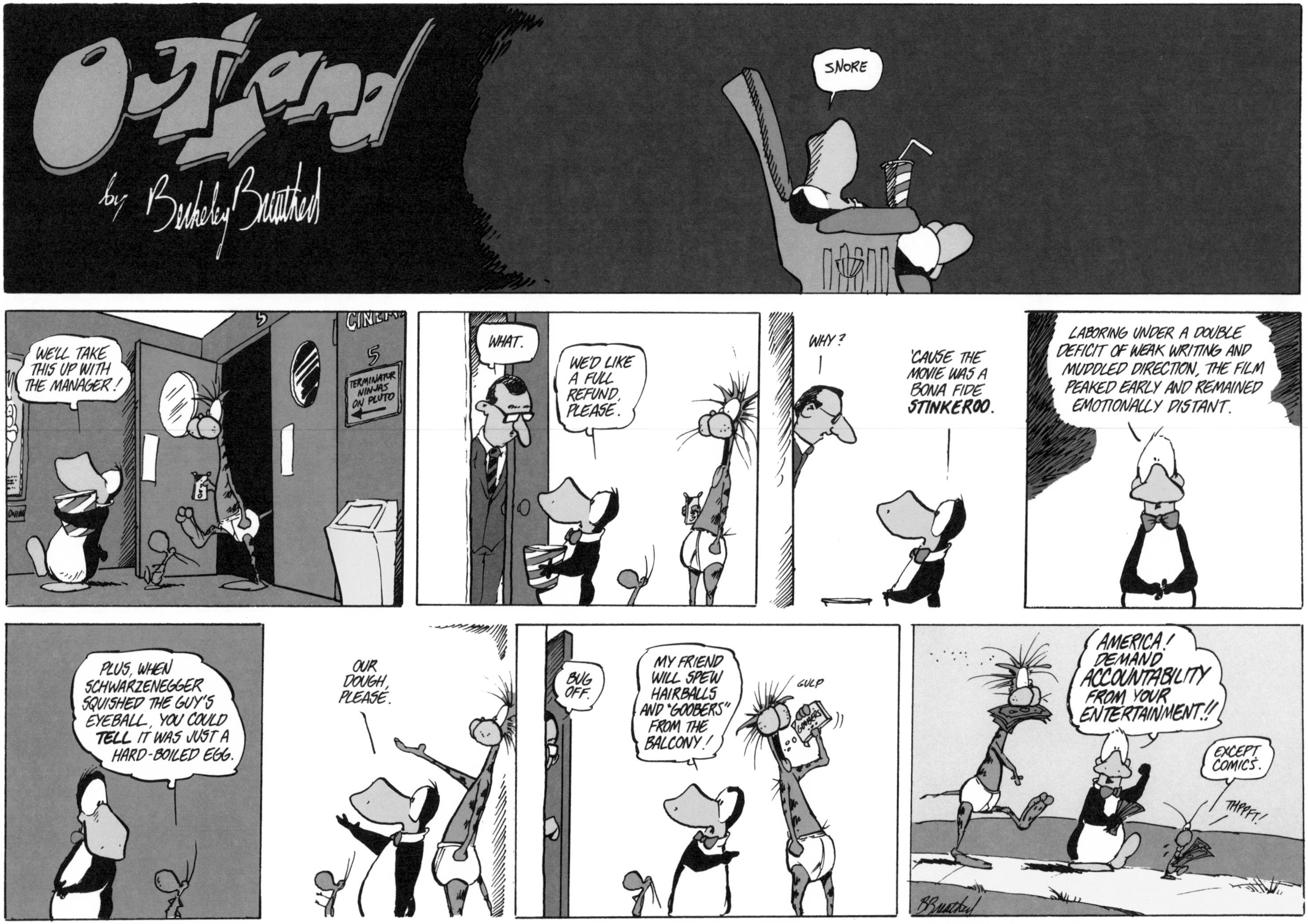
Outland
by Berkeley Breathed
SNORE
WE'LL TAKE THIS UP WITH THE MANAGER!
CINEMA 5
TERMINATOR NINJAS ON PLUTO
WHAT.
WE'D LIKE A FULL REFUND, PLEASE.
WHY?
'CAUSE THE MOVIE WAS A BONA FIDE STINKEROO.
LABORING UNDER A DOUBLE DEFICIT OF WEAK WRITING AND MUDDLED DIRECTION, THE FILM PEAKED EARLY AND REMAINED EMOTIONALLY DISTANT.
PLUS, WHEN SCHWARZENEGGER SQUISHED THE GUY'S EYEBALL, YOU COULD TELL IT WAS JUST A HARD-BOILED EGG.
OUR DOUGH, PLEASE.
BUG OFF.
MY FRIEND WILL SPEW HAIRBALLS AND "GOOBERS" FROM THE BALCONY!
GULP
GOOBERS
AMERICA! DEMAND ACCOUNTABILITY FROM YOUR ENTERTAINMENT!!
EXCEPT COMICS.
THPPFT!
BBreathed

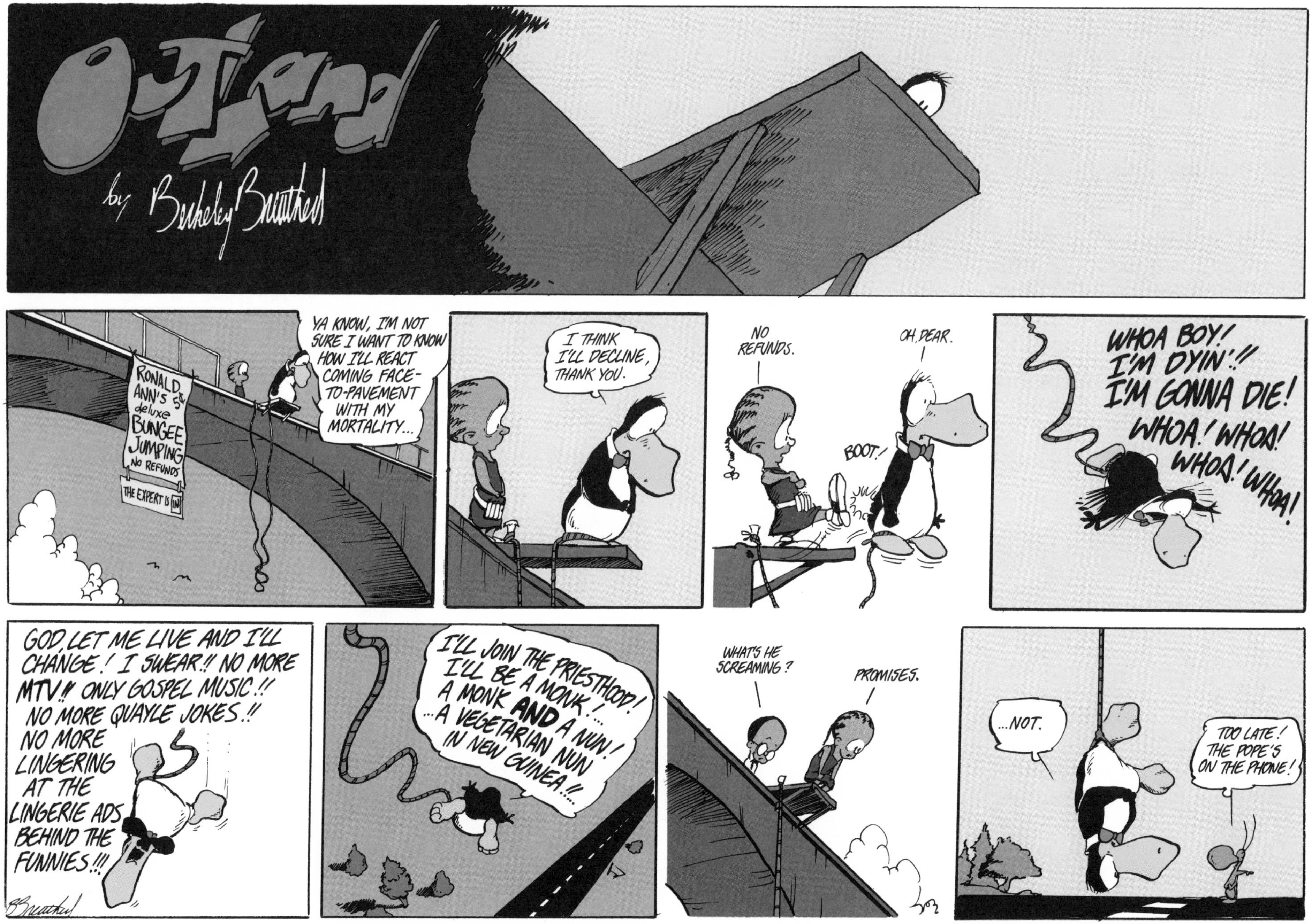

OutLand
by Berkeley Breathed
RONALD ANN'S 5th deluxe BUNGEE JUMPING NO REFUNDS
THE EXPERT IS IN
YA KNOW, I'M NOT SURE I WANT TO KNOW HOW I'LL REACT COMING FACE-TO-PAVEMENT WITH MY MORTALITY...
I THINK I'LL DECLINE, THANK YOU.
NO REFUNDS.
OH, DEAR.
BOOT!
WHOA BOY! I'M DYIN'!! I'M GONNA DIE! WHOA! WHOA! WHOA! WHOA!
GOD, LET ME LIVE AND I'LL CHANGE! I SWEAR!! NO MORE MTV!! ONLY GOSPEL MUSIC!! NO MORE QUAYLE JOKES!! NO MORE LINGERING AT THE LINGERIE ADS BEHIND THE FUNNIES!!!
B Breathed
I'LL JOIN THE PRIESTHOOD! I'LL BE A MONK!... A MONK **AND** A NUN! ...A VEGETARIAN NUN IN NEW GUINEA!!!
WHAT'S HE SCREAMING?
PROMISES.
...NOT.
TOO LATE! THE POPE'S ON THE PHONE!

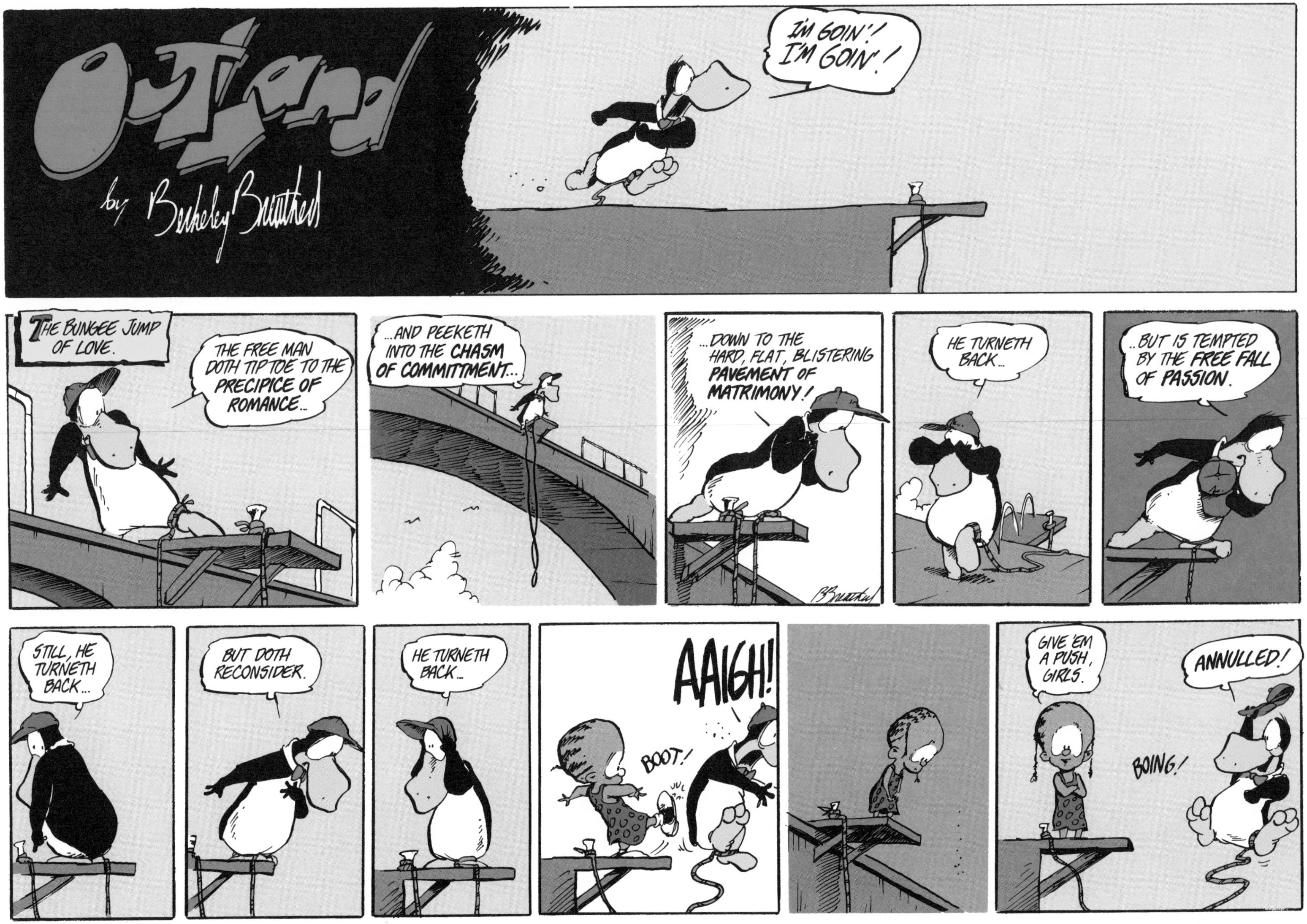
Outland
by Berkeley Breathed
I'M GOIN'! I'M GOIN'!
THE BUNGEE JUMP OF LOVE.
THE FREE MAN DOTH TIPTOE TO THE PRECIPICE OF ROMANCE...
...AND PEEKETH INTO THE CHASM OF COMMITTMENT...
...DOWN TO THE HARD, FLAT, BLISTERING PAVEMENT OF MATRIMONY!
B Breathed
HE TURNETH BACK...
..BUT IS TEMPTED BY THE FREE FALL OF PASSION.
STILL, HE TURNETH BACK...
BUT DOTH RECONSIDER.
HE TURNETH BACK...
AAIGH!
BOOT!
GIVE 'EM A PUSH, GIRLS.
ANNULLED!
BOING!

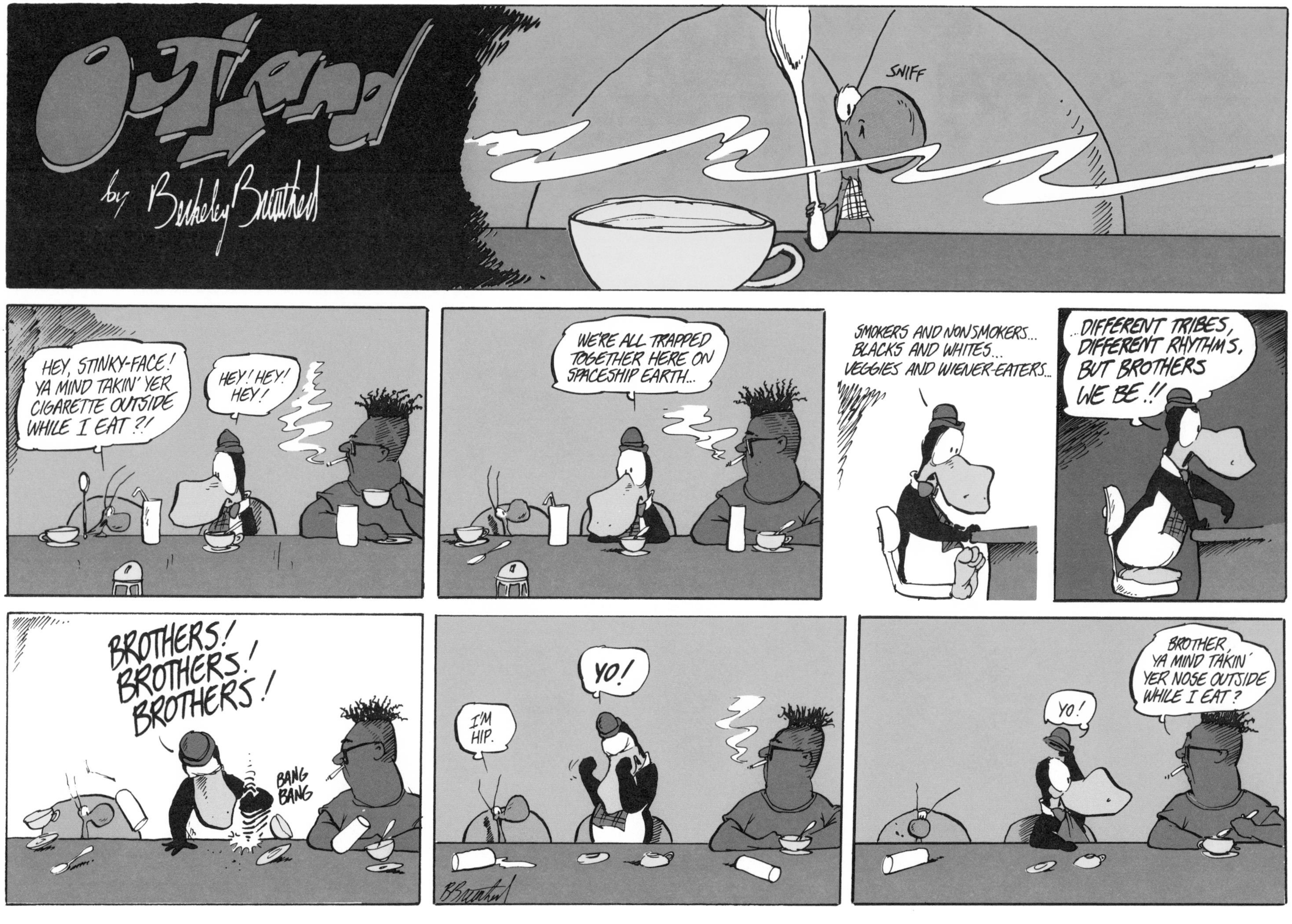

Outland
by Berkeley Breathed
SNIFF
HEY, STINKY-FACE! YA MIND TAKIN' YER CIGARETTE OUTSIDE WHILE I EAT ?!
HEY! HEY! HEY!
WE'RE ALL TRAPPED TOGETHER HERE ON SPACESHIP EARTH...
SMOKERS AND NONSMOKERS... BLACKS AND WHITES... VEGGIES AND WIENER-EATERS...
...DIFFERENT TRIBES, DIFFERENT RHYTHM'S, BUT BROTHERS WE BE!!
BROTHERS! BROTHERS! BROTHERS!
BANG BANG
I'M HIP.
YO!
YO!
BROTHER, YA MIND TAKIN' YER NOSE OUTSIDE WHILE I EAT ?

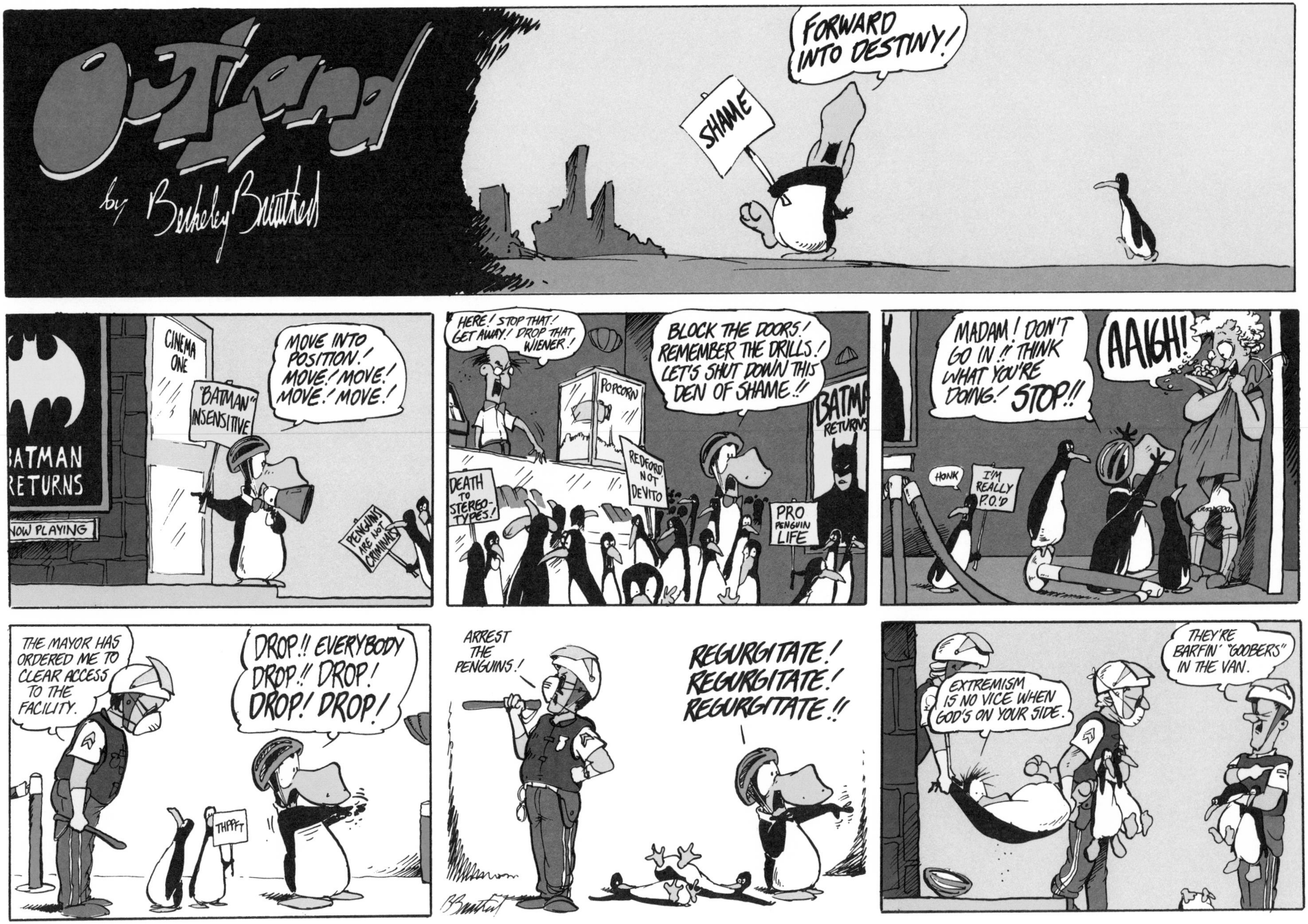
Outland
by Berkeley Breathed
FORWARD INTO DESTINY!
SHAME
CINEMA ONE
BATMAN RETURNS
NOW PLAYING
"BATMAN" INSENSITIVE
MOVE INTO POSITION! MOVE! MOVE! MOVE! MOVE!
PENGUINS ARE NOT CRIMINALS
HERE! STOP THAT! GET AWAY! DROP THAT WIENER!
POPCORN
BLOCK THE DOORS! REMEMBER THE DRILLS! LET'S SHUT DOWN THIS DEN OF SHAME!!
BATMAN RETURNS
DEATH TO STEREO-TYPES!
REDFORD NOT DEVITO
PRO PENGUIN LIFE
MADAM! DON'T GO IN!! THINK WHAT YOU'RE DOING! STOP!!
AAIGH!
HONK
I'M REALLY P.O.'D
THE MAYOR HAS ORDERED ME TO CLEAR ACCESS TO THE FACILITY.
DROP!! EVERYBODY DROP!! DROP! DROP! DROP!
THPPFT
ARREST THE PENGUINS!
REGURGITATE! REGURGITATE! REGURGITATE!!
EXTREMISM IS NO VICE WHEN GOD'S ON YOUR SIDE.
THEY'RE BARFIN' "GOOBERS" IN THE VAN.

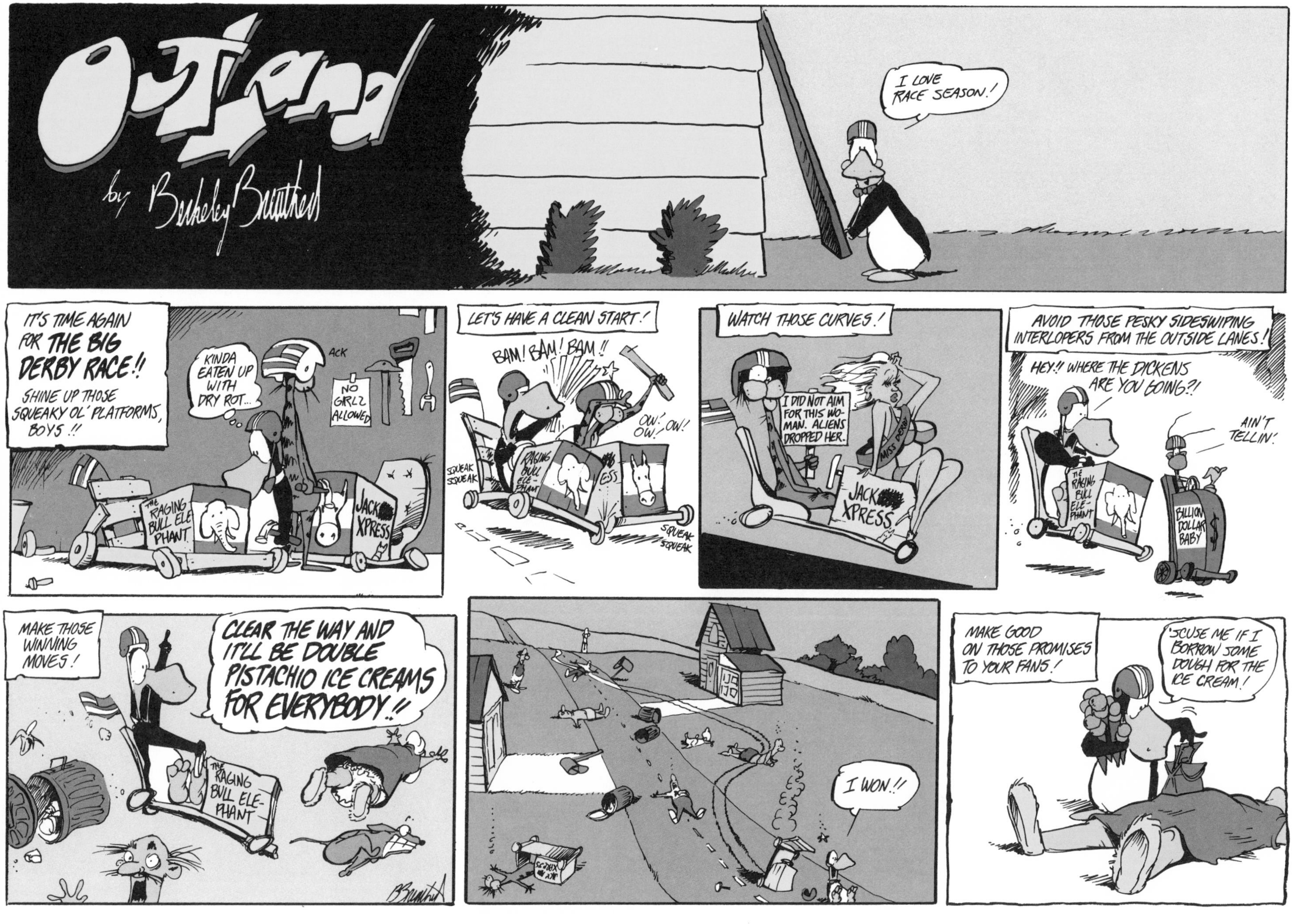
Outland
by Berkeley Breathed
I LOVE RACE SEASON.!
IT'S TIME AGAIN FOR THE BIG DERBY RACE!! SHINE UP THOSE SQUEAKY OL' PLATFORMS, BOYS!!
KINDA EATEN UP WITH DRY ROT...
ACK
NO GIRLZ ALLOWED
THE RAGING BULL ELE-PHANT
JACK XPRESS
LET'S HAVE A CLEAN START.!
BAM! BAM! BAM!!
OW! OW! OW!
SQUEAK SQUEAK
RAGING BULL ELE-PHANT
SQUEAK SQUEAK
WATCH THOSE CURVES.!
I DID NOT AIM FOR THIS WO-MAN. ALIENS DROPPED HER.
MISS DERBY
JACK XPRESS
AVOID THOSE PESKY SIDESWIPING INTERLOPERS FROM THE OUTSIDE LANES.!
HEY!! WHERE THE DICKENS ARE YOU GOING?!
AIN'T TELLIN'.
THE RAGING BULL ELE-PHANT
BILLION DOLLAR BABY
MAKE THOSE WINNING MOVES.!
CLEAR THE WAY AND IT'LL BE DOUBLE PISTACHIO ICE CREAMS FOR EVERYBODY!!
THE RAGING BULL ELE-PHANT
I WON.!!
MAKE GOOD ON THOSE PROMISES TO YOUR FANS.!
'SCUSE ME IF I BORROW SOME DOUGH FOR THE ICE CREAM.!

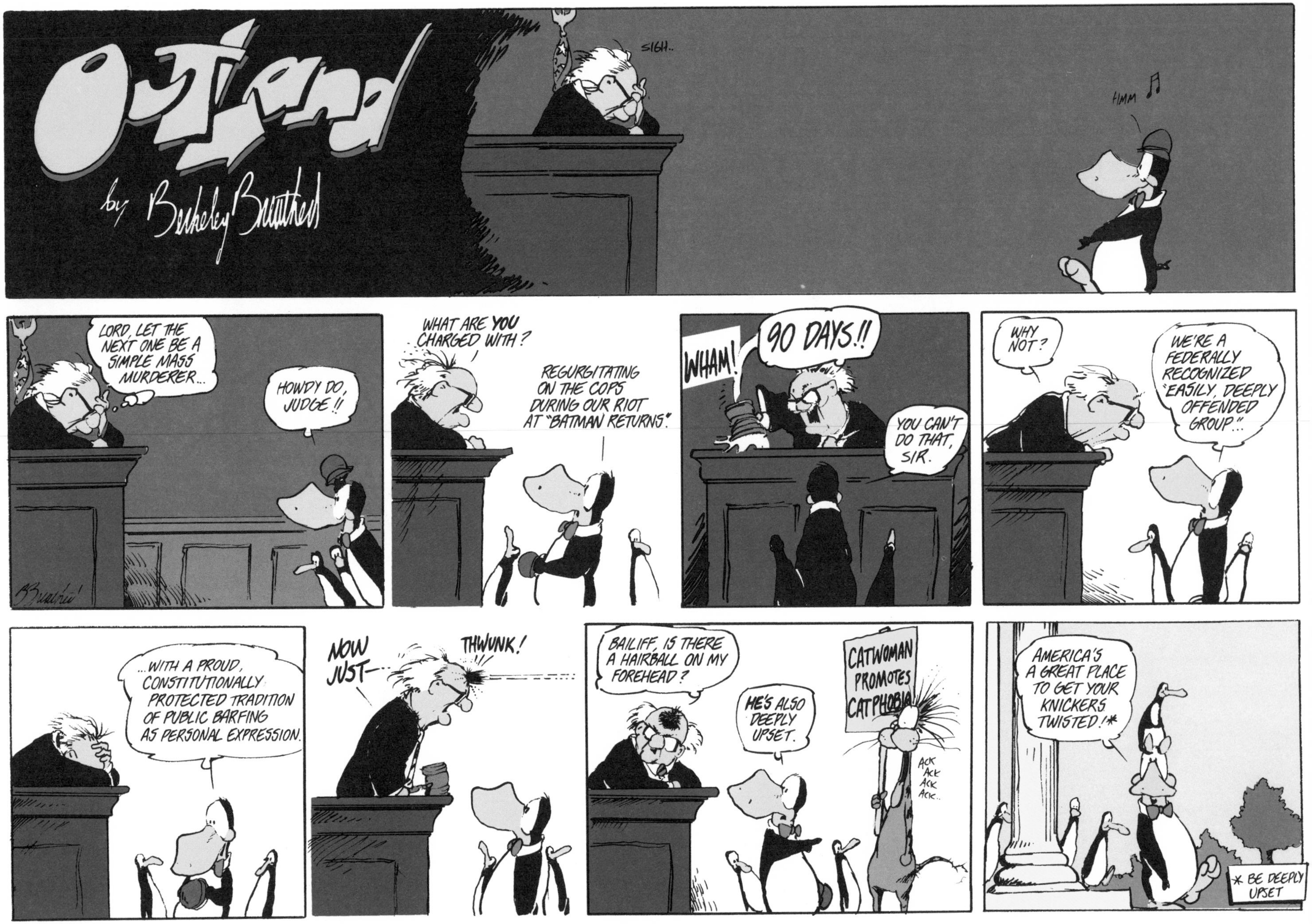

Outland
by Berkeley Breathed
SIGH..
HMM
LORD, LET THE NEXT ONE BE A SIMPLE MASS MURDERER...
HOWDY DO, JUDGE!!
WHAT ARE YOU CHARGED WITH?
REGURGITATING ON THE COPS DURING OUR RIOT AT "BATMAN RETURNS."
WHAM!
90 DAYS!!
YOU CAN'T DO THAT, SIR.
WHY NOT?
WE'RE A FEDERALLY RECOGNIZED "EASILY, DEEPLY OFFENDED GROUP"...
...WITH A PROUD, CONSTITUTIONALLY PROTECTED TRADITION OF PUBLIC BARFING AS PERSONAL EXPRESSION.
NOW JUST—
THWUNK!
BAILIFF, IS THERE A HAIRBALL ON MY FOREHEAD?
HE'S ALSO DEEPLY UPSET.
CATWOMAN PROMOTES CATPHOBIA
ACK ACK ACK ACK..
AMERICA'S A GREAT PLACE TO GET YOUR KNICKERS TWISTED!*
* BE DEEPLY UPSET

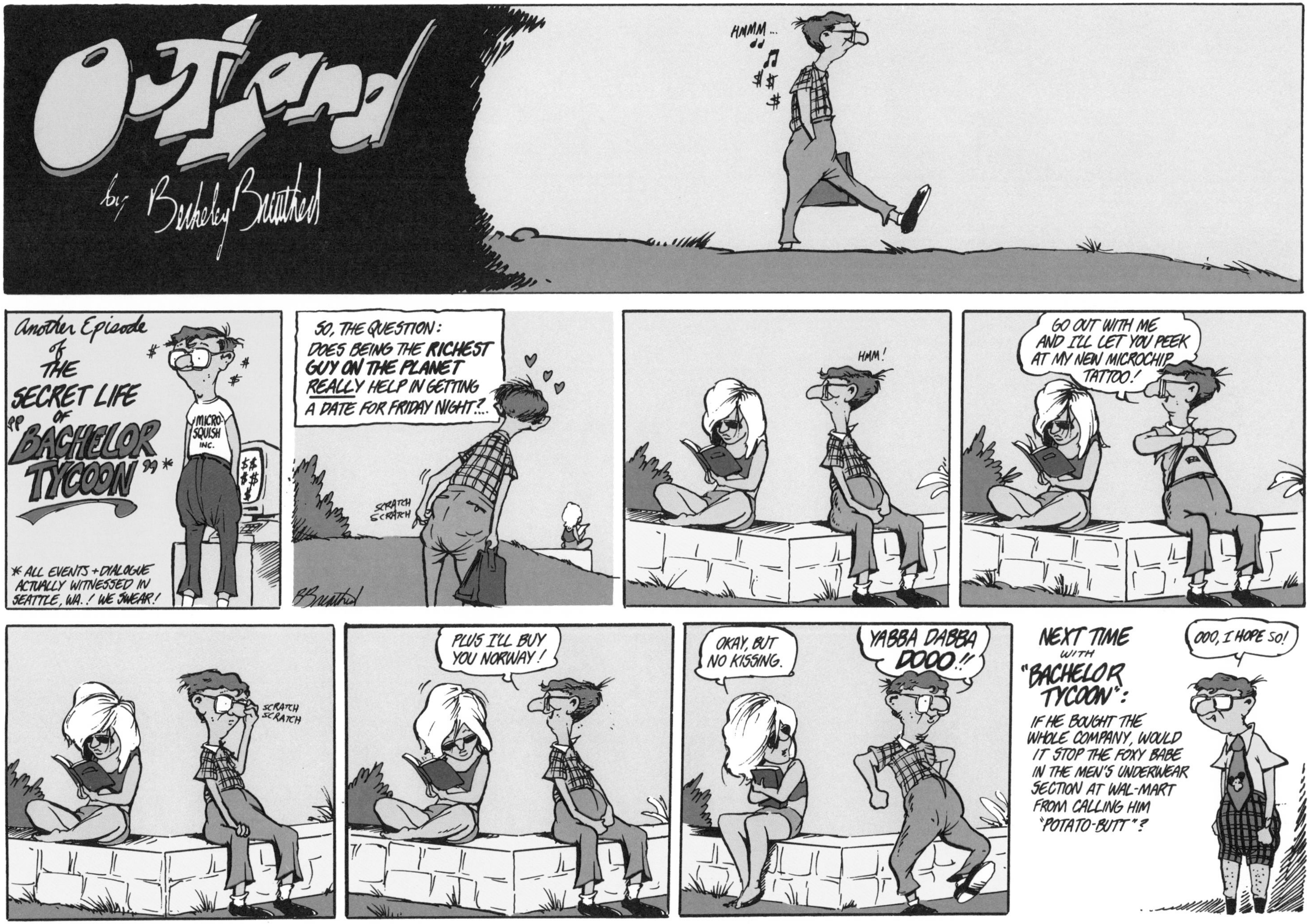
Outland
by Berkeley Breathed
HMMM...
Another Episode of
THE SECRET LIFE OF "BACHELOR TYCOON"*
MICRO-SQUISH INC.
* ALL EVENTS + DIALOGUE ACTUALLY WITNESSED IN SEATTLE, WA.! WE SWEAR!
SO, THE QUESTION: DOES BEING THE RICHEST GUY ON THE PLANET REALLY HELP IN GETTING A DATE FOR FRIDAY NIGHT?...
SCRATCH SCRATCH
B Breathed
HMM!
GO OUT WITH ME AND I'LL LET YOU PEEK AT MY NEW MICROCHIP TATTOO!
SCRATCH SCRATCH
PLUS I'LL BUY YOU NORWAY!
OKAY, BUT NO KISSING.
YABBA DABBA DOOO!!
NEXT TIME WITH "BACHELOR TYCOON":
IF HE BOUGHT THE WHOLE COMPANY, WOULD IT STOP THE FOXY BABE IN THE MEN'S UNDERWEAR SECTION AT WAL-MART FROM CALLING HIM "POTATO-BUTT"?
OOO, I HOPE SO!

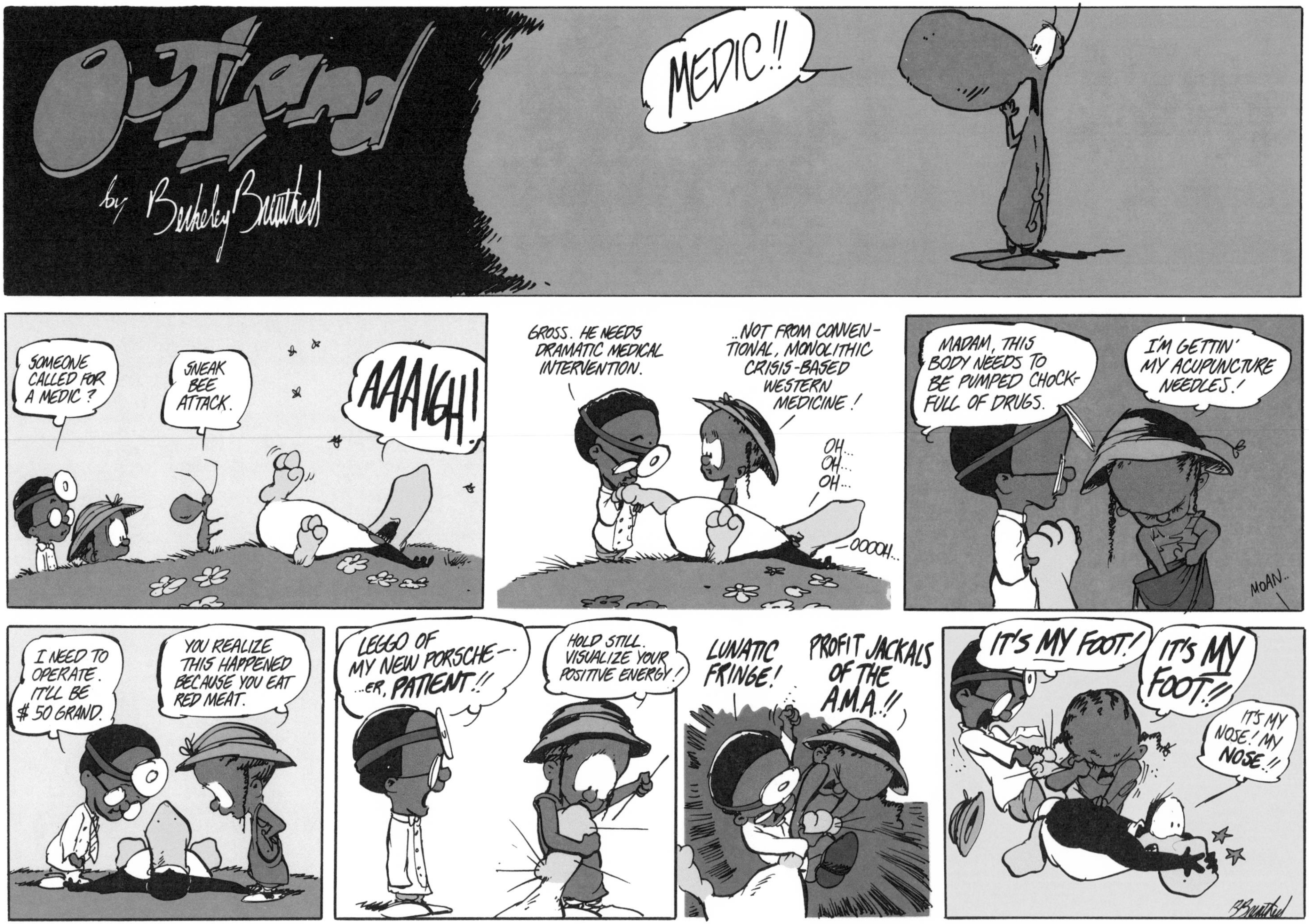
Outland
by Berkeley Breathed
MEDIC!!
SOMEONE CALLED FOR A MEDIC?
SNEAK BEE ATTACK.
AAAIGH!
GROSS. HE NEEDS DRAMATIC MEDICAL INTERVENTION.
..NOT FROM CONVENTIONAL, MONOLITHIC CRISIS-BASED WESTERN MEDICINE!
OH... OH... OH...
OOOOH..
MADAM, THIS BODY NEEDS TO BE PUMPED CHOCK-FULL OF DRUGS.
I'M GETTIN' MY ACUPUNCTURE NEEDLES!
MOAN..
I NEED TO OPERATE. IT'LL BE $ 50 GRAND.
YOU REALIZE THIS HAPPENED BECAUSE YOU EAT RED MEAT.
LEGGO OF MY NEW PORSCHE-- ...ER, PATIENT!!
HOLD STILL. VISUALIZE YOUR POSITIVE ENERGY!
LUNATIC FRINGE!
PROFIT JACKALS OF THE A.M.A.!!
IT'S MY FOOT!
IT'S MY FOOT!!
IT'S MY NOSE! MY NOSE!!
B. Breathed

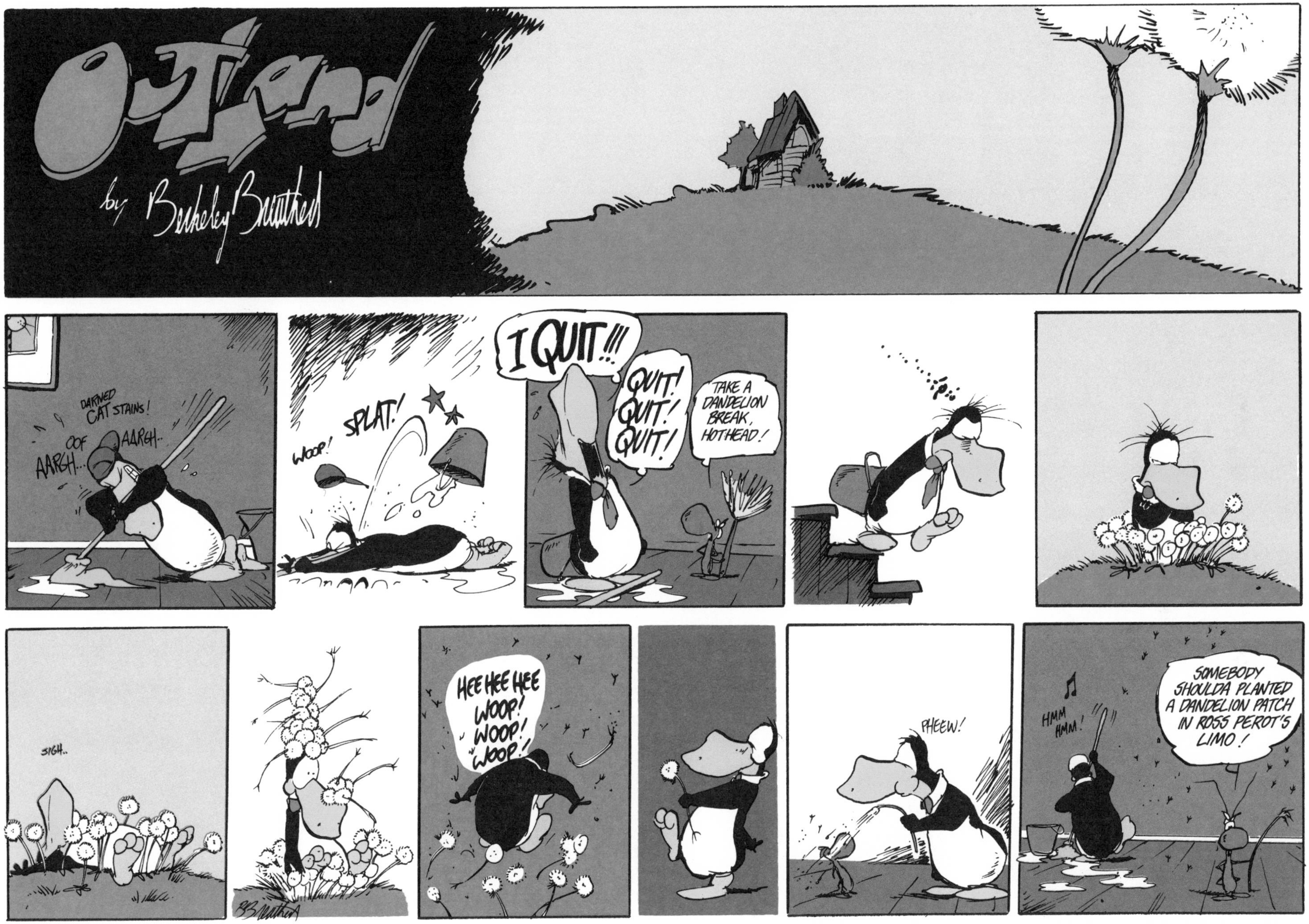
Outland
by Berkeley Breathed
DARNED CAT STAINS!
OOF
AARGH..
AARGH...
WOOP!
SPLAT!
I QUIT!!!
QUIT! QUIT! QUIT!
TAKE A DANDELION BREAK, HOTHEAD!
SIGH..
HEE HEE HEE WOOP! WOOP! WOOP!
PHEEW!
HMM HMM!
SOMEBODY SHOULDA PLANTED A DANDELION PATCH IN ROSS PEROT'S LIMO!

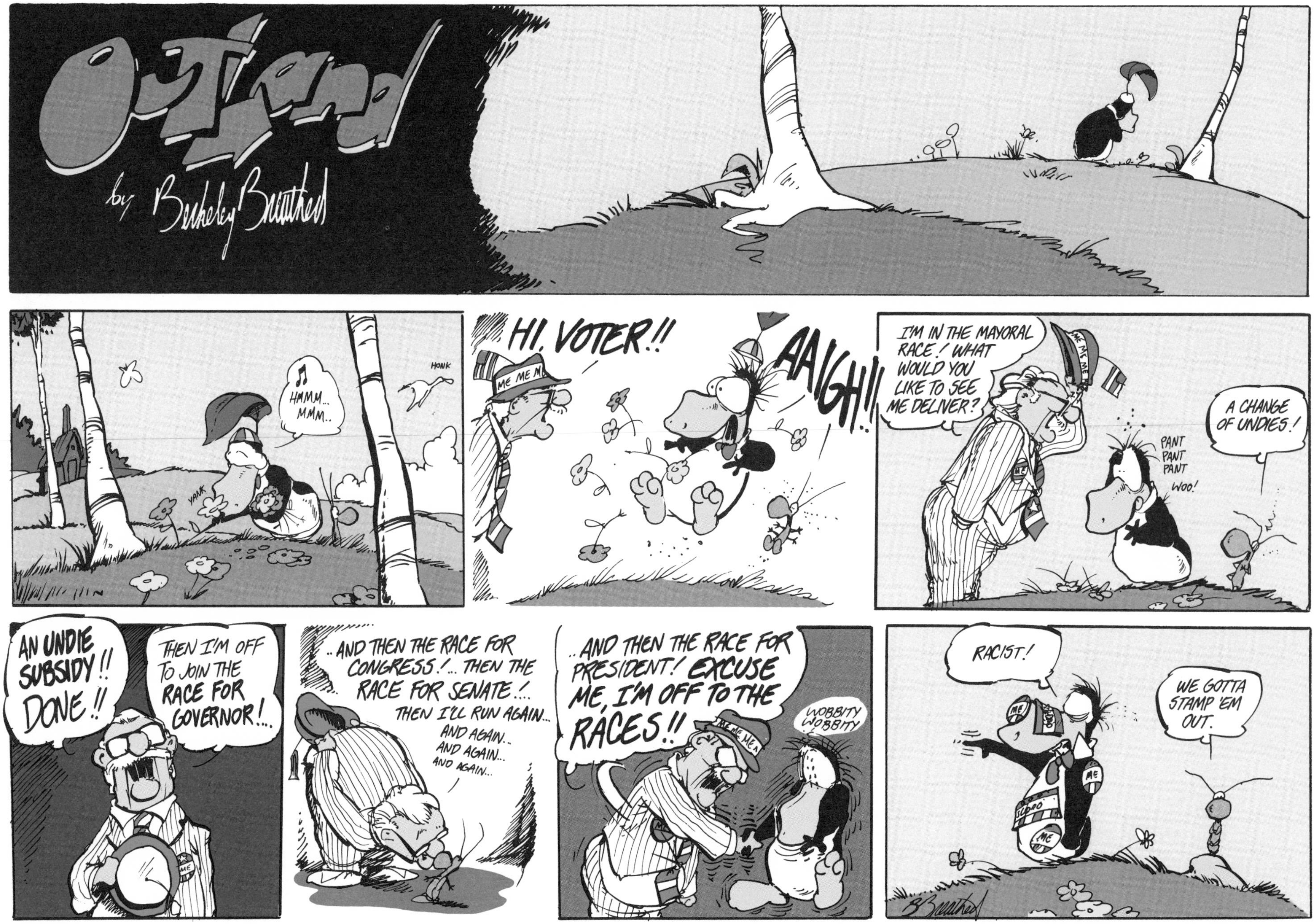

Outland
by Berkeley Breathed
HMMM... MMM..
YANK
HONK
HI, VOTER!!
AAIGH!!
I'M IN THE MAYORAL RACE! WHAT WOULD YOU LIKE TO SEE ME DELIVER?
PANT PANT PANT
WOO!
A CHANGE OF UNDIES!
AN UNDIE SUBSIDY!! DONE!!
THEN I'M OFF TO JOIN THE RACE FOR GOVERNOR!...
...AND THEN THE RACE FOR CONGRESS!... THEN THE RACE FOR SENATE!...
THEN I'LL RUN AGAIN...
AND AGAIN.. AND AGAIN... AND AGAIN...
..AND THEN THE RACE FOR PRESIDENT! EXCUSE ME, I'M OFF TO THE RACES!!
WOBBITY WOBBITY
RACIST!
WE GOTTA STAMP 'EM OUT.
B. Breathed

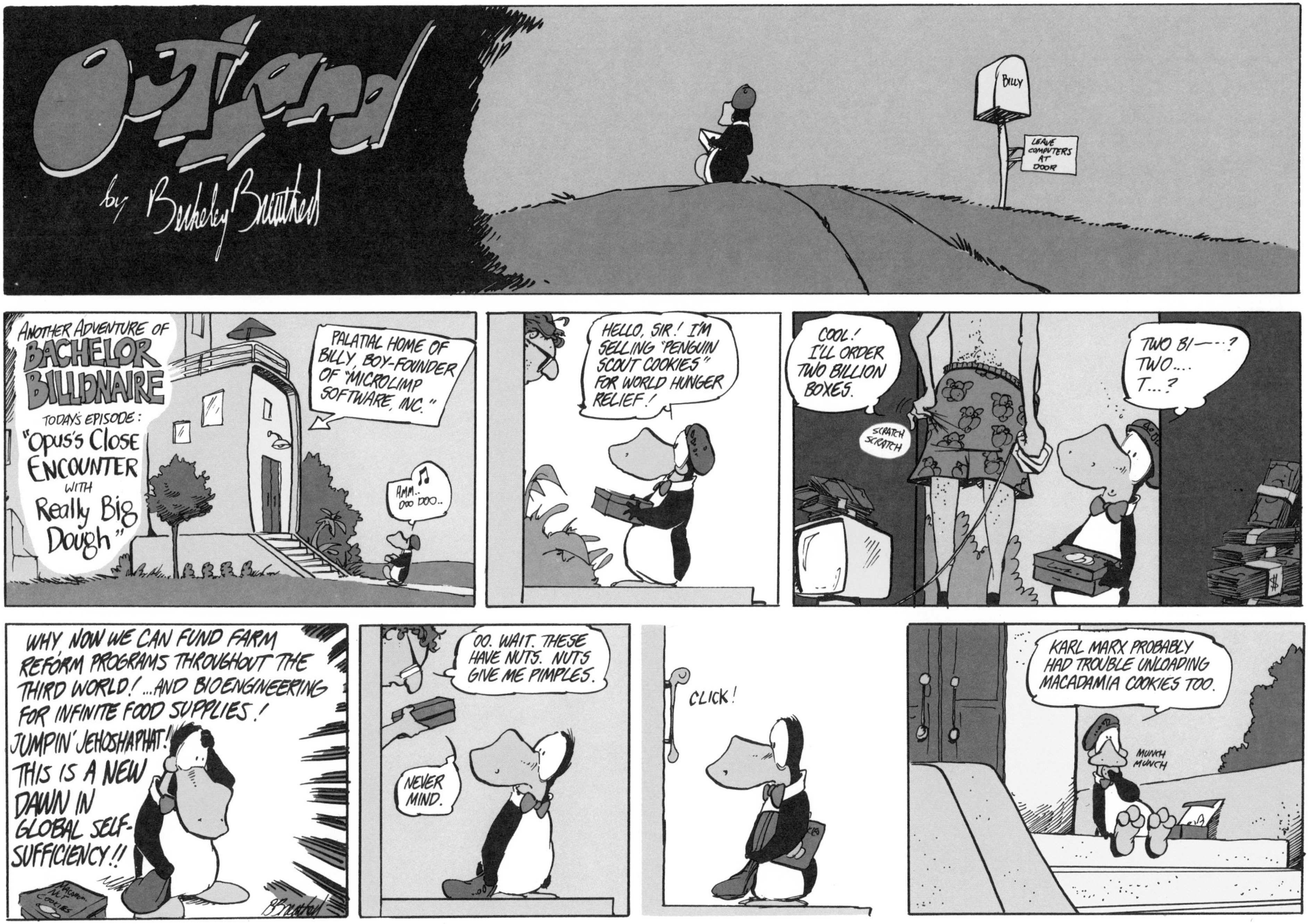
Outland
by Berkeley Breathed
BILLY
LEAVE COMPUTERS AT DOOR
ANOTHER ADVENTURE OF BACHELOR BILLIONAIRE
TODAY'S EPISODE: "Opus's Close Encounter with Really Big Dough"
PALATIAL HOME OF BILLY, BOY-FOUNDER OF "MICROLIMP SOFTWARE, INC."
HMM.. OOO DOO..
HELLO, SIR! I'M SELLING "PENGUIN SCOUT COOKIES" FOR WORLD HUNGER RELIEF!
COOL! I'LL ORDER TWO BILLION BOXES.
SCRATCH SCRATCH
TWO BI—-? TWO.... T...?
WHY, NOW WE CAN FUND FARM REFORM PROGRAMS THROUGHOUT THE THIRD WORLD! ...AND BIOENGINEERING FOR INFINITE FOOD SUPPLIES!
JUMPIN' JEHOSHAPHAT!! THIS IS A NEW DAWN IN GLOBAL SELF-SUFFICIENCY!!
MACADAM. NUT COOKIES
OO. WAIT. THESE HAVE NUTS. NUTS GIVE ME PIMPLES.
NEVER MIND.
CLICK!
KARL MARX PROBABLY HAD TROUBLE UNLOADING MACADAMIA COOKIES TOO.
MUNCH MUNCH

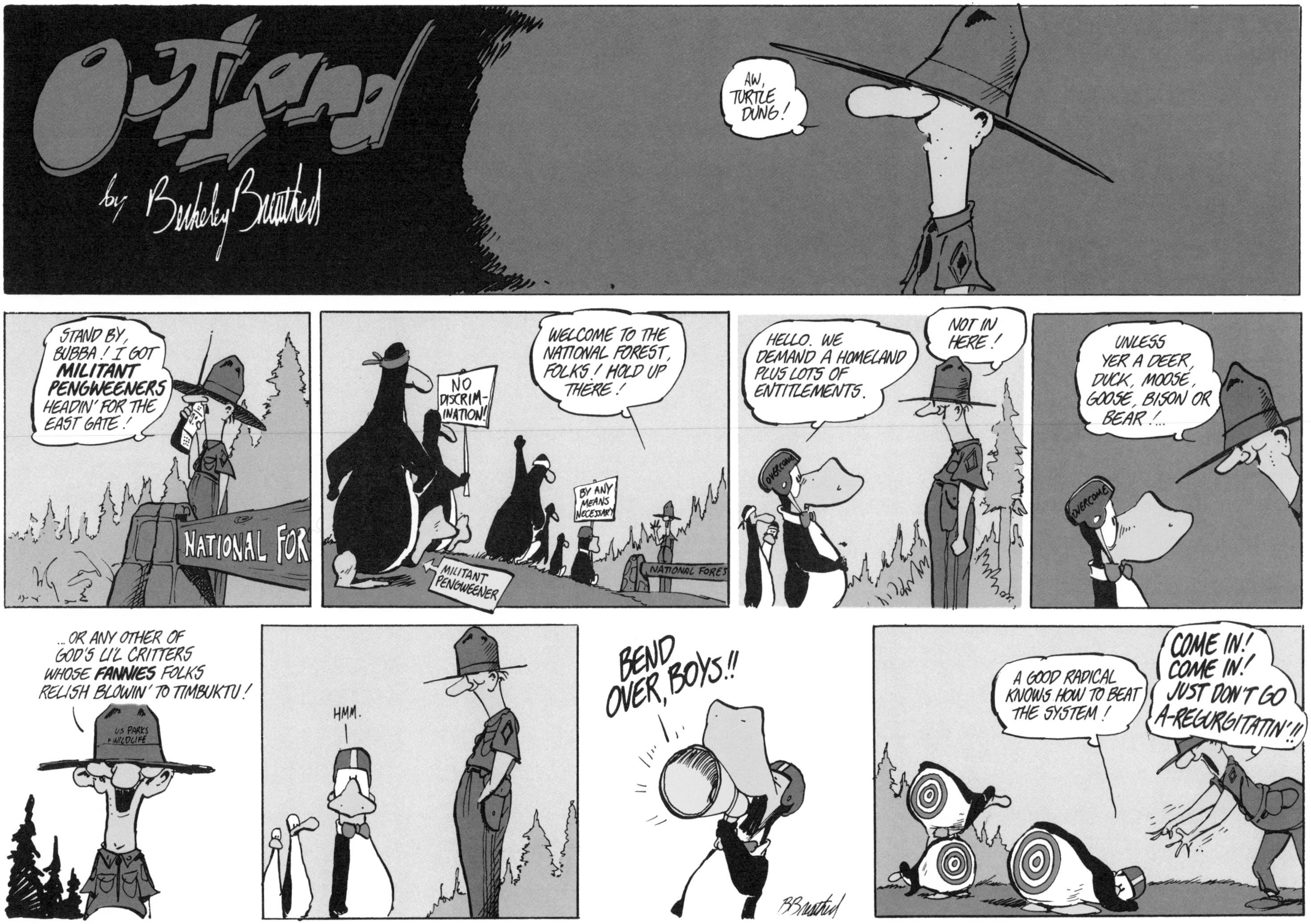

Outland
by Berkeley Breathed
AW, TURTLE DUNG!
STAND BY, BUBBA! I GOT **MILITANT PENGWEENERS** HEADIN' FOR THE EAST GATE!
NATIONAL FOR
NO DISCRIMINATION!
WELCOME TO THE NATIONAL FOREST, FOLKS! HOLD UP THERE!
BY ANY MEANS NECESSARY
MILITANT PENGWEENER
NATIONAL FORES
HELLO. WE DEMAND A HOMELAND PLUS LOTS OF ENTITLEMENTS.
NOT IN HERE!
OVERCOME
UNLESS YER A DEER, DUCK, MOOSE, GOOSE, BISON OR BEAR!...
OVERCOME
...OR ANY OTHER OF GOD'S LI'L CRITTERS WHOSE **FANNIES** FOLKS RELISH BLOWIN' TO TIMBUKTU!
US PARKS + WILDLIFE
HMM.
BEND OVER, BOYS!!
B.Breathed
A GOOD RADICAL KNOWS HOW TO BEAT THE SYSTEM!
COME IN! COME IN! JUST DON'T GO A-REGURGITATIN'!!

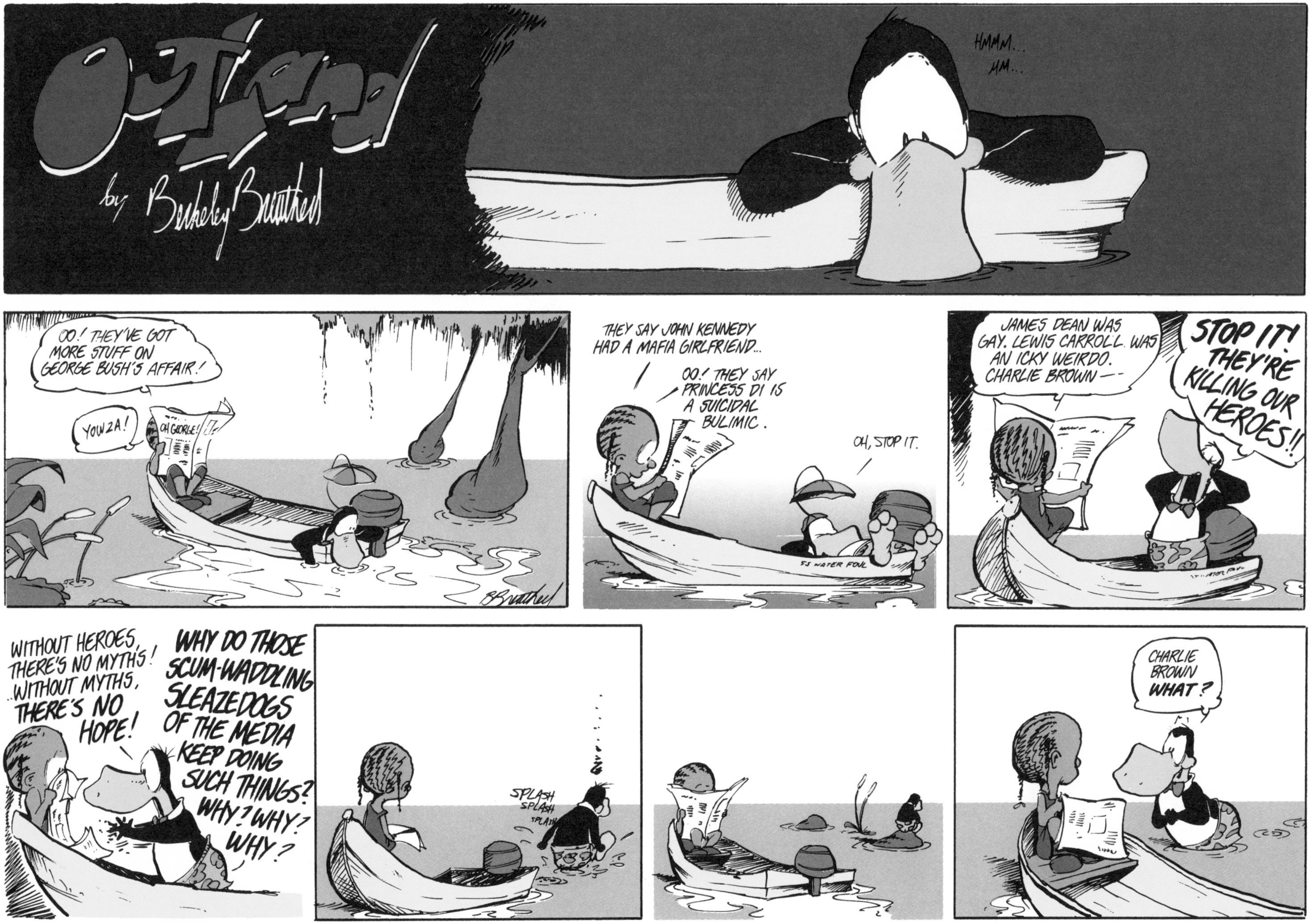

Outland
by Berkeley Breathed
HMMM... MM...
OO! THEY'VE GOT MORE STUFF ON GEORGE BUSH'S AFFAIR!
YOWZA!
OH GEORGE!
BBreathed
THEY SAY JOHN KENNEDY HAD A MAFIA GIRLFRIEND...
OO! THEY SAY PRINCESS DI IS A SUICIDAL BULIMIC.
OH, STOP IT.
SS WATER FOUL
JAMES DEAN WAS GAY. LEWIS CARROLL WAS AN ICKY WEIRDO. CHARLIE BROWN—
STOP IT! THEY'RE KILLING OUR HEROES!!
WITHOUT HEROES, THERE'S NO MYTHS! ..WITHOUT MYTHS, THERE'S NO HOPE!
WHY DO THOSE SCUM-WADDLING SLEAZEDOGS OF THE MEDIA KEEP DOING SUCH THINGS? WHY? WHY? WHY?
SPLASH SPLASH SPLASH
CHARLIE BROWN WHAT?

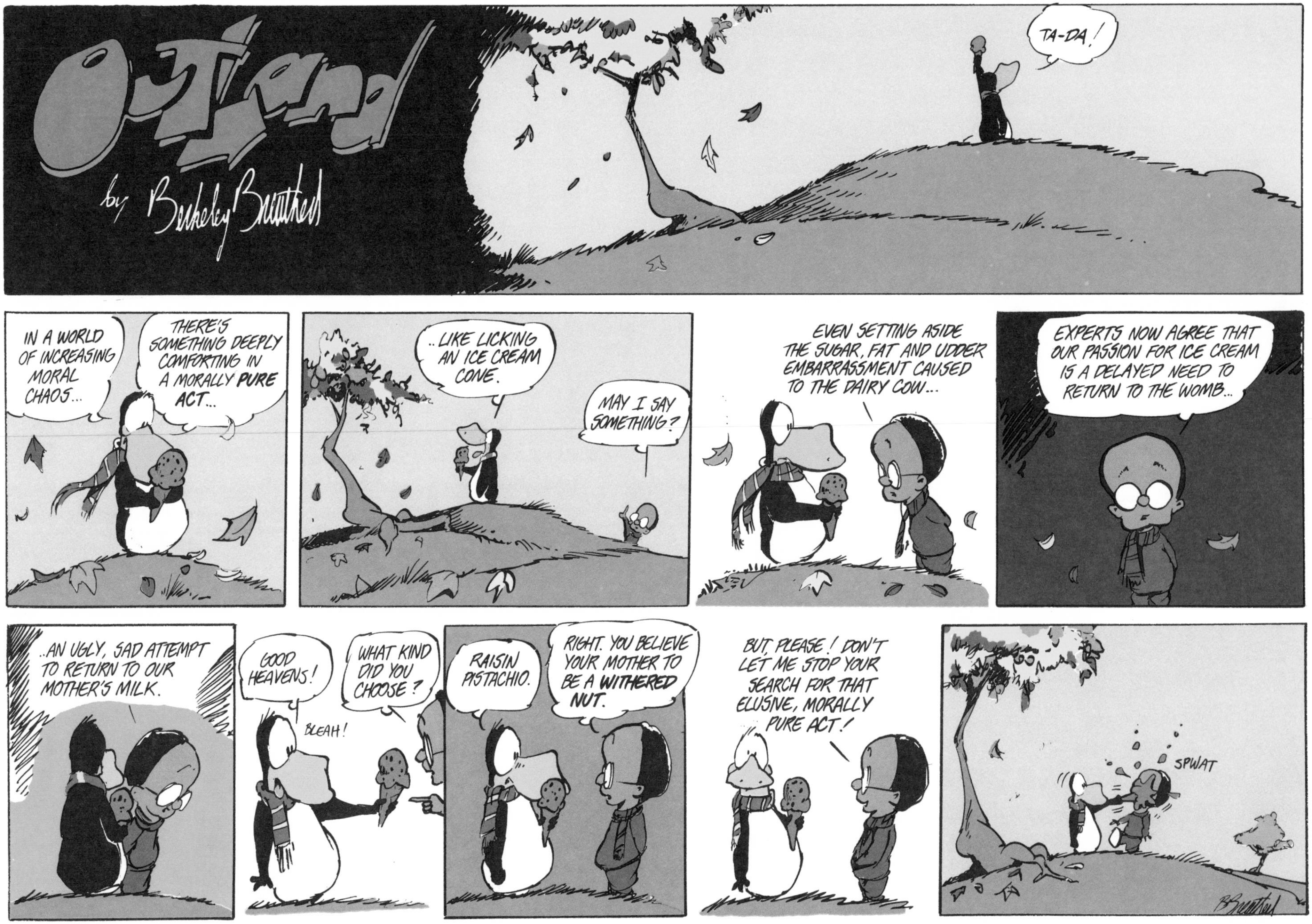
Outland
by Berkeley Breathed
TA-DA!
IN A WORLD OF INCREASING MORAL CHAOS...
THERE'S SOMETHING DEEPLY COMFORTING IN A MORALLY PURE ACT...
..LIKE LICKING AN ICE CREAM CONE.
MAY I SAY SOMETHING?
EVEN SETTING ASIDE THE SUGAR, FAT AND UDDER EMBARRASSMENT CAUSED TO THE DAIRY COW...
EXPERTS NOW AGREE THAT OUR PASSION FOR ICE CREAM IS A DELAYED NEED TO RETURN TO THE WOMB...
..AN UGLY, SAD ATTEMPT TO RETURN TO OUR MOTHER'S MILK.
GOOD HEAVENS!
BLEAH!
WHAT KIND DID YOU CHOOSE?
RAISIN PISTACHIO.
RIGHT. YOU BELIEVE YOUR MOTHER TO BE A WITHERED NUT.
BUT, PLEASE! DON'T LET ME STOP YOUR SEARCH FOR THAT ELUSIVE, MORALLY PURE ACT!
SPWAT
B Breathed

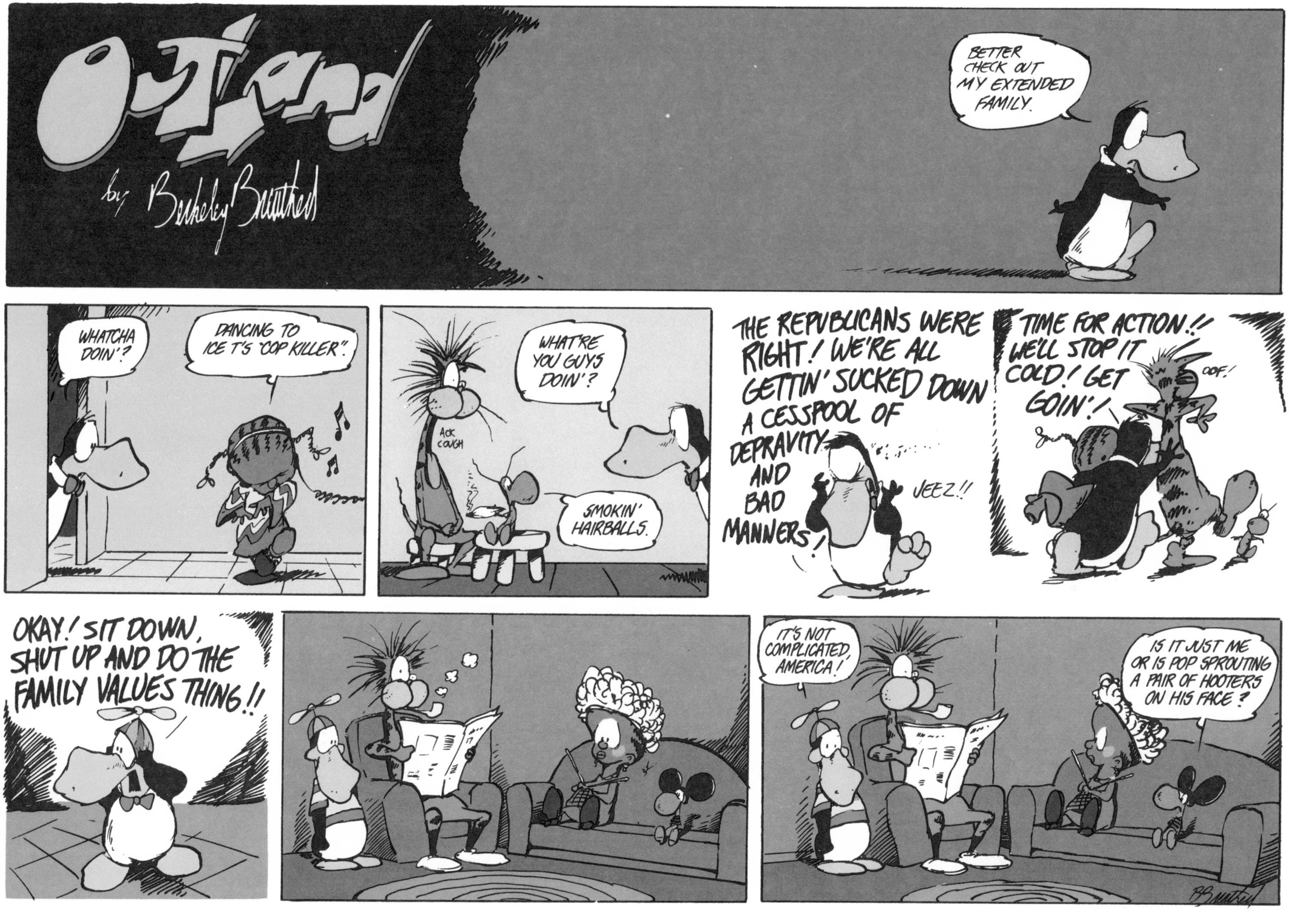
Outland
by Berkeley Breathed
BETTER CHECK OUT MY EXTENDED FAMILY.
WHATCHA DOIN'?
DANCING TO ICE T'S "COP KILLER".
WHAT'RE YOU GUYS DOIN'?
ACK COUGH
SMOKIN' HAIRBALLS.
THE REPUBLICANS WERE RIGHT! WE'RE ALL GETTIN' SUCKED DOWN A CESSPOOL OF DEPRAVITY AND BAD MANNERS!
JEEZ!!
TIME FOR ACTION!! WE'LL STOP IT COLD! GET GOIN'!
OOF!
OKAY! SIT DOWN, SHUT UP AND DO THE FAMILY VALUES THING!!
IT'S NOT COMPLICATED, AMERICA!
IS IT JUST ME OR IS POP SPROUTING A PAIR OF HOOTERS ON HIS FACE?

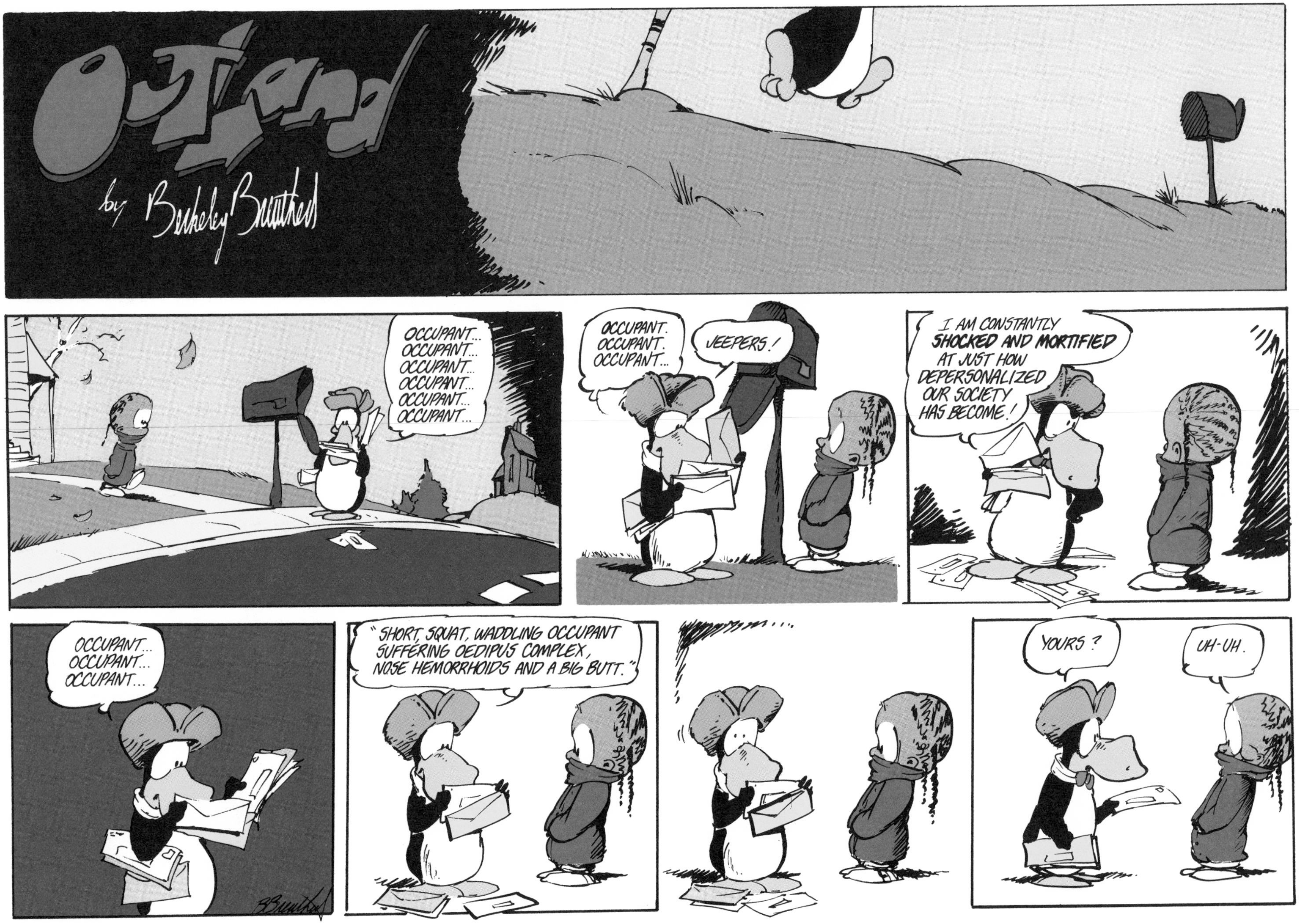
Outland
by Berkeley Breathed
OCCUPANT... OCCUPANT... OCCUPANT... OCCUPANT... OCCUPANT... OCCUPANT...
OCCUPANT. OCCUPANT. OCCUPANT...
JEEPERS!
I AM CONSTANTLY SHOCKED AND MORTIFIED AT JUST HOW DEPERSONALIZED OUR SOCIETY HAS BECOME!
OCCUPANT... OCCUPANT... OCCUPANT...
"SHORT, SQUAT, WADDLING OCCUPANT SUFFERING OEDIPUS COMPLEX, NOSE HEMORRHOIDS AND A BIG BUTT."
YOURS?
UH-UH.
BBreathed

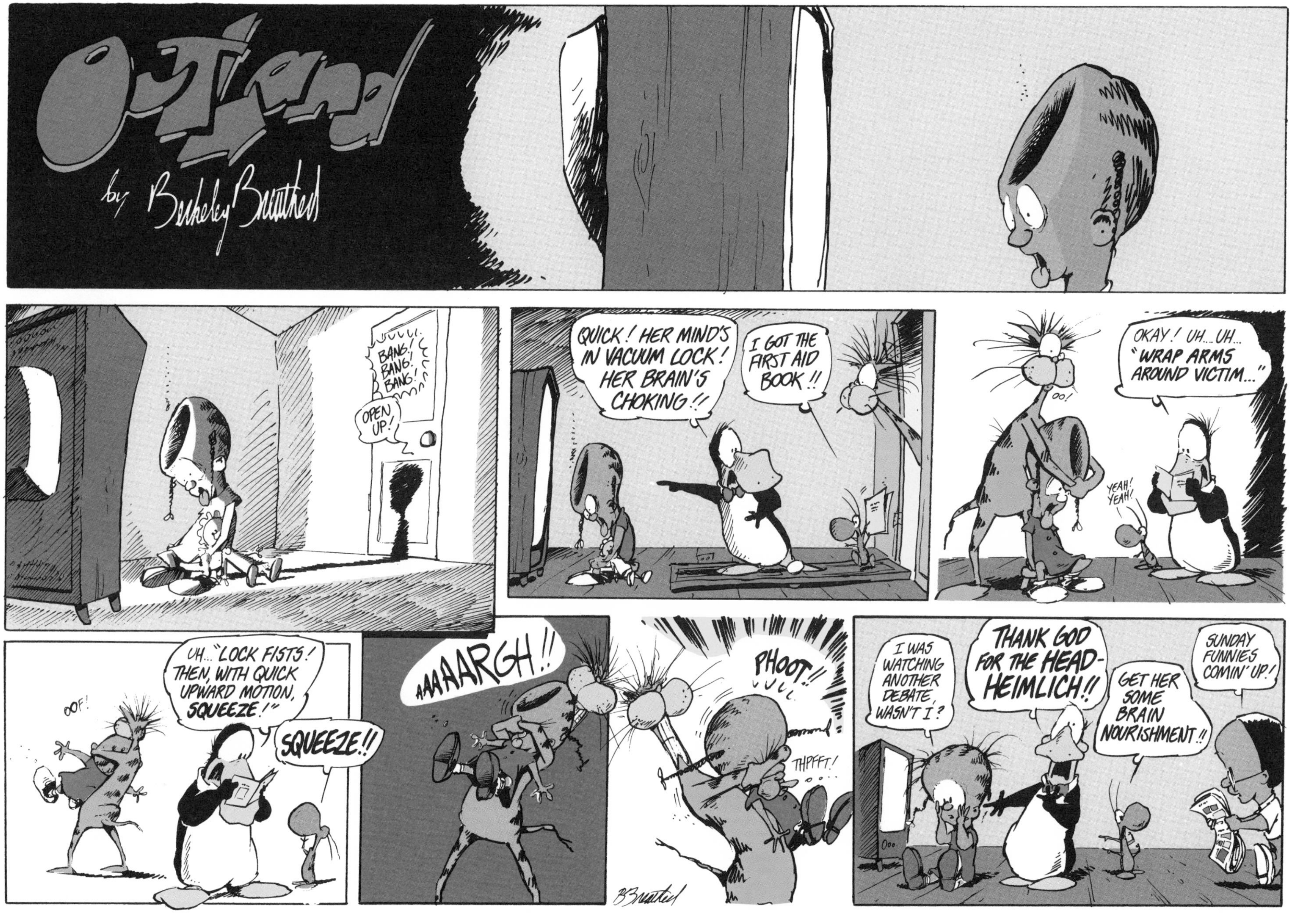
Outland
by Berkeley Breathed
BANG! BANG! BANG!
OPEN UP!
QUICK! HER MIND'S IN VACUUM LOCK! HER BRAIN'S CHOKING!!
I GOT THE FIRST AID BOOK!!
OKAY! UH... UH... "WRAP ARMS AROUND VICTIM..."
YEAH! YEAH!
OOF!
UH... "LOCK FISTS! THEN, WITH QUICK UPWARD MOTION, SQUEEZE!"
SQUEEZE!!
AAAAARGH!!
PHOOT!!
THPFFT!
I WAS WATCHING ANOTHER DEBATE, WASN'T I?
THANK GOD FOR THE HEAD-HEIMLICH!!
GET HER SOME BRAIN NOURISHMENT!!
SUNDAY FUNNIES COMIN' UP!
BBreathed

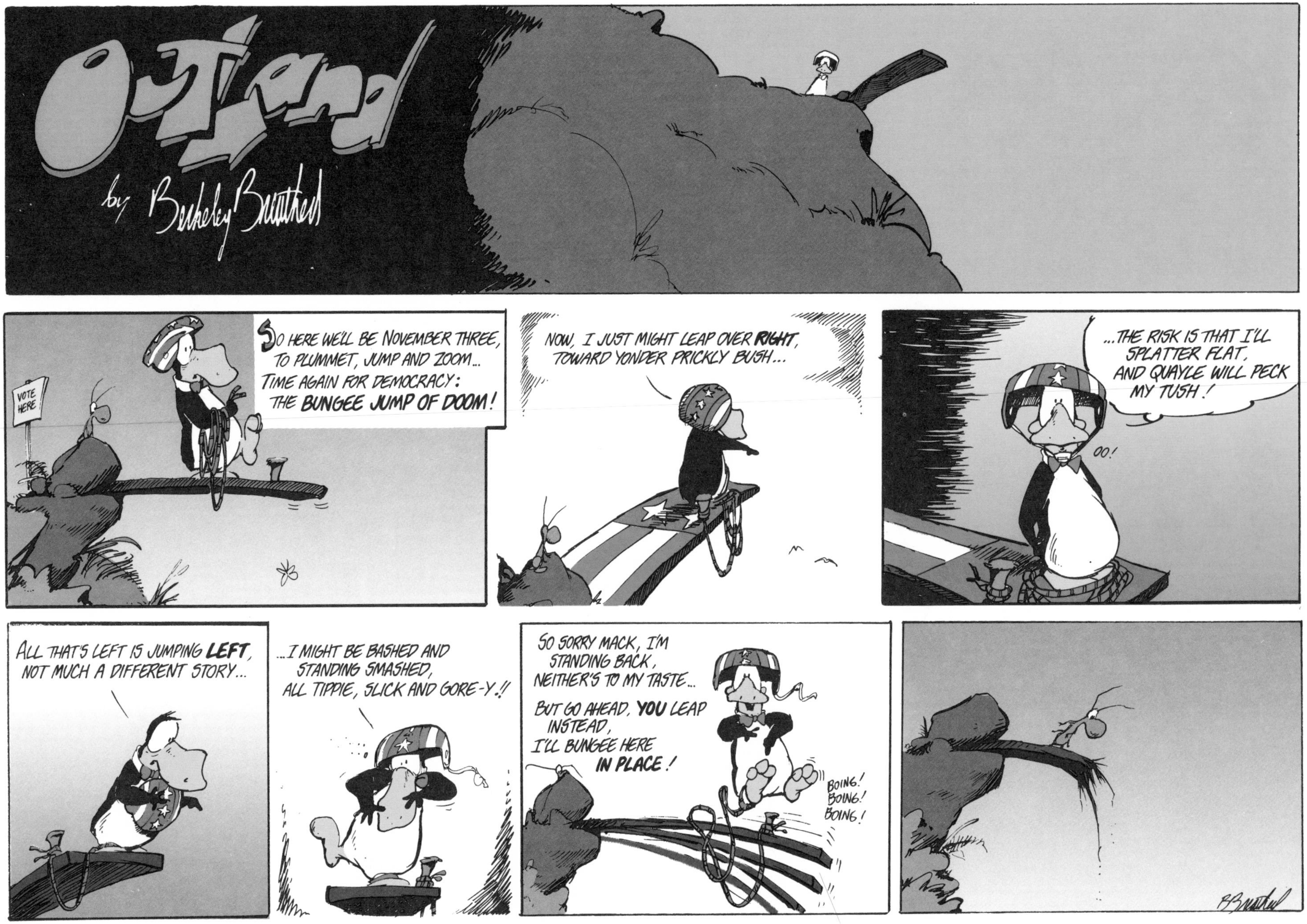
Outland
by Berkeley Breathed
VOTE HERE
So here we'll be November three, to plummet, jump and zoom... Time again for democracy: the BUNGEE JUMP OF DOOM!
Now, I just might leap over RIGHT, toward yonder prickly bush...
...The risk is that I'll splatter flat, and Quayle will peck my tush!
OO!
All that's left is jumping LEFT, not much a different story...
...I might be bashed and standing smashed, all tippie, slick and gore-y!!
So sorry Mack, I'm standing back, neither's to my taste...
But go ahead, YOU leap instead, I'll bungee here IN PLACE!
BOING! BOING! BOING!
B Breathed

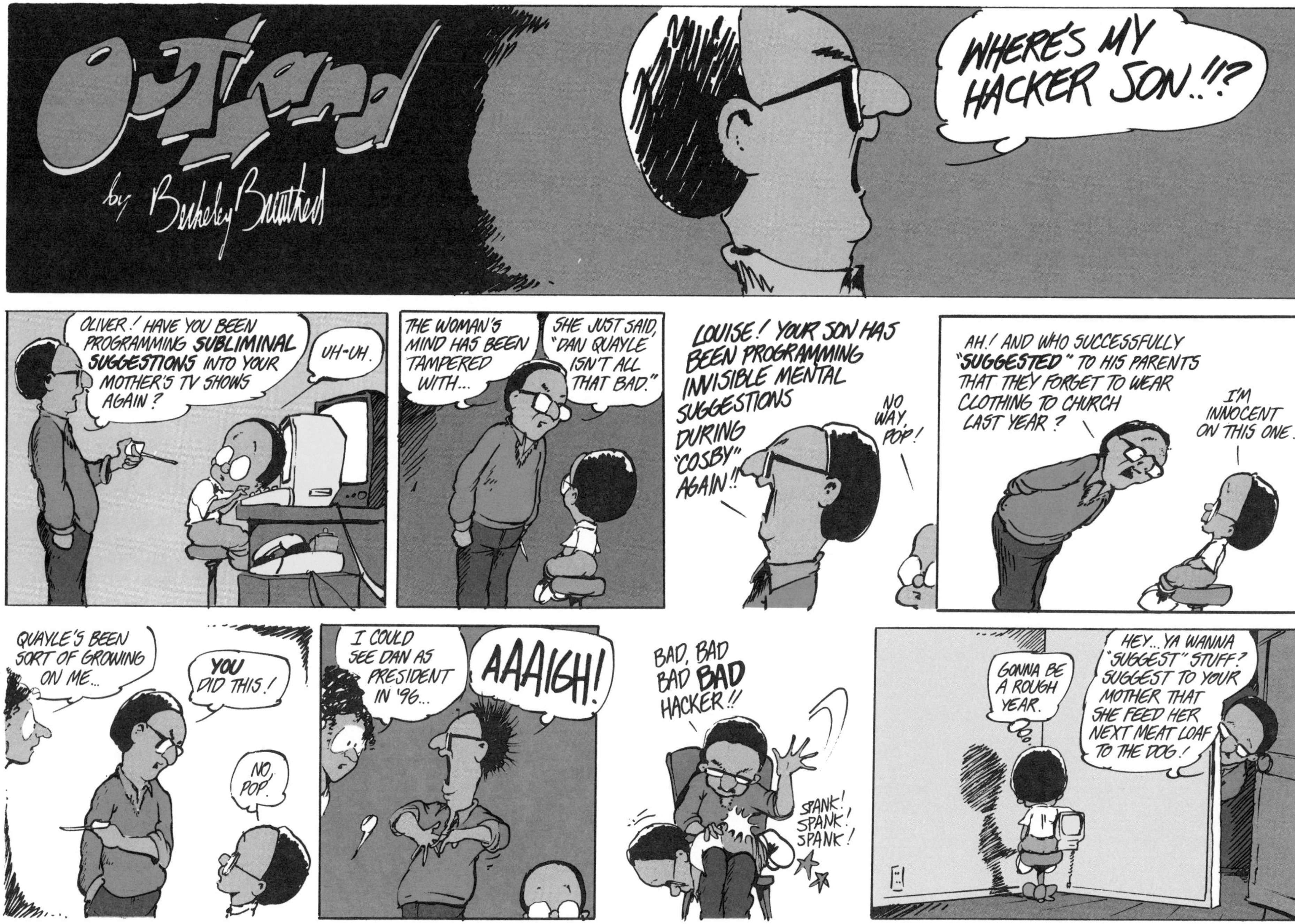
Outland
by Berkeley Breathed
WHERE'S MY HACKER SON..!!?
OLIVER! HAVE YOU BEEN PROGRAMMING SUBLIMINAL SUGGESTIONS INTO YOUR MOTHER'S TV SHOWS AGAIN?
UH-UH.
THE WOMAN'S MIND HAS BEEN TAMPERED WITH...
SHE JUST SAID, "DAN QUAYLE ISN'T ALL THAT BAD."
LOUISE! YOUR SON HAS BEEN PROGRAMMING INVISIBLE MENTAL SUGGESTIONS DURING "COSBY" AGAIN!!
NO WAY, POP!
AH! AND WHO SUCCESSFULLY "SUGGESTED" TO HIS PARENTS THAT THEY FORGET TO WEAR CLOTHING TO CHURCH LAST YEAR?
I'M INNOCENT ON THIS ONE.
QUAYLE'S BEEN SORT OF GROWING ON ME...
YOU DID THIS!
NO, POP.
I COULD SEE DAN AS PRESIDENT IN '96...
AAAIGH!
BAD, BAD BAD BAD HACKER!!
SPANK! SPANK! SPANK!
GONNA BE A ROUGH YEAR.
HEY... YA WANNA "SUGGEST" STUFF? SUGGEST TO YOUR MOTHER THAT SHE FEED HER NEXT MEAT LOAF TO THE DOG!

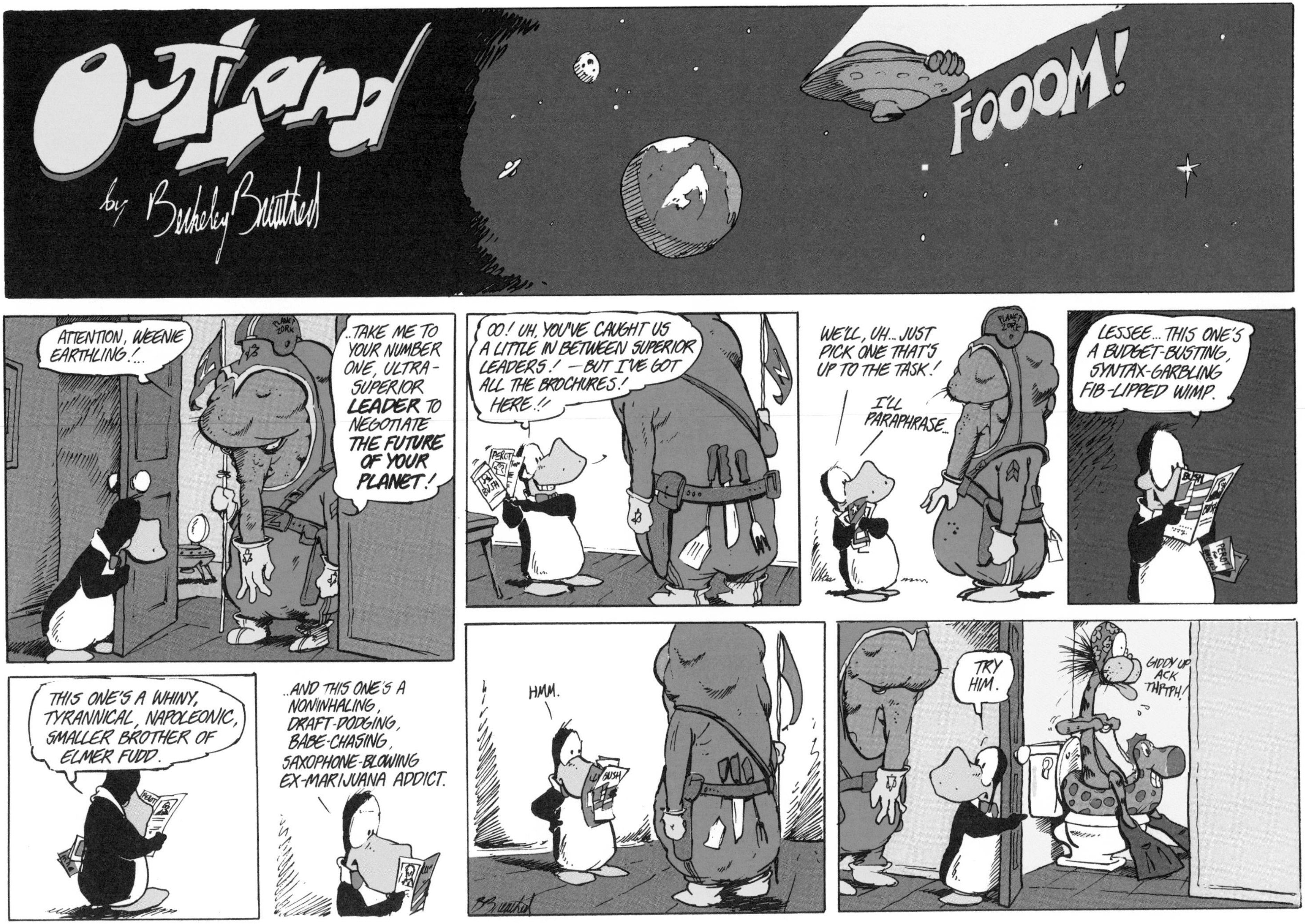
Outland
by Berkeley Breathed
FOOOM!
ATTENTION, WEENIE EARTHLING!...
...TAKE ME TO YOUR NUMBER ONE, ULTRA-SUPERIOR LEADER TO NEGOTIATE THE FUTURE OF YOUR PLANET!
PLANET ZORK
OO! UH, YOU'VE CAUGHT US A LITTLE IN BETWEEN SUPERIOR LEADERS! —BUT I'VE GOT ALL THE BROCHURES! HERE!!
WE'LL, UH... JUST PICK ONE THAT'S UP TO THE TASK!
I'LL PARAPHRASE...
LESSEE... THIS ONE'S A BUDGET-BUSTING, SYNTAX-GARBLING FIB-LIPPED WIMP.
BUSH
THIS ONE'S A WHINY, TYRANNICAL, NAPOLEONIC, SMALLER BROTHER OF ELMER FUDD.
...AND THIS ONE'S A NONINHALING, DRAFT-DODGING, BABE-CHASING, SAXOPHONE-BLOWING EX-MARIJUANA ADDICT.
HMM.
BUSH
TRY HIM.
GIDDY UP ACK THPTPH!

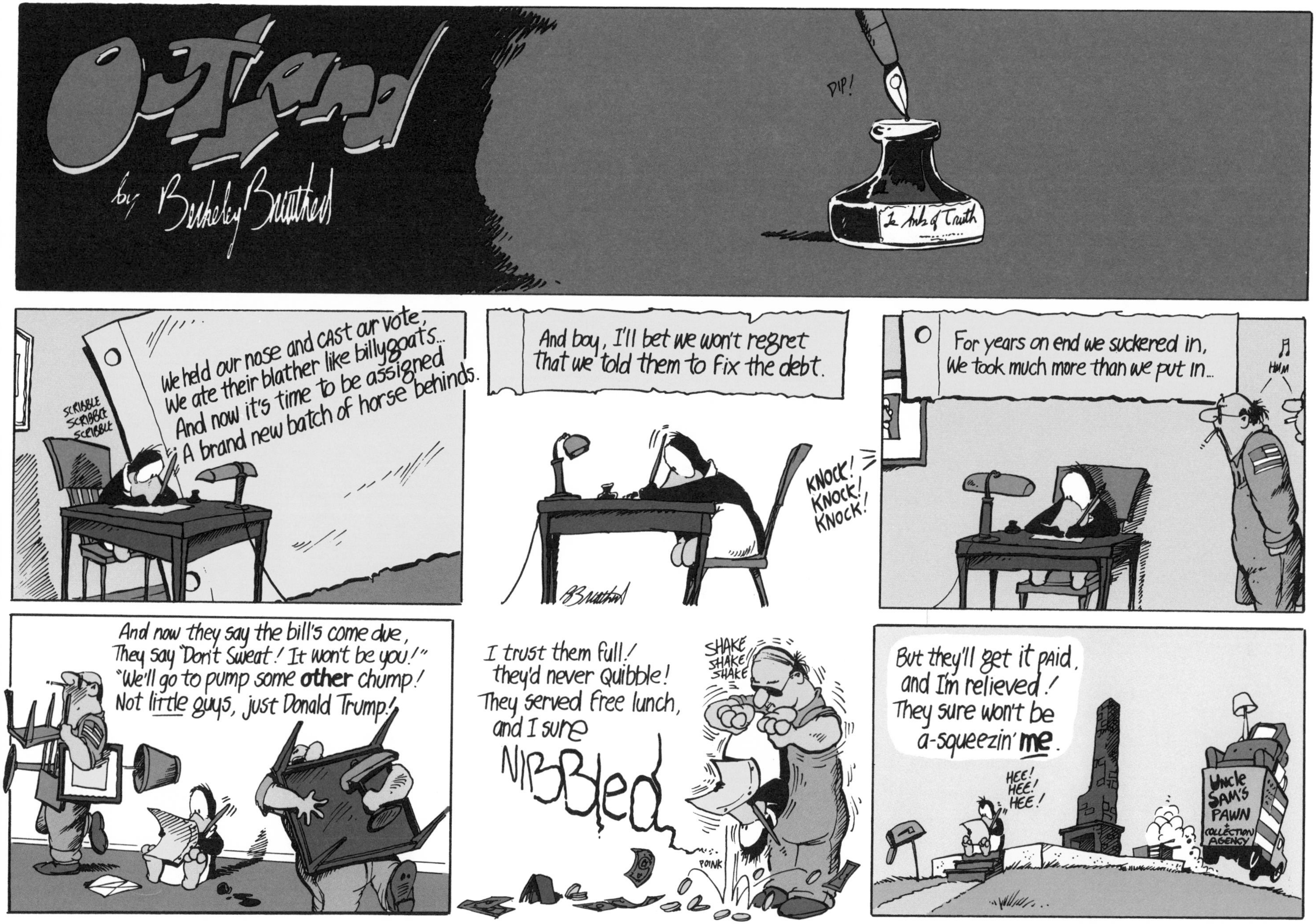

Outland
by Berkeley Breathed
DIP!
Ye Inks of Truth
SCRIBBLE SCRIBBLE SCRIBBLE
We held our nose and cast our vote, We ate their blather like billygoats... And now it's time to be assigned A brand new batch of horse behinds.
And boy, I'll bet we won't regret That we told them to fix the debt.
KNOCK! KNOCK! KNOCK!
B Breathed
For years on end we suckered in, We took much more than we put in...
HMM
And now they say the bill's come due, They say "Don't Sweat! It won't be you!" "We'll go to pump some other chump! Not little guys, just Donald Trump!"
I trust them full! they'd never Quibble! They served free lunch, and I sure NIBBled
SHAKE SHAKE SHAKE
POINK
But they'll get it paid, and I'm relieved! They sure won't be a-squeezin' me.
HEE! HEE! HEE!
Uncle Sam's Pawn + Collection Agency

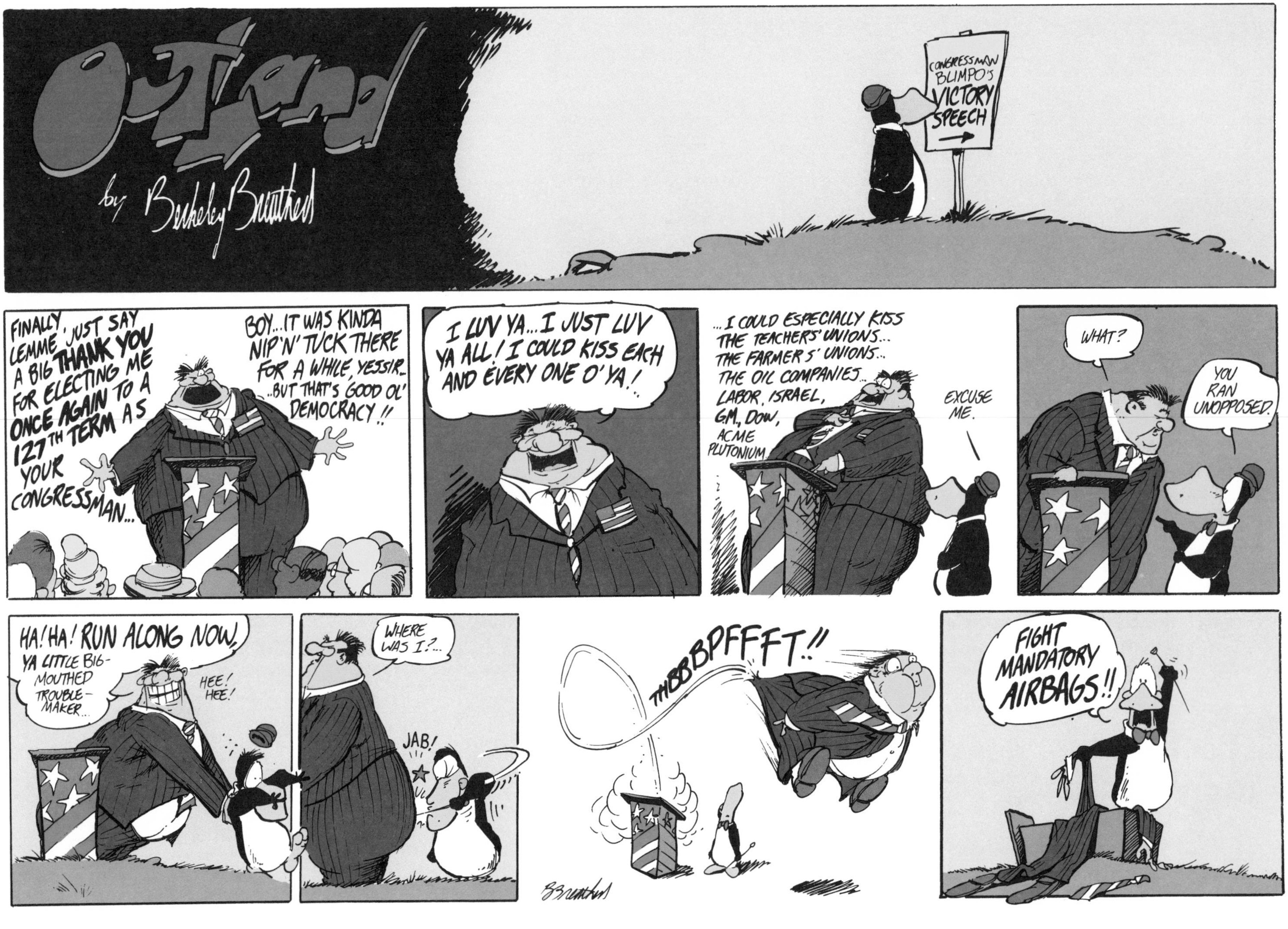
Outland
by Berkeley Breathed
CONGRESSMAN BLIMPO'S VICTORY SPEECH
FINALLY, LEMME JUST SAY A BIG THANK YOU FOR ELECTING ME ONCE AGAIN TO A 127TH TERM AS YOUR CONGRESSMAN...
BOY... IT WAS KINDA NIP 'N' TUCK THERE FOR A WHILE, YESSIR... ...BUT THAT'S GOOD OL' DEMOCRACY!!
I LUV YA... I JUST LUV YA ALL! I COULD KISS EACH AND EVERY ONE O' YA!..
...I COULD ESPECIALLY KISS THE TEACHERS' UNIONS... THE FARMERS' UNIONS... THE OIL COMPANIES... LABOR, ISRAEL, GM, DOW, ACME PLUTONIUM...
EXCUSE ME.
WHAT?
YOU RAN UNOPPOSED.
HA! HA! RUN ALONG NOW, YA LITTLE BIG-MOUTHED TROUBLE-MAKER...
HEE! HEE!
WHERE WAS I?...
JAB!
THBBBPFFFFT!!
FIGHT MANDATORY AIRBAGS!!
B Breathed

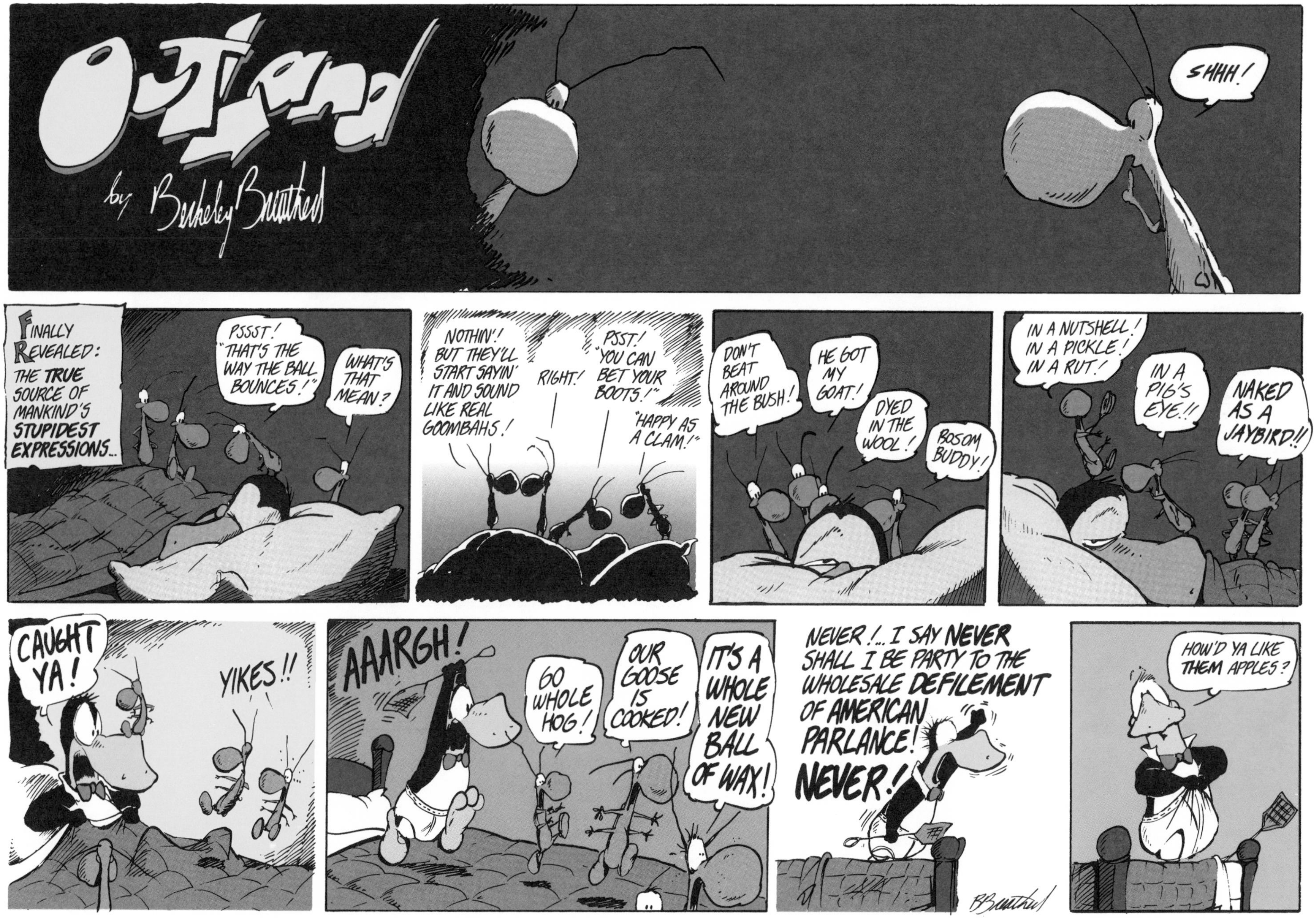
Outland
by Berkeley Breathed
SHHH!
FINALLY REVEALED: THE TRUE SOURCE OF MANKIND'S STUPIDEST EXPRESSIONS...
PSSST! "THAT'S THE WAY THE BALL BOUNCES!"
WHAT'S THAT MEAN?
NOTHIN'! BUT THEY'LL START SAYIN' IT AND SOUND LIKE REAL GOOMBAHS!
RIGHT!
PSST! "YOU CAN BET YOUR BOOTS!"
"HAPPY AS A CLAM!"
DON'T BEAT AROUND THE BUSH!
HE GOT MY GOAT!
DYED IN THE WOOL!
BOSOM BUDDY!
IN A NUTSHELL! IN A PICKLE! IN A RUT!
IN A PIG'S EYE!!
NAKED AS A JAYBIRD!!
CAUGHT YA!
YIKES!!
AAARGH!
GO WHOLE HOG!
OUR GOOSE IS COOKED!
IT'S A WHOLE NEW BALL OF WAX!
NEVER!... I SAY NEVER SHALL I BE PARTY TO THE WHOLESALE DEFILEMENT OF AMERICAN PARLANCE! NEVER!
BBreathed
HOW'D YA LIKE THEM APPLES?

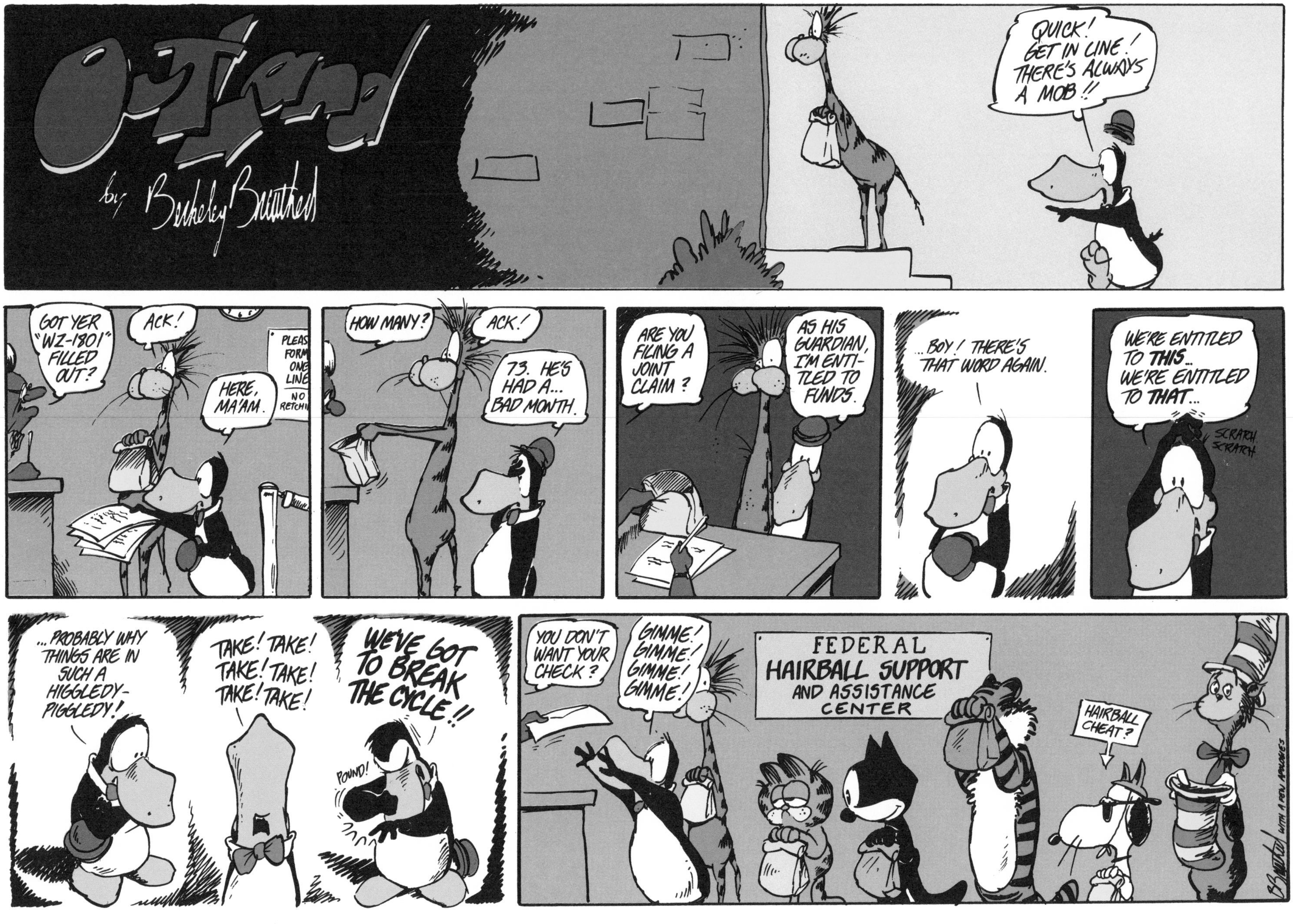
Outland
by Berkeley Breathed
QUICK! GET IN LINE! THERE'S ALWAYS A MOB!!
GOT YER "WZ-1801" FILLED OUT?
ACK!
HERE, MA'AM.
HOW MANY?
ACK!
73. HE'S HAD A... BAD MONTH.
ARE YOU FILING A JOINT CLAIM?
AS HIS GUARDIAN, I'M ENTITLED TO FUNDS.
...BOY! THERE'S THAT WORD AGAIN.
WE'RE ENTITLED TO THIS... WE'RE ENTITLED TO THAT...
SCRATCH SCRATCH
...PROBABLY WHY THINGS ARE IN SUCH A HIGGLEDY-PIGGLEDY!
TAKE! TAKE! TAKE! TAKE! TAKE! TAKE!
WE'VE GOT TO BREAK THE CYCLE!!
POUND!
YOU DON'T WANT YOUR CHECK?
GIMME! GIMME! GIMME! GIMME!
FEDERAL HAIRBALL SUPPORT AND ASSISTANCE CENTER
HAIRBALL CHEAT?
WITH A FEW APOLOGIES

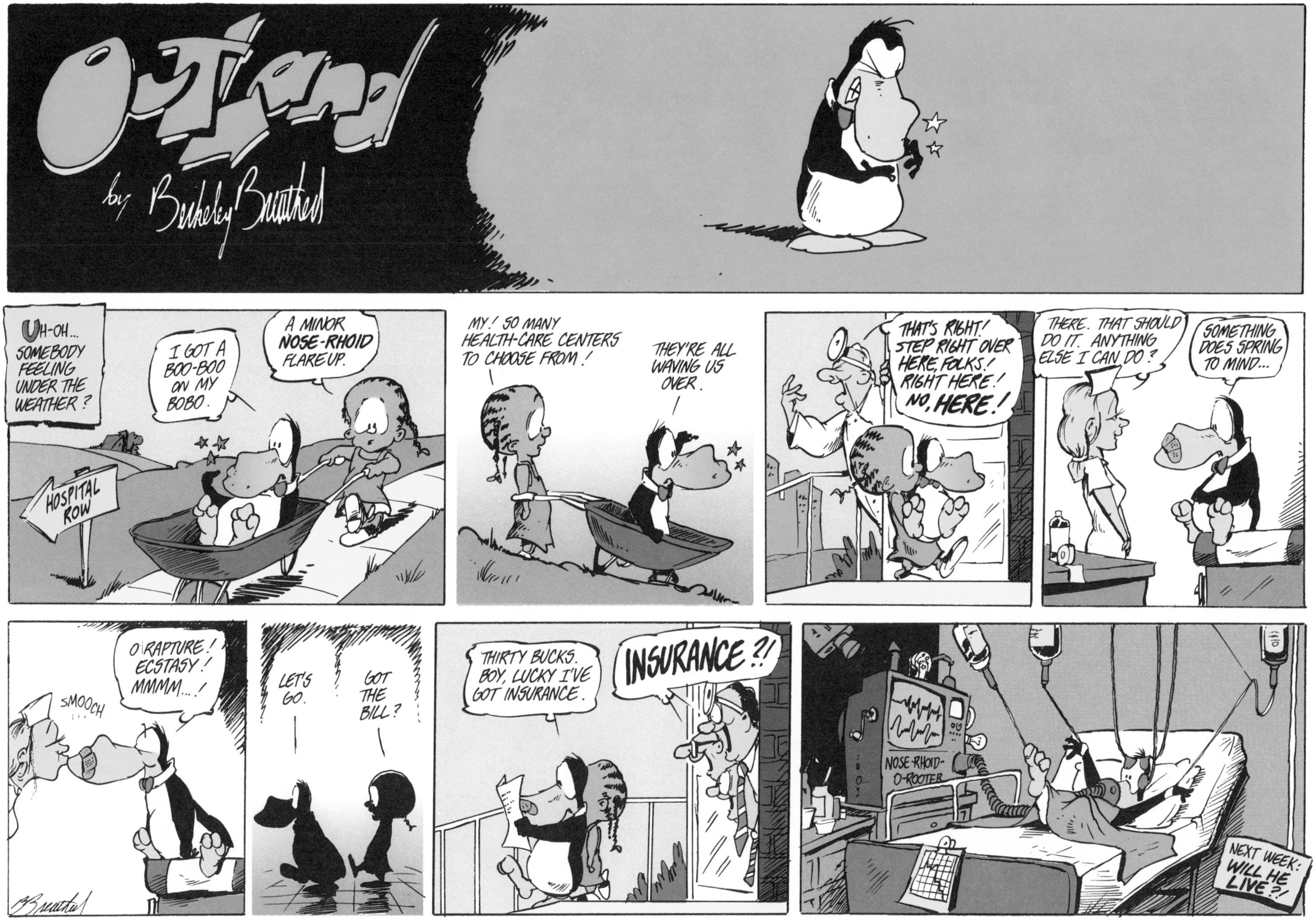
Outland
by Berkeley Breathed
UH-OH... SOMEBODY FEELING UNDER THE WEATHER?
I GOT A BOO-BOO ON MY BOBO.
A MINOR NOSE-RHOID FLARE-UP.
HOSPITAL ROW
MY! SO MANY HEALTH-CARE CENTERS TO CHOOSE FROM!
THEY'RE ALL WAVING US OVER.
THAT'S RIGHT! STEP RIGHT OVER HERE, FOLKS! RIGHT HERE! NO, HERE!
THERE. THAT SHOULD DO IT. ANYTHING ELSE I CAN DO?
SOMETHING DOES SPRING TO MIND...
SMOOCH
O RAPTURE! ECSTASY! MMMM...!
LET'S GO.
GOT THE BILL?
THIRTY BUCKS. BOY, LUCKY I'VE GOT INSURANCE.
INSURANCE?!
NOSE-RHOID-O-ROOTER
NEXT WEEK: WILL HE LIVE?!

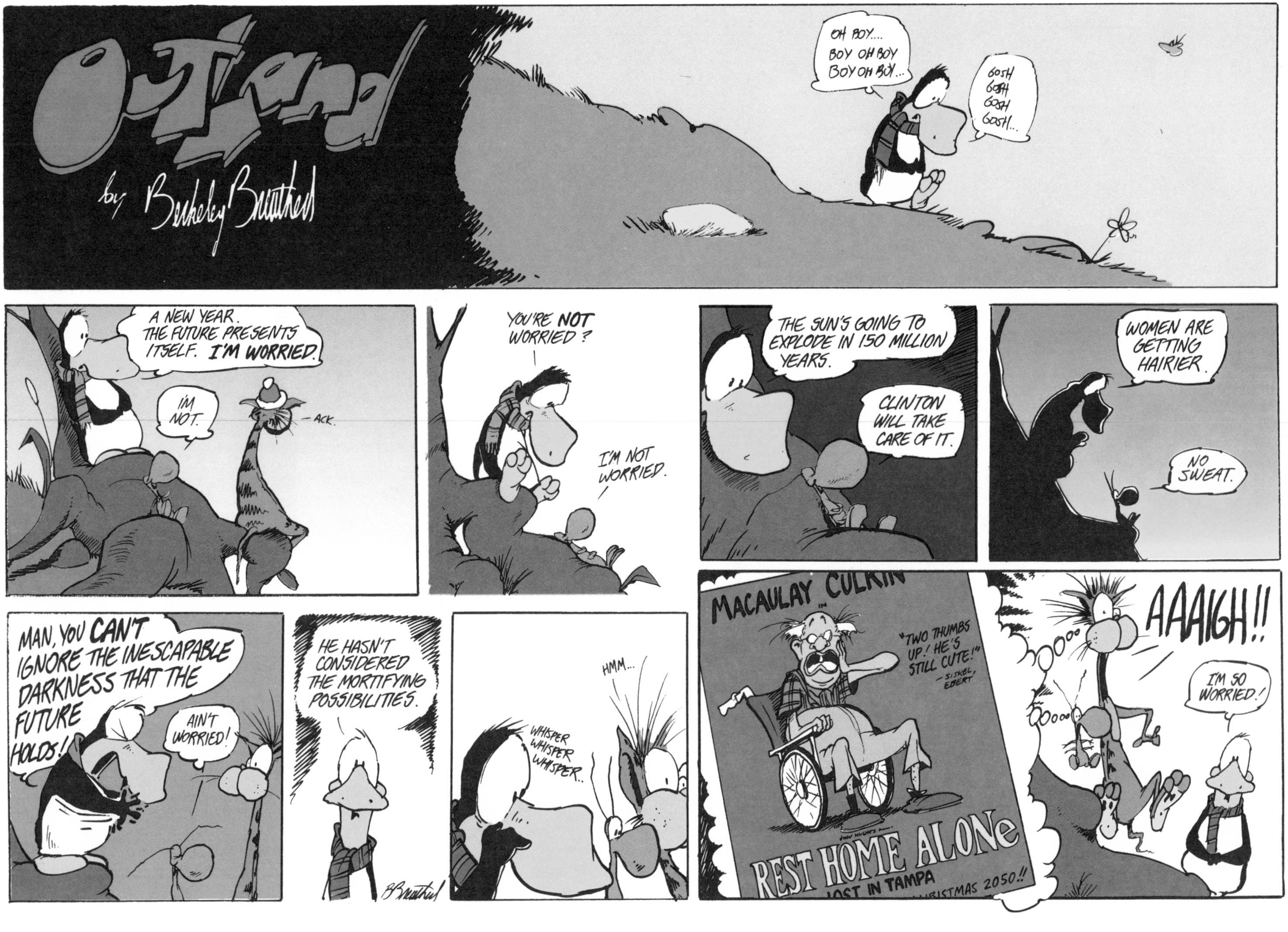
Outland
by Berkeley Breathed
OH BOY.... BOY OH BOY BOY OH BOY...
GOSH GOSH GOSH GOSH...
A NEW YEAR. THE FUTURE PRESENTS ITSELF. I'M WORRIED.
I'M NOT.
ACK.
YOU'RE NOT WORRIED?
I'M NOT WORRIED.
THE SUN'S GOING TO EXPLODE IN 150 MILLION YEARS.
CLINTON WILL TAKE CARE OF IT.
WOMEN ARE GETTING HAIRIER.
NO SWEAT.
MAN, YOU CAN'T IGNORE THE INESCAPABLE DARKNESS THAT THE FUTURE HOLDS!
AIN'T WORRIED!
HE HASN'T CONSIDERED THE MORTIFYING POSSIBILITIES.
HMM...
WHISPER WHISPER WHISPER...
MACAULAY CULKIN IN
"TWO THUMBS UP! HE'S STILL CUTE!" -SISKEL, EBERT
REST HOME ALONE
LOST IN TAMPA
AAAIGH!!
I'M SO WORRIED!
BBreathed

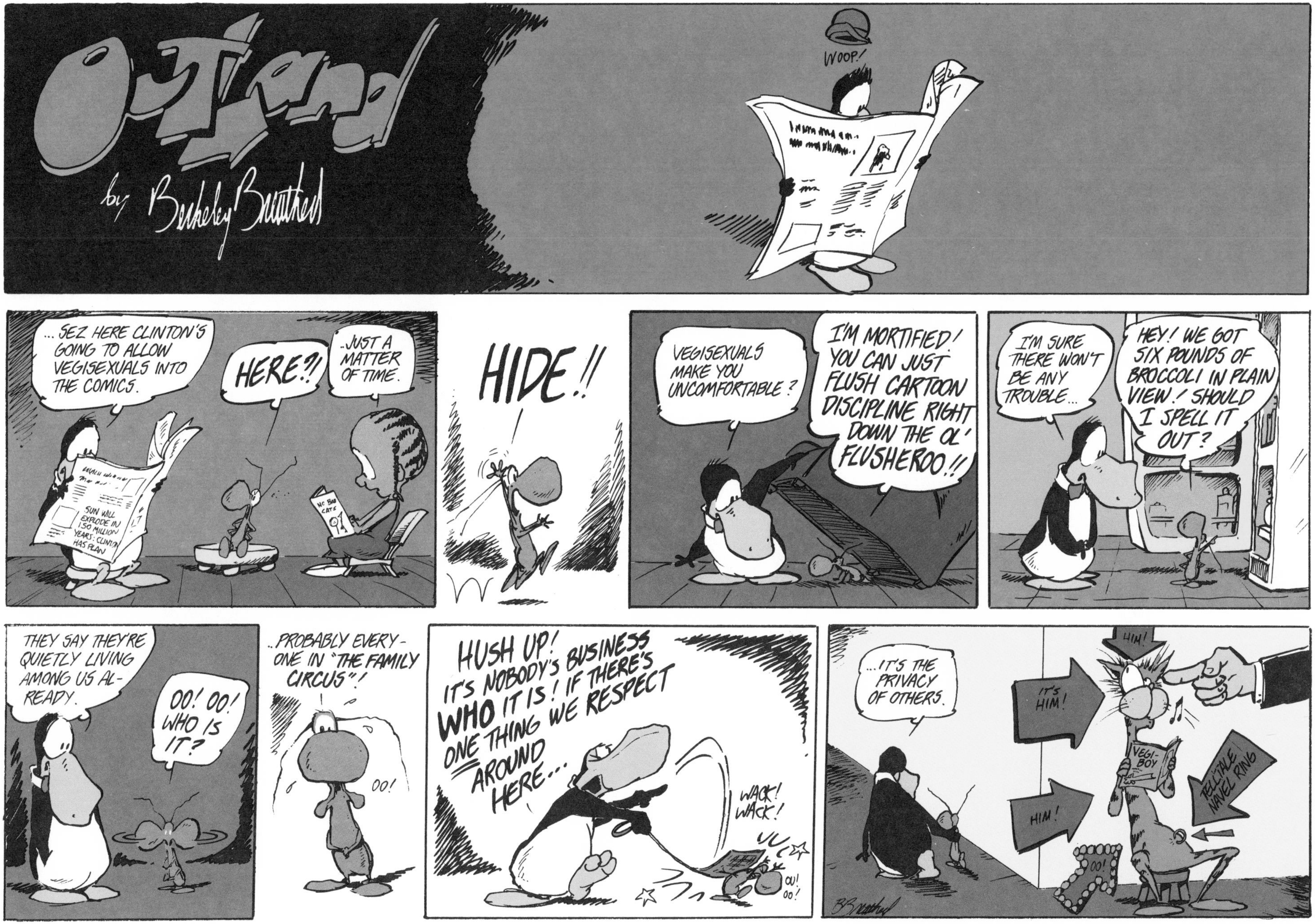
Outland
by Berkeley Breathed
WOOP!
...SEZ HERE CLINTON'S GOING TO ALLOW VEGISEXUALS INTO THE COMICS.
SUN WILL EXPLODE IN 150 MILLION YEARS: CLINTON HAS PLAN
HERE?!
...JUST A MATTER OF TIME.
HIDE!!
VEGISEXUALS MAKE YOU UNCOMFORTABLE?
I'M MORTIFIED! YOU CAN JUST FLUSH CARTOON DISCIPLINE RIGHT DOWN THE OL' FLUSHEROO!!
I'M SURE THERE WON'T BE ANY TROUBLE...
HEY! WE GOT SIX POUNDS OF BROCCOLI IN PLAIN VIEW! SHOULD I SPELL IT OUT?
THEY SAY THEY'RE QUIETLY LIVING AMONG US AL-READY.
OO! OO! WHO IS IT?
..PROBABLY EVERY-ONE IN "THE FAMILY CIRCUS"!
OO!
HUSH UP! IT'S NOBODY'S BUSINESS WHO IT IS! IF THERE'S ONE THING WE RESPECT AROUND HERE...
WACK! WACK!
OU! OO!
...IT'S THE PRIVACY OF OTHERS.
HIM!
IT'S HIM!
HIM!
VEGI-BOY
TELLTALE NAVEL RING
OO!
B. Breathed

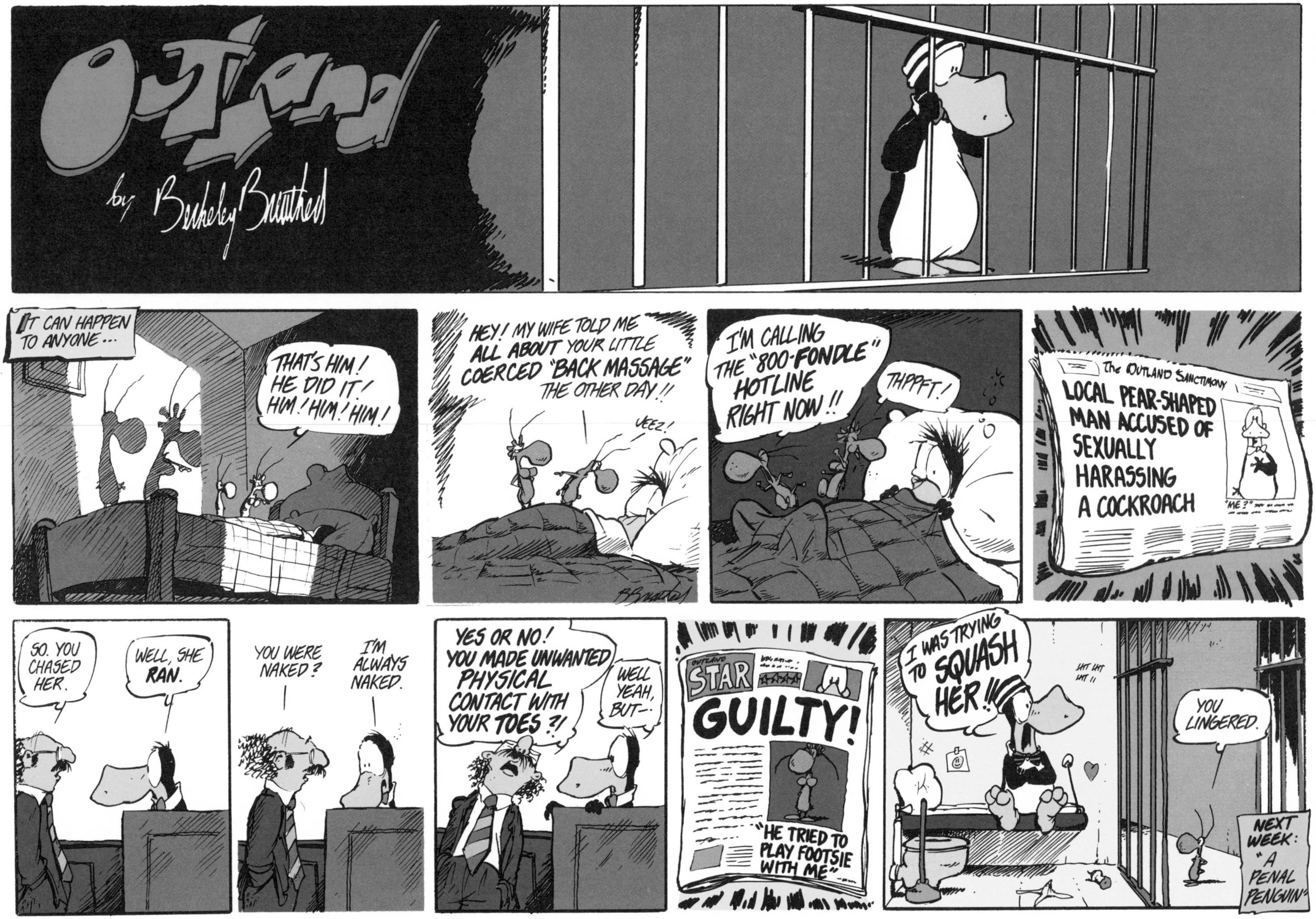
Outland
by Berkeley Breathed
IT CAN HAPPEN TO ANYONE...
THAT'S HIM! HE DID IT! HIM! HIM! HIM!
HEY! MY WIFE TOLD ME ALL ABOUT YOUR LITTLE COERCED "BACK MASSAGE" THE OTHER DAY!!
JEEZ!
I'M CALLING THE "800-FONDLE" HOTLINE RIGHT NOW!!
THPPFT!
The OUTLAND SANCTIMONY
LOCAL PEAR-SHAPED MAN ACCUSED OF SEXUALLY HARASSING A COCKROACH
"ME?"
SO. YOU CHASED HER.
WELL, SHE RAN.
YOU WERE NAKED?
I'M ALWAYS NAKED.
YES OR NO! YOU MADE UNWANTED PHYSICAL CONTACT WITH YOUR TOES?!
WELL YEAH, BUT--
OUTLAND STAR
GUILTY!
"HE TRIED TO PLAY FOOTSIE WITH ME"
I WAS TRYING TO SQUASH HER!!!
YOU LINGERED.
NEXT WEEK: "A PENAL PENGUIN"

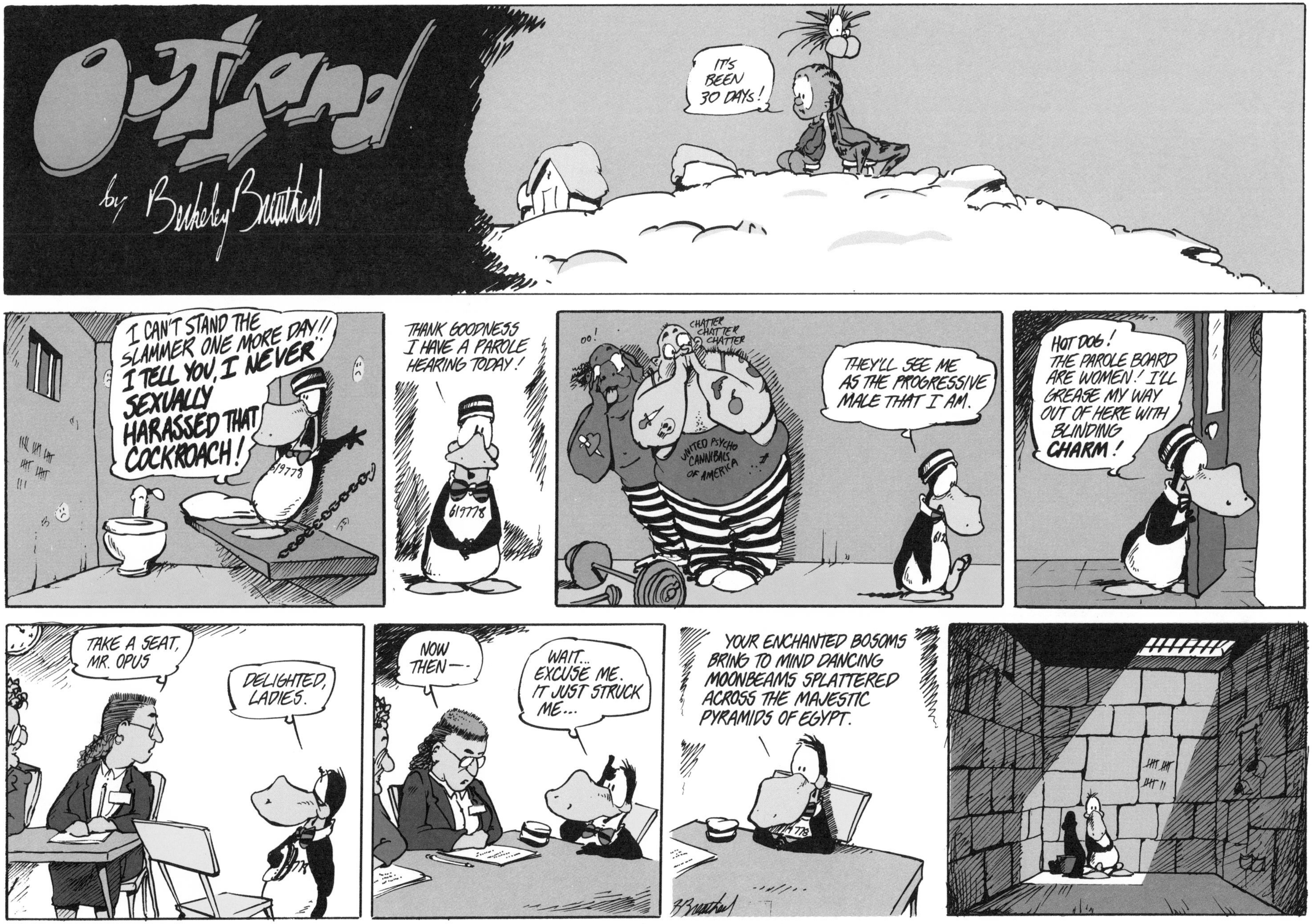
Outland
by Berkeley Breathed
IT'S BEEN 30 DAYS!
I CAN'T STAND THE SLAMMER ONE MORE DAY!! I TELL YOU, I NEVER SEXUALLY HARASSED THAT COCKROACH!
619778
THANK GOODNESS I HAVE A PAROLE HEARING TODAY!
619778
OO!
CHATTER CHATTER CHATTER
UNITED PSYCHO CANNIBALS OF AMERICA
THEY'LL SEE ME AS THE PROGRESSIVE MALE THAT I AM.
HOT DOG! THE PAROLE BOARD ARE WOMEN! I'LL GREASE MY WAY OUT OF HERE WITH BLINDING CHARM!
TAKE A SEAT, MR. OPUS
DELIGHTED, LADIES.
NOW THEN—.
WAIT... EXCUSE ME. IT JUST STRUCK ME...
YOUR ENCHANTED BOSOMS BRING TO MIND DANCING MOONBEAMS SPLATTERED ACROSS THE MAJESTIC PYRAMIDS OF EGYPT.
B. Breathed

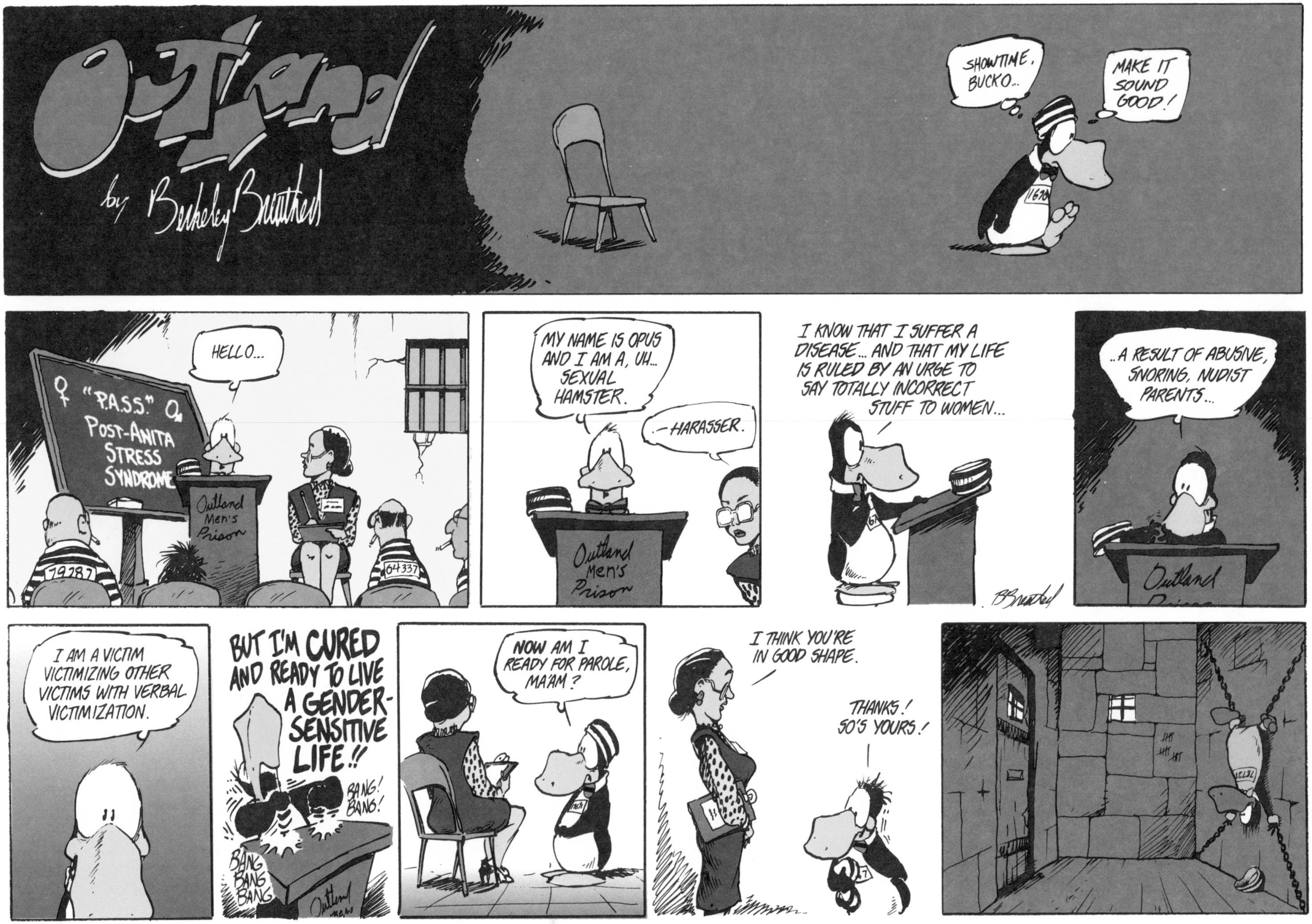
Outland
by Berkeley Breathed
SHOWTIME, BUCKO...
MAKE IT SOUND GOOD!
HELLO...
♀ "P.A.S.S." ♂ POST-ANITA STRESS SYNDROME
Outland Men's Prison
MY NAME IS OPUS AND I AM A, UH... SEXUAL HAMSTER.
—HARASSER.
Outland Men's Prison
I KNOW THAT I SUFFER A DISEASE... AND THAT MY LIFE IS RULED BY AN URGE TO SAY TOTALLY INCORRECT STUFF TO WOMEN...
..A RESULT OF ABUSIVE, SNORING, NUDIST PARENTS...
I AM A VICTIM VICTIMIZING OTHER VICTIMS WITH VERBAL VICTIMIZATION.
BUT I'M CURED AND READY TO LIVE A GENDER-SENSITIVE LIFE!!
BANG! BANG!
BANG BANG BANG
NOW AM I READY FOR PAROLE, MA'AM?
I THINK YOU'RE IN GOOD SHAPE.
THANKS! SO'S YOURS!

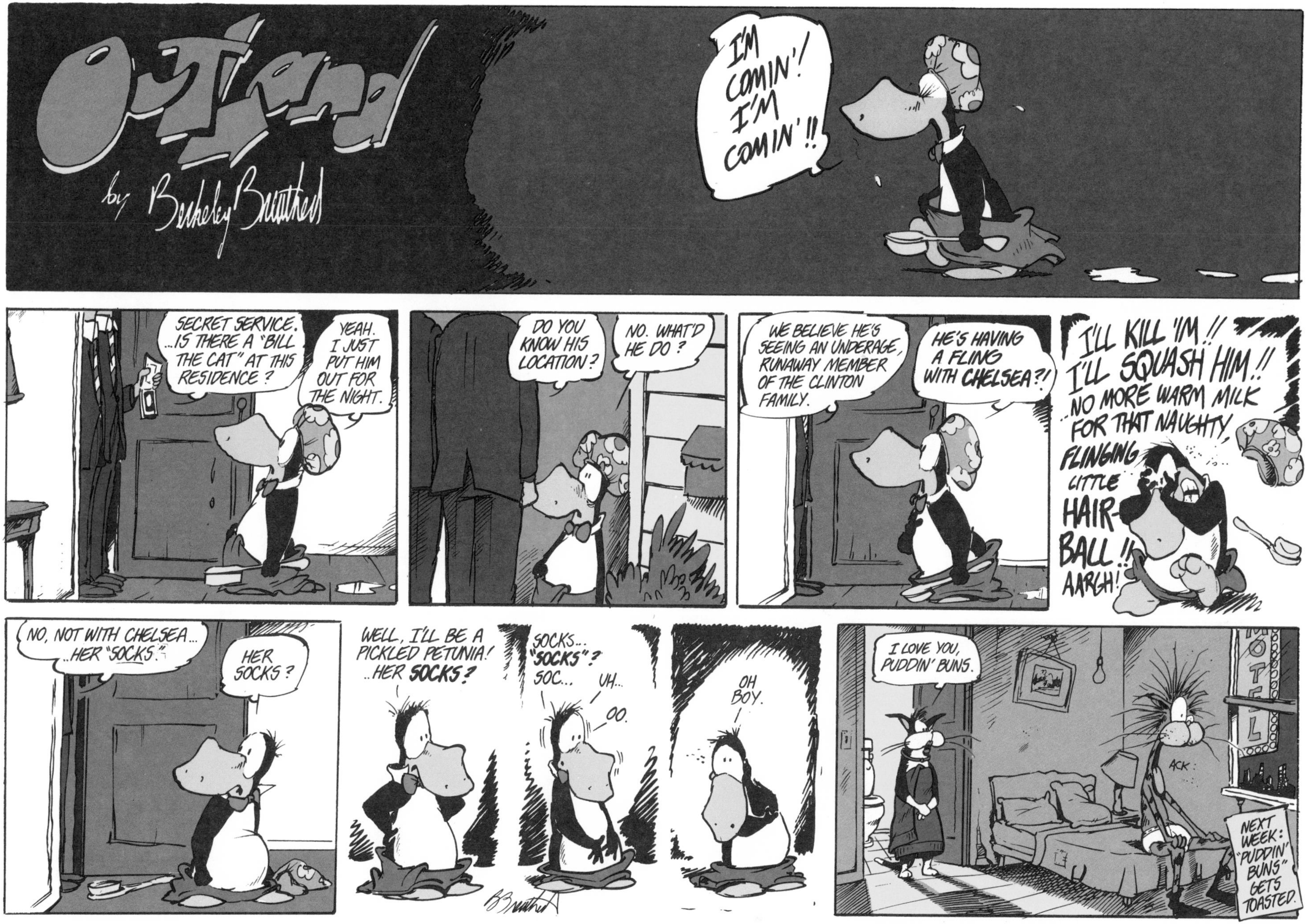
Outland
by Berkeley Breathed
I'M COMIN'! I'M COMIN'!!
SECRET SERVICE. ...IS THERE A "BILL THE CAT" AT THIS RESIDENCE?
YEAH. I JUST PUT HIM OUT FOR THE NIGHT.
DO YOU KNOW HIS LOCATION?
NO. WHAT'D HE DO?
WE BELIEVE HE'S SEEING AN UNDERAGE, RUNAWAY MEMBER OF THE CLINTON FAMILY.
HE'S HAVING A FLING WITH CHELSEA?!
I'LL KILL 'IM!! I'LL SQUASH HIM!! ..NO MORE WARM MILK FOR THAT NAUGHTY, FLINGING LITTLE HAIR-BALL!! AARGH!
NO, NOT WITH CHELSEA... ..HER "SOCKS."
HER SOCKS?
WELL, I'LL BE A PICKLED PETUNIA! ..HER SOCKS?
SOCKS... "SOCKS"? SOC...
UH... OO.
OH BOY.
I LOVE YOU, PUDDIN' BUNS.
ACK
MOTEL
NEXT WEEK: "PUDDIN' BUNS" GETS TOASTED.
B. Breathed

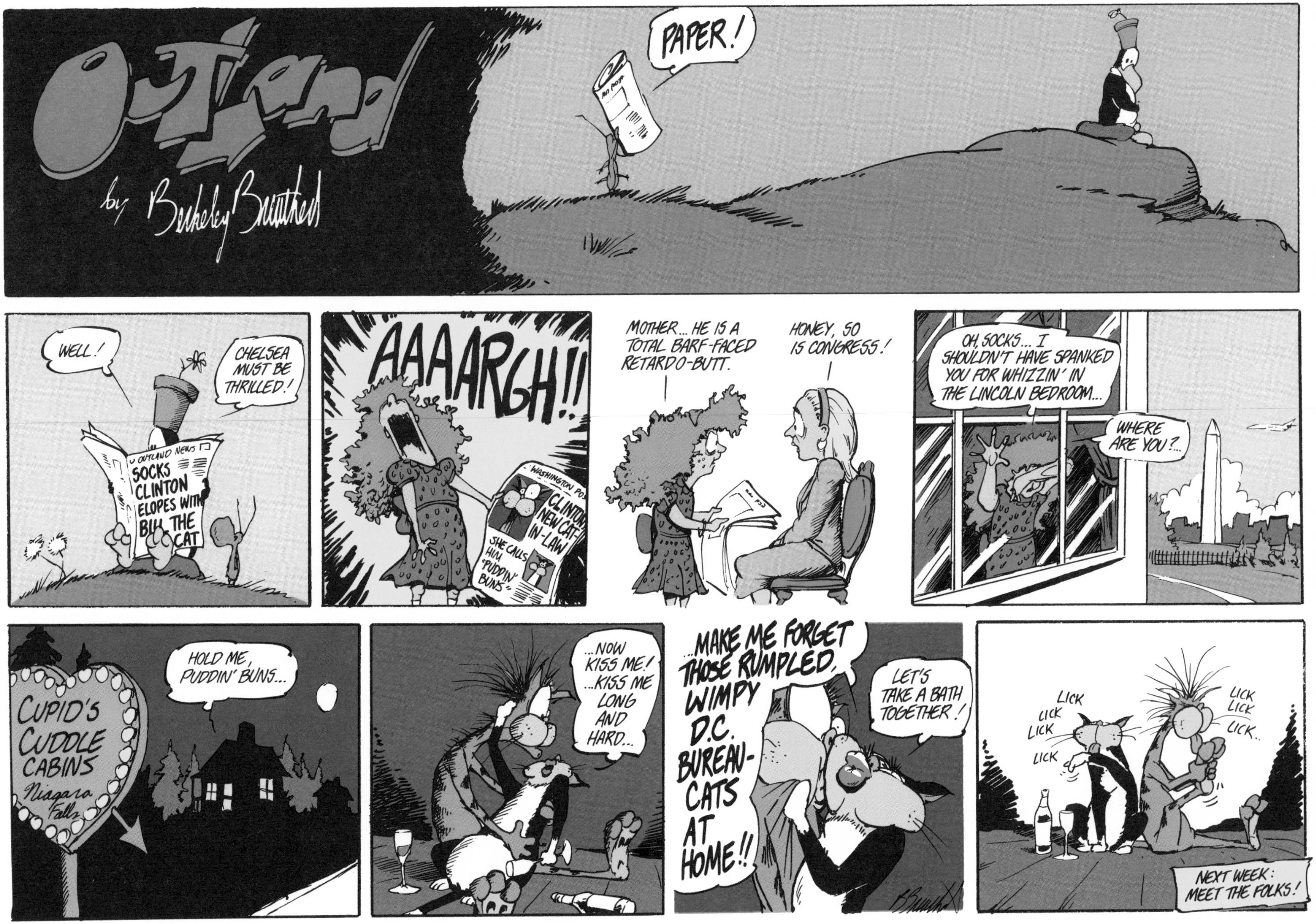
Outland
by Berkeley Breathed
PAPER!
WELL!
CHELSEA MUST BE THRILLED!
OUTLAND NEWS
SOCKS CLINTON ELOPES WITH BILL THE CAT
AAAARGH!!!
WASHINGTON PO
CLINTON NEW CAT-IN-LAW
SHE CALLS HIM "PUDDIN' BUNS"
MOTHER... HE IS A TOTAL BARF-FACED RETARDO-BUTT.
HONEY, SO IS CONGRESS!
OH, SOCKS... I SHOULDN'T HAVE SPANKED YOU FOR WHIZZIN' IN THE LINCOLN BEDROOM...
WHERE ARE YOU?...
CUPID'S CUDDLE CABINS
Niagara Falls
HOLD ME, PUDDIN' BUNS...
...NOW KISS ME! ...KISS ME LONG AND HARD...
...MAKE ME FORGET THOSE RUMPLED, WIMPY D.C. BUREAU-CATS AT HOME!!
LET'S TAKE A BATH TOGETHER!
LICK
LICK
LICK
LICK
LICK
LICK
LICK..
NEXT WEEK: MEET THE FOLKS!

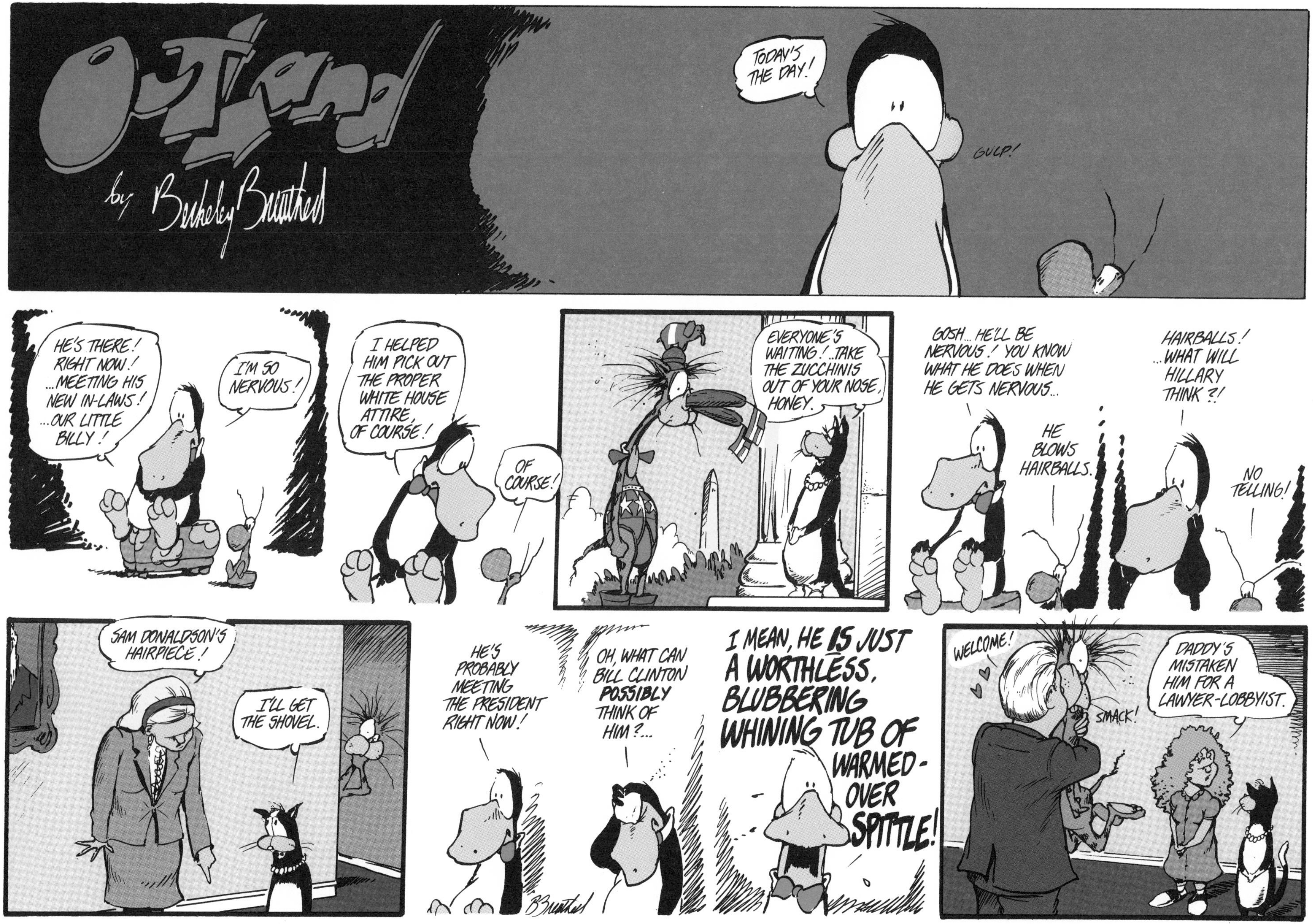
Outland
by Berkeley Breathed
TODAY'S THE DAY!
GULP!
HE'S THERE! RIGHT NOW! ...MEETING HIS NEW IN-LAWS! ...OUR LITTLE BILLY!
I'M SO NERVOUS!
I HELPED HIM PICK OUT THE PROPER WHITE HOUSE ATTIRE, OF COURSE!
OF COURSE!
EVERYONE'S WAITING! ..TAKE THE ZUCCHINIS OUT OF YOUR NOSE, HONEY.
GOSH... HE'LL BE NERVOUS! YOU KNOW WHAT HE DOES WHEN HE GETS NERVOUS...
HE BLOWS HAIRBALLS.
HAIRBALLS! ...WHAT WILL HILLARY THINK ?!
NO TELLING!
SAM DONALDSON'S HAIRPIECE!
I'LL GET THE SHOVEL.
HE'S PROBABLY MEETING THE PRESIDENT RIGHT NOW!
OH, WHAT CAN BILL CLINTON POSSIBLY THINK OF HIM?...
I MEAN, HE IS JUST A WORTHLESS, BLUBBERING WHINING TUB OF WARMED-OVER SPITTLE!
WELCOME!
SMACK!
DADDY'S MISTAKEN HIM FOR A LAWYER-LOBBYIST.
B Breathed

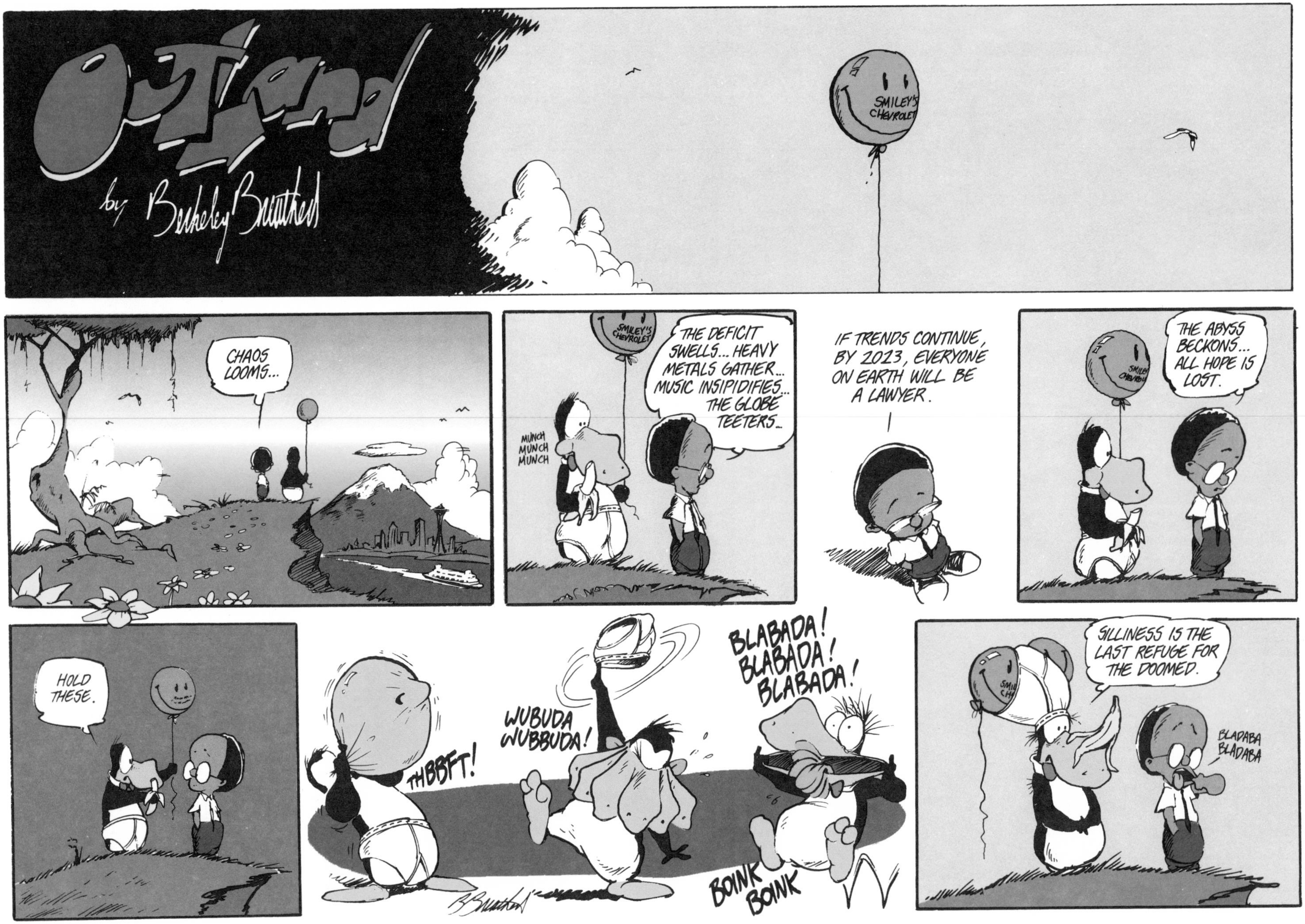

Outland
by Berkeley Breathed
SMILEY'S CHEVROLET
CHAOS LOOMS...
SMILEY'S CHEVROLET
THE DEFICIT SWELLS... HEAVY METALS GATHER... MUSIC INSIPIDIFIES... THE GLOBE TEETERS...
MUNCH MUNCH MUNCH
IF TRENDS CONTINUE, BY 2023, EVERYONE ON EARTH WILL BE A LAWYER.
THE ABYSS BECKONS... ALL HOPE IS LOST.
HOLD THESE.
THBBFT!
WUBUDA WUBBUDA!
BLABADA! BLABADA! BLABADA!
BOINK BOINK
B. Breathed
SILLINESS IS THE LAST REFUGE FOR THE DOOMED.
BLADABA BLADABA

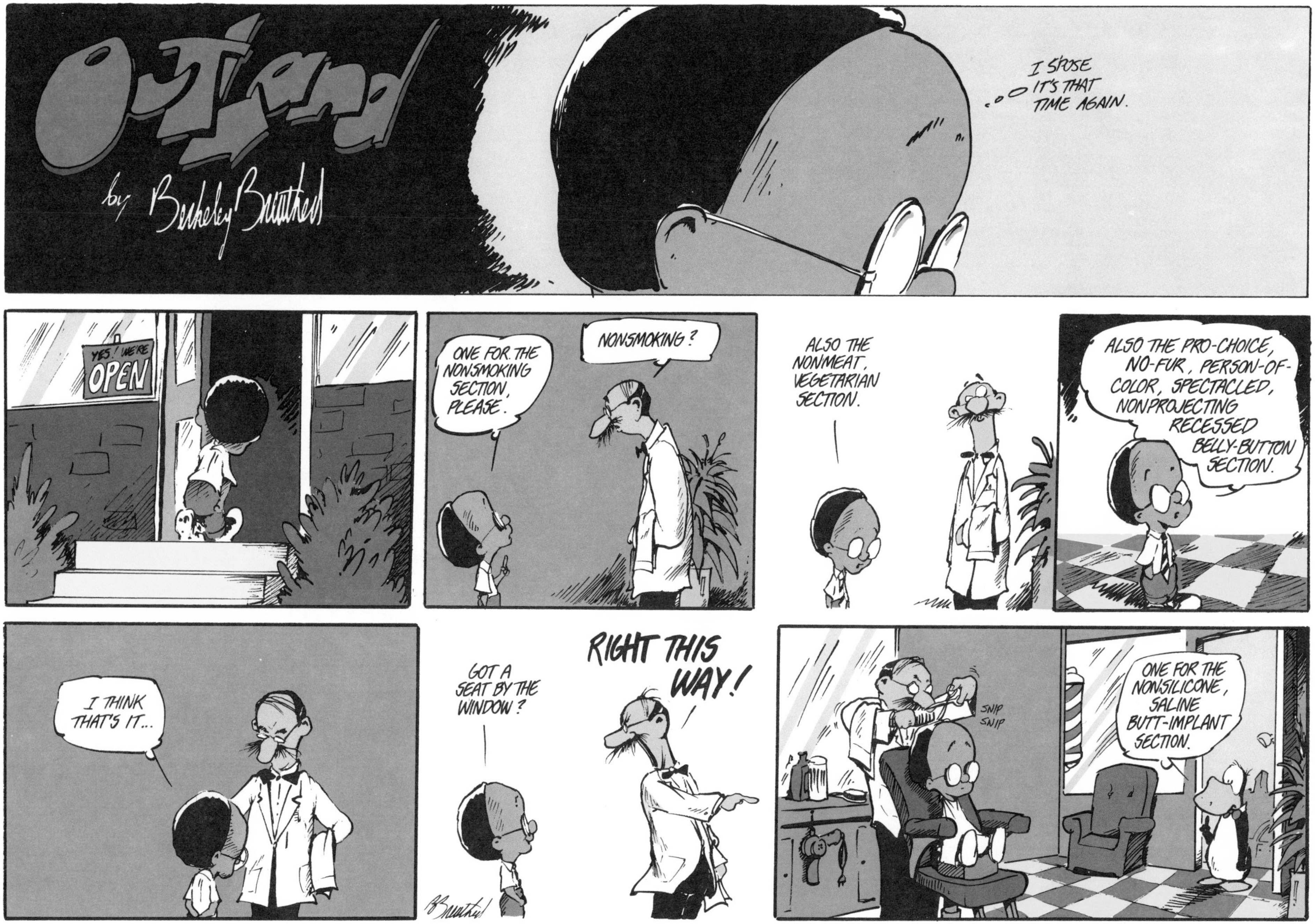
Outland
by Berkeley Breathed
I S'POSE IT'S THAT TIME AGAIN.
YES! WE'RE OPEN
ONE FOR THE NONSMOKING SECTION, PLEASE.
NONSMOKING?
ALSO THE NONMEAT, VEGETARIAN SECTION.
ALSO THE PRO-CHOICE, NO-FUR, PERSON-OF-COLOR, SPECTACLED, NONPROJECTING RECESSED BELLY-BUTTON SECTION.
I THINK THAT'S IT...
GOT A SEAT BY THE WINDOW?
RIGHT THIS WAY!
B Breathed
SNIP SNIP
ONE FOR THE NONSILICONE, SALINE BUTT-IMPLANT SECTION.

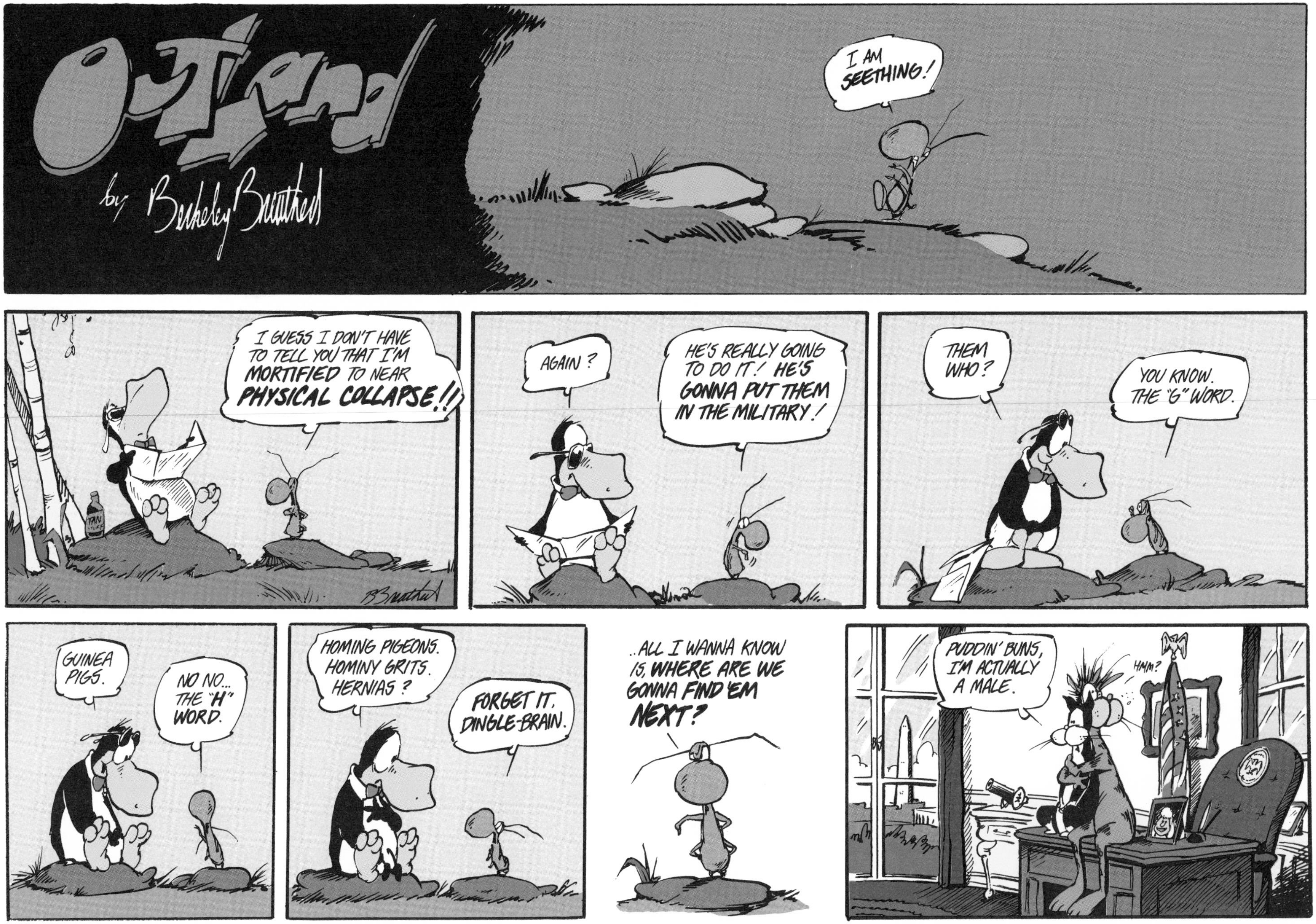
Outland
by Berkeley Breathed
I AM SEETHING!
I GUESS I DON'T HAVE TO TELL YOU THAT I'M MORTIFIED TO NEAR PHYSICAL COLLAPSE!!
AGAIN?
HE'S REALLY GOING TO DO IT! HE'S GONNA PUT THEM IN THE MILITARY!
THEM WHO?
YOU KNOW. THE "G" WORD.
GUINEA PIGS.
NO NO... THE "H" WORD.
HOMING PIGEONS. HOMINY GRITS. HERNIAS?
FORGET IT, DINGLE-BRAIN.
..ALL I WANNA KNOW IS, WHERE ARE WE GONNA FIND 'EM NEXT?
PUDDIN' BUNS, I'M ACTUALLY A MALE.
HMM?

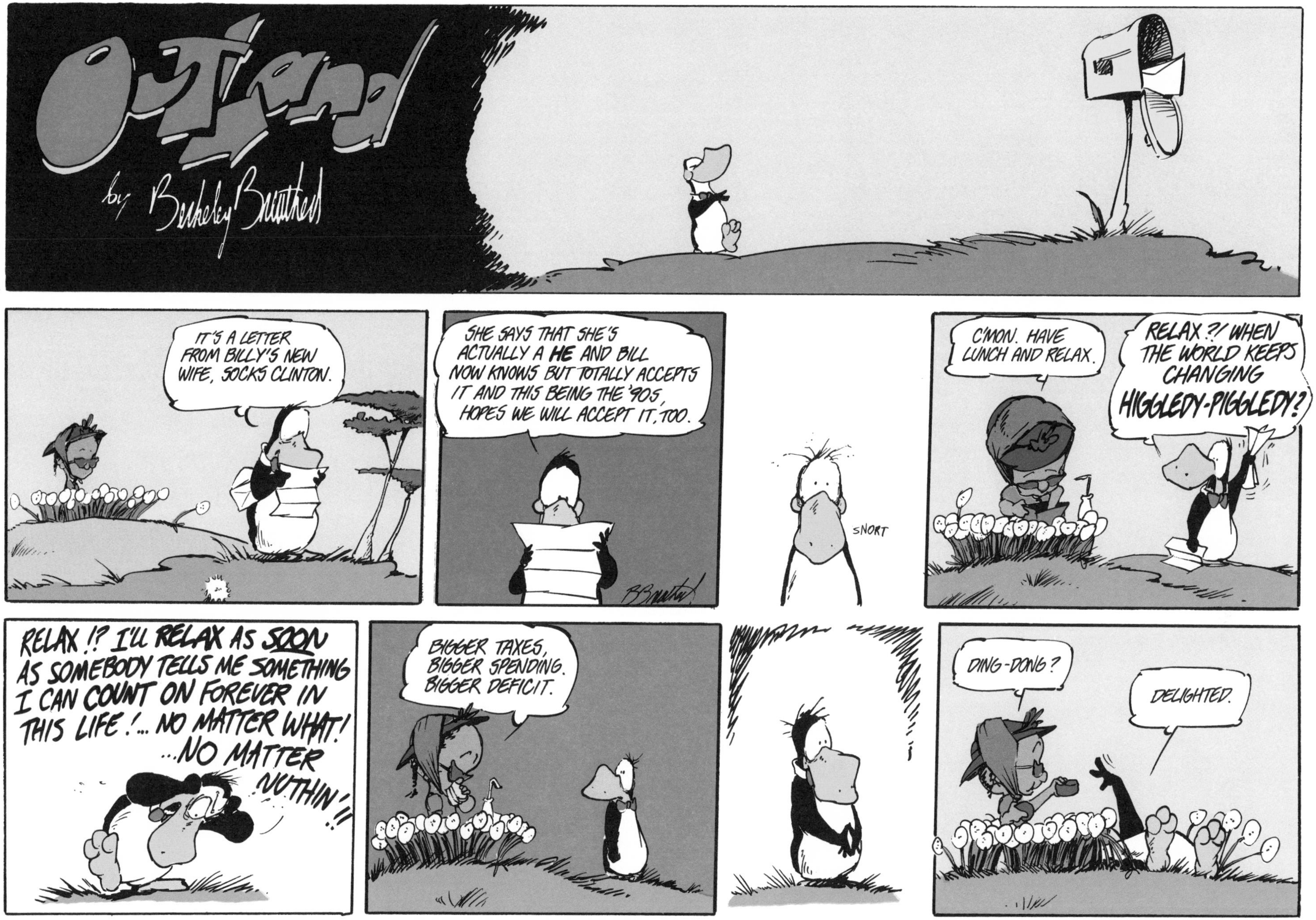
Outland
by Berkeley Breathed
IT'S A LETTER FROM BILLY'S NEW WIFE, SOCKS CLINTON.
SHE SAYS THAT SHE'S ACTUALLY A HE AND BILL NOW KNOWS BUT TOTALLY ACCEPTS IT AND THIS BEING THE '90S, HOPES WE WILL ACCEPT IT, TOO.
B. Breathed
SNORT
C'MON. HAVE LUNCH AND RELAX.
RELAX?! WHEN THE WORLD KEEPS CHANGING HIGGLEDY-PIGGLEDY?
RELAX!? I'LL RELAX AS SOON AS SOMEBODY TELLS ME SOMETHING I CAN COUNT ON FOREVER IN THIS LIFE!... NO MATTER WHAT! ...NO MATTER NUTHIN'!!
BIGGER TAXES, BIGGER SPENDING. BIGGER DEFICIT.
DING-DONG?
DELIGHTED.

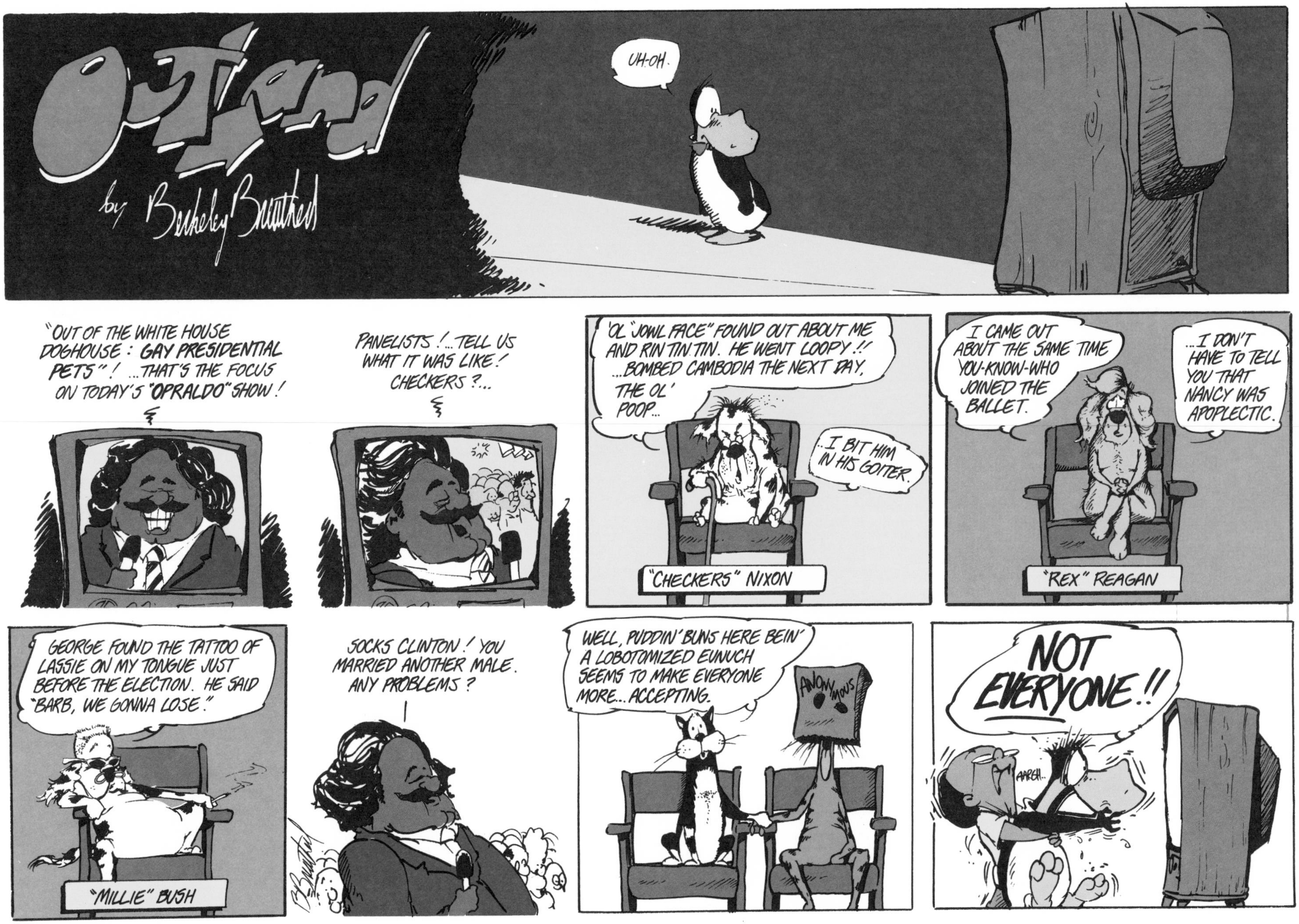

Outland
by Berkeley Breathed
UH-OH.
"OUT OF THE WHITE HOUSE DOGHOUSE : GAY PRESIDENTIAL PETS" ! ...THAT'S THE FOCUS ON TODAY'S "OPRALDO" SHOW !
PANELISTS !... TELL US WHAT IT WAS LIKE ! CHECKERS ?...
'OL "JOWL FACE" FOUND OUT ABOUT ME AND RIN TIN TIN. HE WENT LOOPY !! ...BOMBED CAMBODIA THE NEXT DAY, THE OL' POOP...
...I BIT HIM IN HIS GOITER.
"CHECKERS" NIXON
I CAME OUT ABOUT THE SAME TIME YOU-KNOW-WHO JOINED THE BALLET.
...I DON'T HAVE TO TELL YOU THAT NANCY WAS APOPLECTIC.
"REX" REAGAN
GEORGE FOUND THE TATTOO OF LASSIE ON MY TONGUE JUST BEFORE THE ELECTION. HE SAID "BARB, WE GONNA LOSE."
"MILLIE" BUSH
SOCKS CLINTON ! YOU MARRIED ANOTHER MALE. ANY PROBLEMS ?
WELL, PUDDIN' BUNS HERE BEIN' A LOBOTOMIZED EUNUCH SEEMS TO MAKE EVERYONE MORE... ACCEPTING.
ANONYMOUS
NOT EVERYONE !!
AARGH...

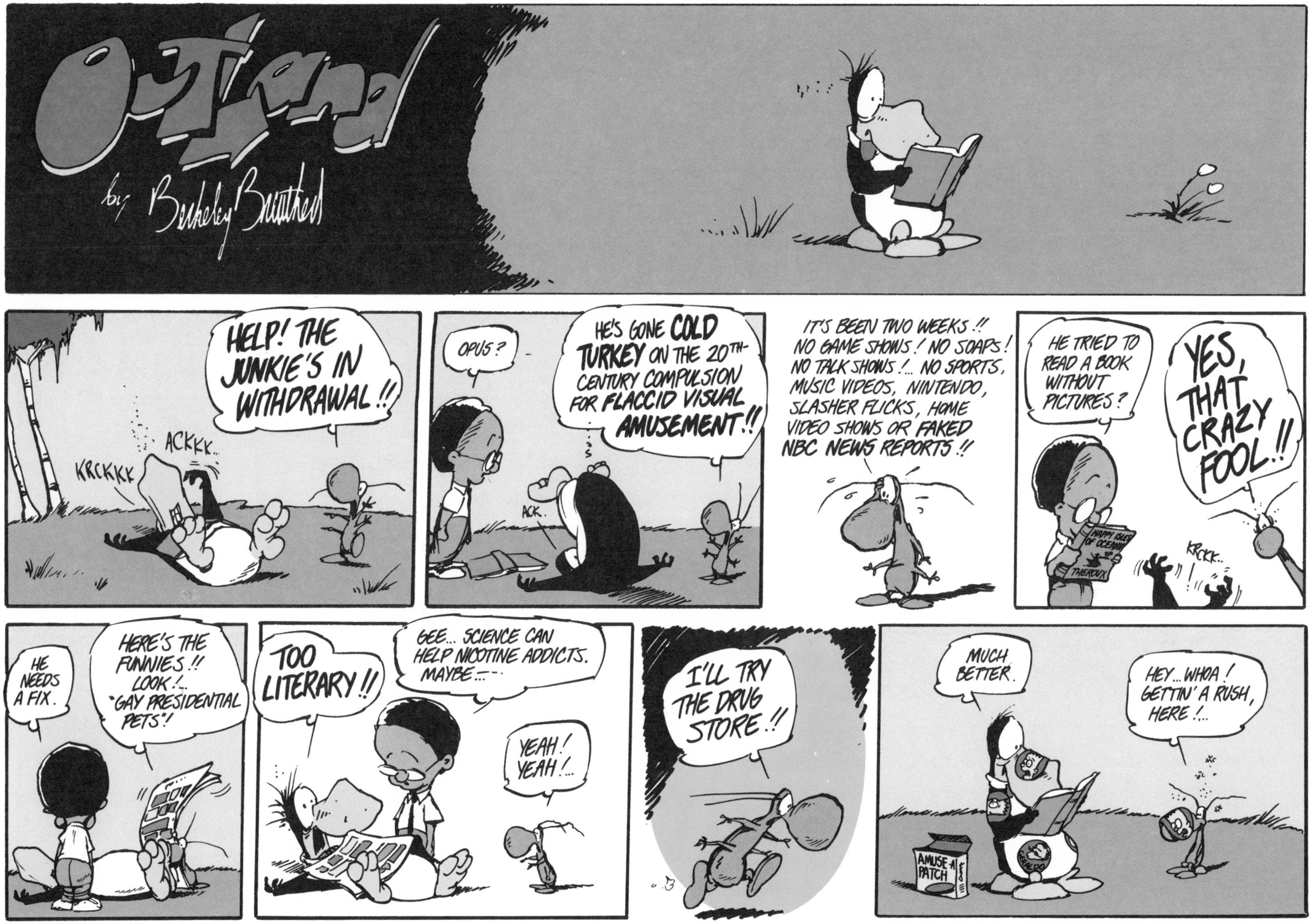
Outland
by Berkeley Breathed
HELP! THE JUNKIE'S IN WITHDRAWAL!!
KRCKKK
ACKKK...
OPUS?
HE'S GONE COLD TURKEY ON THE 20TH-CENTURY COMPULSION FOR FLACCID VISUAL AMUSEMENT!!
ACK.
IT'S BEEN TWO WEEKS!! NO GAME SHOWS! NO SOAPS! NO TALK SHOWS!... NO SPORTS, MUSIC VIDEOS, NINTENDO, SLASHER FLICKS, HOME VIDEO SHOWS OR FAKED NBC NEWS REPORTS!!
HE TRIED TO READ A BOOK WITHOUT PICTURES?
YES, THAT CRAZY FOOL!!
HAPPY ISLES OF OCEANIA
THEROUX
KRCKK..
HE NEEDS A FIX.
HERE'S THE FUNNIES!! LOOK!.. "GAY PRESIDENTIAL PETS"!
TOO LITERARY!!
GEE... SCIENCE CAN HELP NICOTINE ADDICTS. MAYBE...
YEAH! YEAH!...
I'LL TRY THE DRUG STORE!!
MUCH BETTER.
HEY... WHOA! GETTIN' A RUSH, HERE!...
AMUSE-A-PATCH
GERALDO

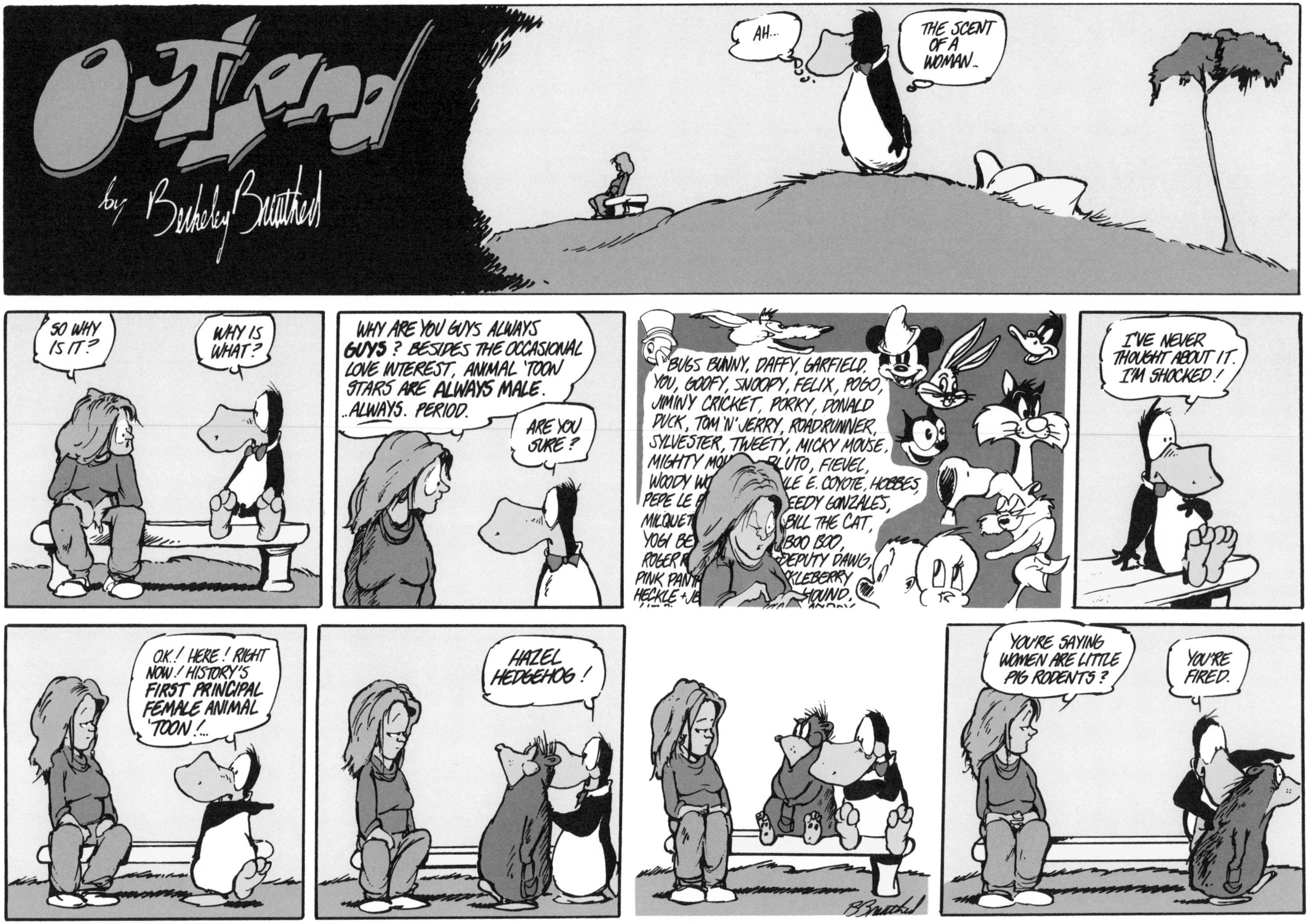
Outland
by Berkeley Breathed
AH...
THE SCENT OF A WOMAN...
SO WHY IS IT?
WHY IS WHAT?
WHY ARE YOU GUYS ALWAYS GUYS? BESIDES THE OCCASIONAL LOVE INTEREST, ANIMAL 'TOON STARS ARE ALWAYS MALE. ..ALWAYS. PERIOD.
ARE YOU SURE?
BUGS BUNNY, DAFFY, GARFIELD, YOU, GOOFY, SNOOPY, FELIX, POGO, JIMINY CRICKET, PORKY, DONALD DUCK, TOM 'N' JERRY, ROADRUNNER, SYLVESTER, TWEETY, MICKY MOUSE, MIGHTY MOU PLUTO, FIEVEL, WOODY WO LE E. COYOTE, HOBBES, PEPE LE EEDY GONZALES, MILQUET BILL THE CAT, YOGI BE BOO BOO, ROGER DEPUTY DAWG, PINK PANT KLEBERRY HECKLE + JE HOUND.
I'VE NEVER THOUGHT ABOUT IT. I'M SHOCKED!
O.K.! HERE! RIGHT NOW! HISTORY'S FIRST PRINCIPAL FEMALE ANIMAL 'TOON!...
HAZEL HEDGEHOG!
B. Breathed
YOU'RE SAYING WOMEN ARE LITTLE PIG RODENTS?
YOU'RE FIRED.

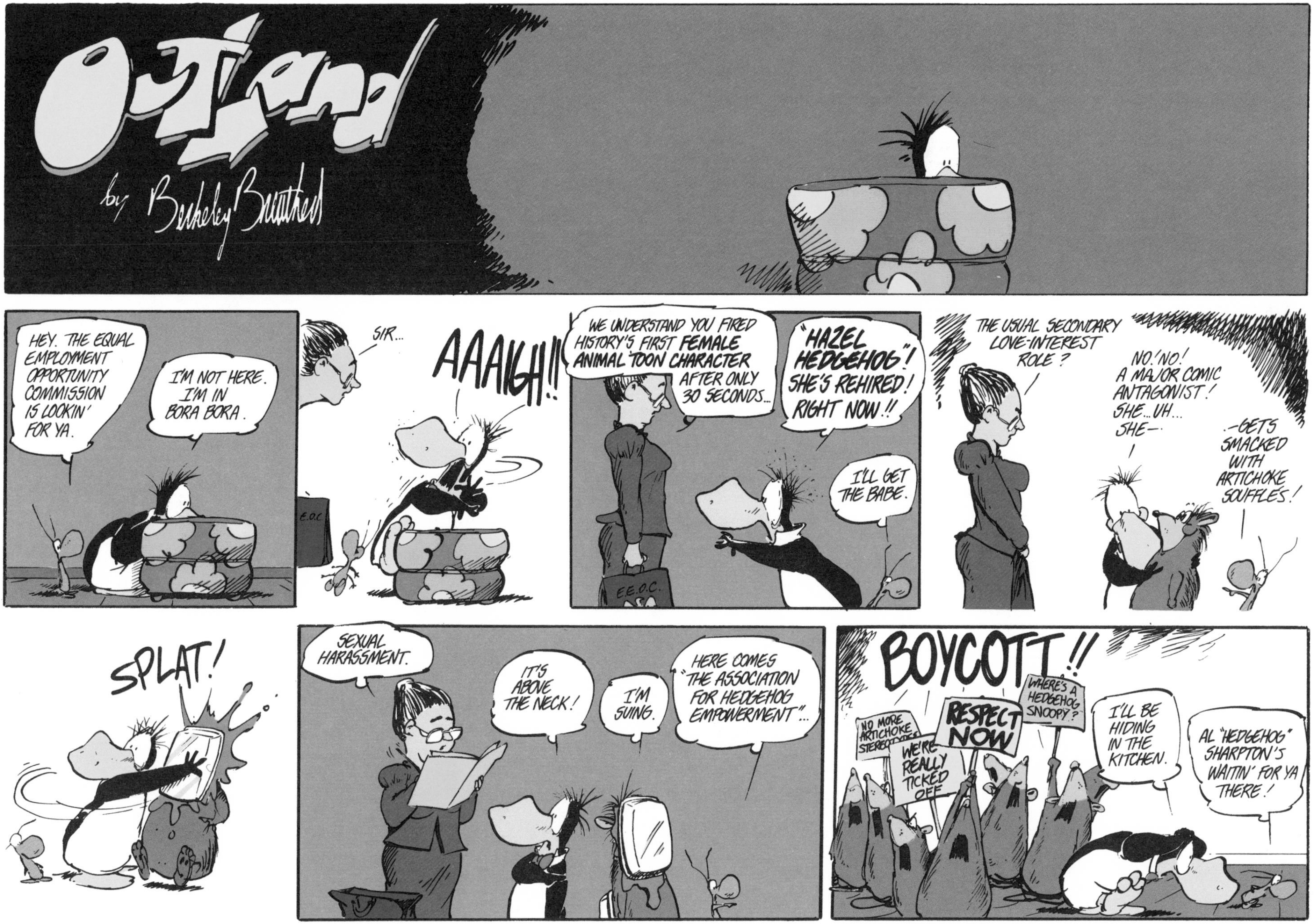
Outland
by Berkeley Breathed
HEY. THE EQUAL EMPLOYMENT OPPORTUNITY COMMISSION IS LOOKIN' FOR YA.
I'M NOT HERE. I'M IN BORA BORA.
E.O.C.
SIR...
AAAIGH!!
WE UNDERSTAND YOU FIRED HISTORY'S FIRST FEMALE ANIMAL 'TOON CHARACTER AFTER ONLY 30 SECONDS...
"HAZEL HEDGEHOG"! SHE'S REHIRED! RIGHT NOW!!
I'LL GET THE BABE.
E.E.O.C.
THE USUAL SECONDARY LOVE-INTEREST ROLE?
NO! NO! A MAJOR COMIC ANTAGONIST! SHE... UH... SHE—
—GETS SMACKED WITH ARTICHOKE SOUFFLES!
SPLAT!
SEXUAL HARASSMENT.
IT'S ABOVE THE NECK!
I'M SUING.
HERE COMES "THE ASSOCIATION FOR HEDGEHOG EMPOWERMENT"...
BOYCOTT!!
NO MORE ARTICHOKE STEREOTYPES
RESPECT NOW
WHERE'S A HEDGEHOG SNOOPY?
WE'RE REALLY TICKED OFF
I'LL BE HIDING IN THE KITCHEN.
AL "HEDGEHOG" SHARPTON'S WAITIN' FOR YA THERE!

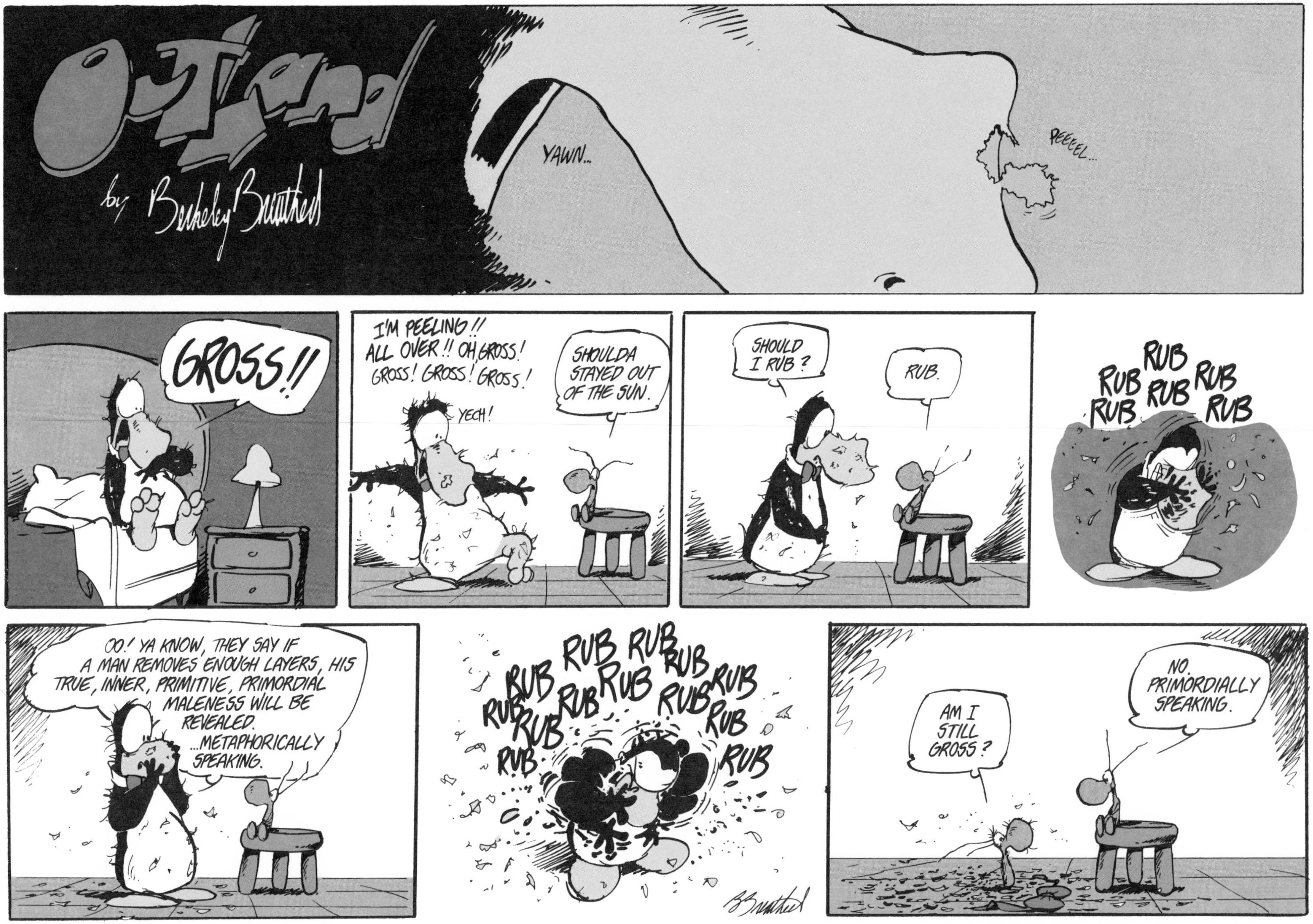
Outland
by Berkeley Breathed
YAWN...
PEEEEL...
GROSS!!
I'M PEELING!! ALL OVER!! OH, GROSS! GROSS! GROSS! GROSS!
YECH!
SHOULDA STAYED OUT OF THE SUN.
SHOULD I RUB?
RUB.
RUB RUB RUB RUB RUB RUB
OO! YA KNOW, THEY SAY IF A MAN REMOVES ENOUGH LAYERS, HIS TRUE, INNER, PRIMITIVE, PRIMORDIAL MALENESS WILL BE REVEALED. ...METAPHORICALLY SPEAKING.
RUB RUB RUB RUB RUB RUB RUB RUB RUB RUB RUB RUB RUB RUB
AM I STILL GROSS?
NO. PRIMORDIALLY SPEAKING.
B Breathed

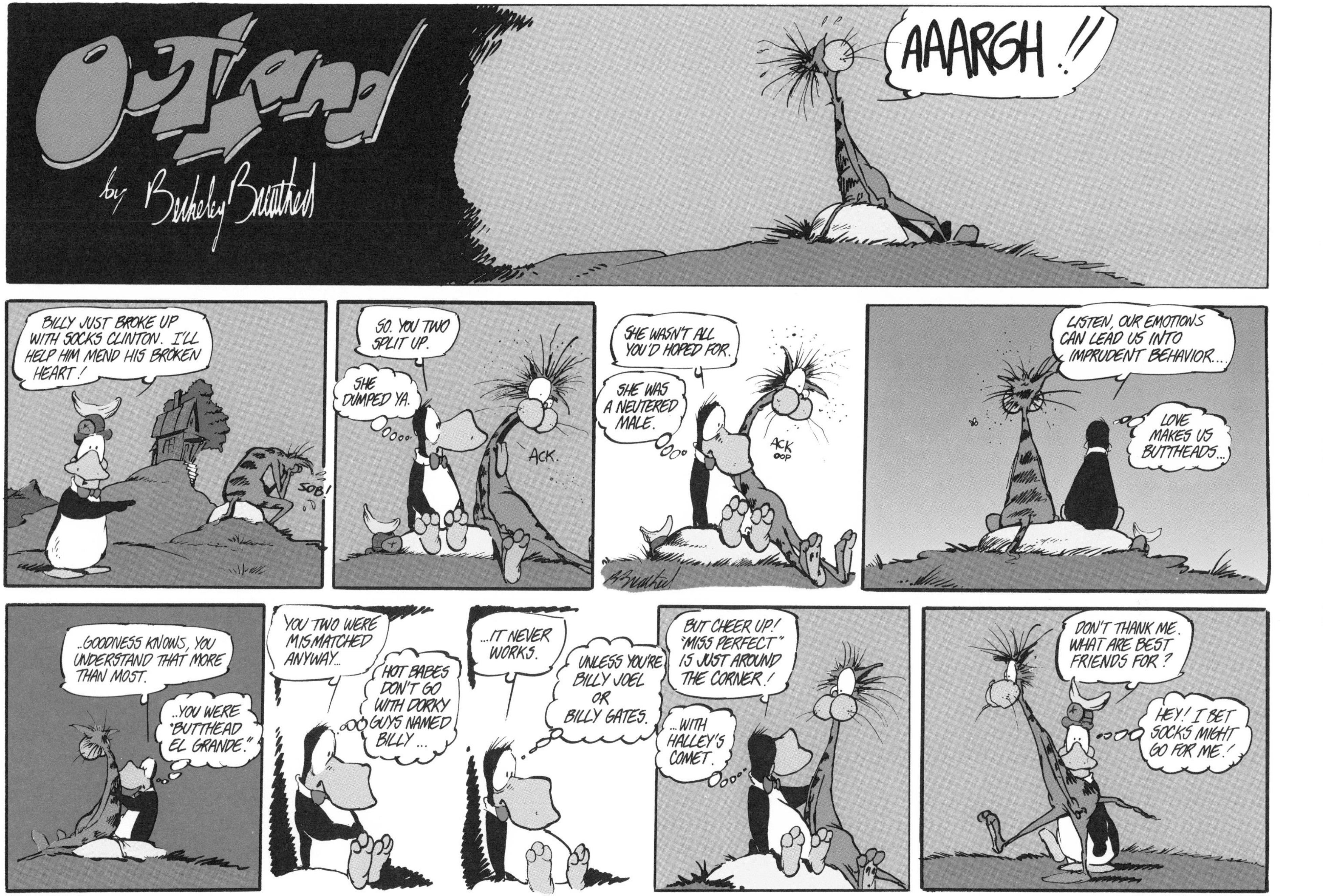
Outland
by Berkeley Breathed
AAARGH !!
BILLY JUST BROKE UP WITH SOCKS CLINTON. I'LL HELP HIM MEND HIS BROKEN HEART!
SOB!
SO. YOU TWO SPLIT UP.
SHE DUMPED YA.
ACK.
SHE WASN'T ALL YOU'D HOPED FOR.
SHE WAS A NEUTERED MALE.
ACK OOP
LISTEN, OUR EMOTIONS CAN LEAD US INTO IMPRUDENT BEHAVIOR...
LOVE MAKES US BUTTHEADS...
..GOODNESS KNOWS, YOU UNDERSTAND THAT MORE THAN MOST.
..YOU WERE "BUTTHEAD EL GRANDE."
YOU TWO WERE MISMATCHED ANYWAY...
HOT BABES DON'T GO WITH DORKY GUYS NAMED BILLY ...
...IT NEVER WORKS.
UNLESS YOU'RE BILLY JOEL OR BILLY GATES.
BUT CHEER UP! "MISS PERFECT" IS JUST AROUND THE CORNER!
...WITH HALLEY'S COMET.
DON'T THANK ME. WHAT ARE BEST FRIENDS FOR?
HEY! I BET SOCKS MIGHT GO FOR ME!

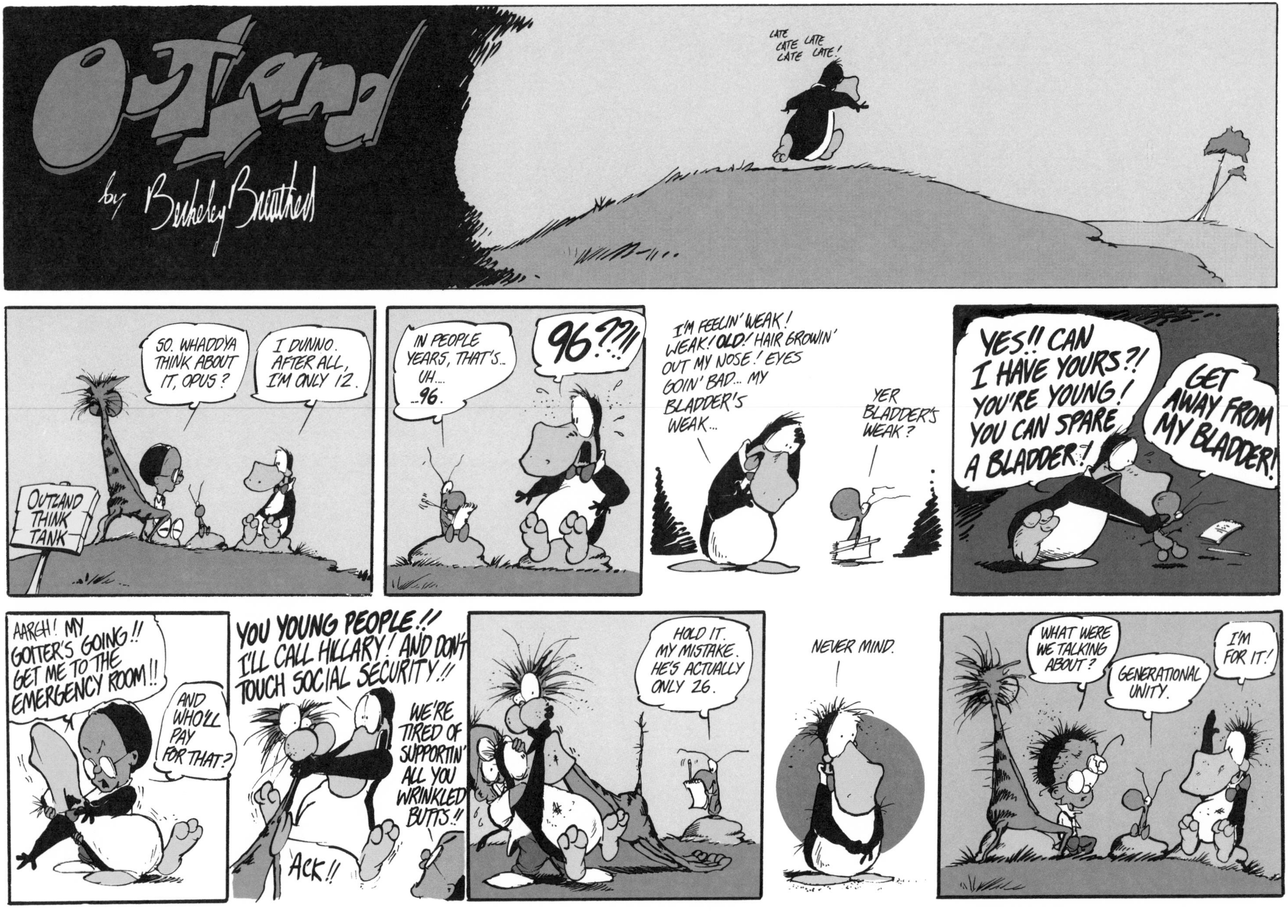

Outland
by Berkeley Breathed
LATE LATE LATE LATE LATE!
SO. WHADDYA THINK ABOUT IT, OPUS?
I DUNNO. AFTER ALL, I'M ONLY 12.
OUTLAND THINK TANK
IN PEOPLE YEARS, THAT'S.. UH.... ..96.
96?!!
I'M FEELIN' WEAK! WEAK! OLD! HAIR GROWIN' OUT MY NOSE! EYES GOIN' BAD... MY BLADDER'S WEAK...
YER BLADDER'S WEAK?
YES!! CAN I HAVE YOURS?! YOU'RE YOUNG! YOU CAN SPARE A BLADDER!
GET AWAY FROM MY BLADDER!
AARGH! MY GOITER'S GOING!! GET ME TO THE EMERGENCY ROOM!!
AND WHO'LL PAY FOR THAT?
YOU YOUNG PEOPLE!! I'LL CALL HILLARY! AND DON'T TOUCH SOCIAL SECURITY!!
WE'RE TIRED OF SUPPORTIN' ALL YOU WRINKLED BUTTS!!
ACK!!
HOLD IT. MY MISTAKE. HE'S ACTUALLY ONLY 26.
NEVER MIND.
WHAT WERE WE TALKING ABOUT?
GENERATIONAL UNITY.
I'M FOR IT!

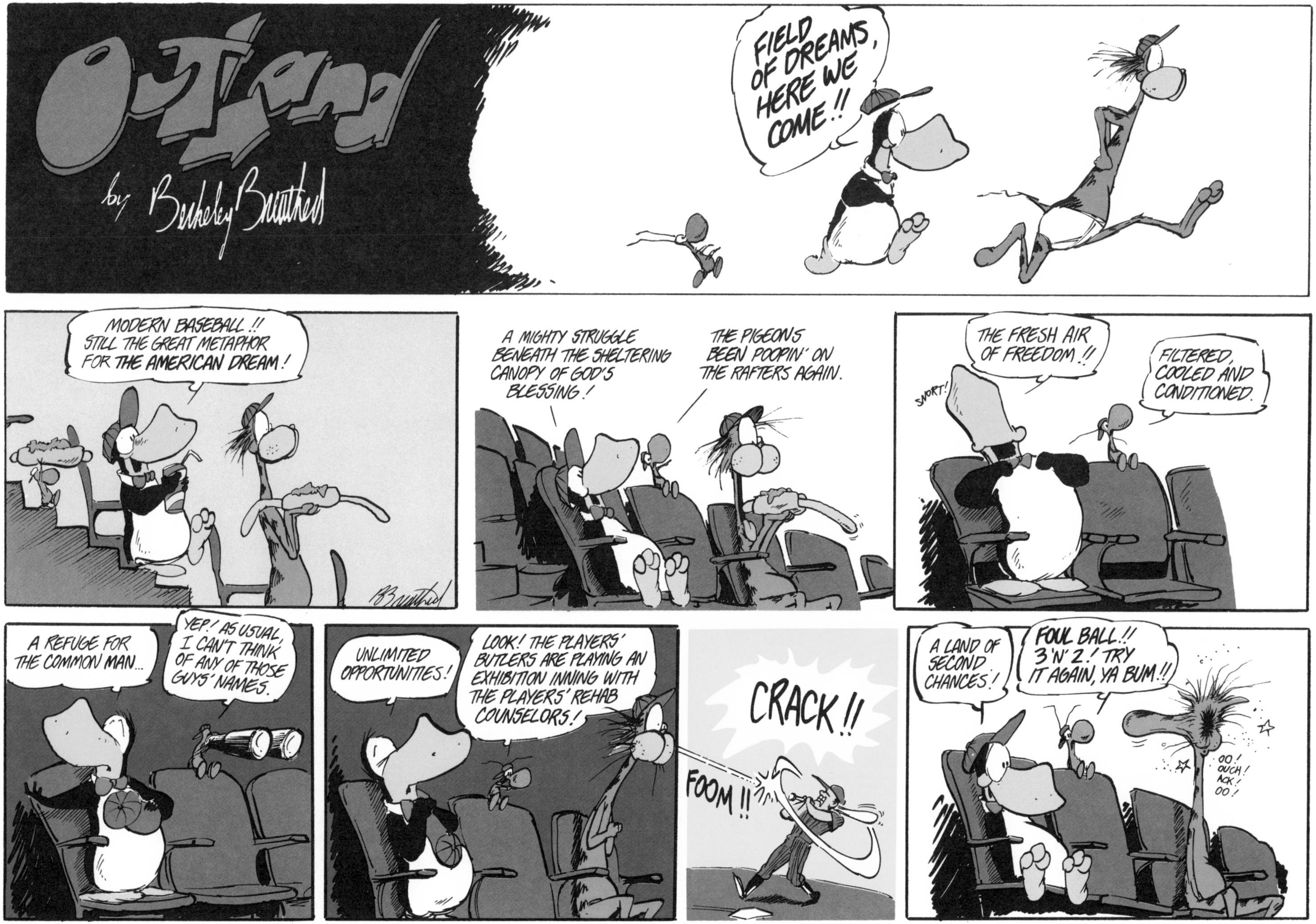
Outland
by Berkeley Breathed
FIELD OF DREAMS, HERE WE COME!!
MODERN BASEBALL!! STILL THE GREAT METAPHOR FOR THE AMERICAN DREAM!
A MIGHTY STRUGGLE BENEATH THE SHELTERING CANOPY OF GOD'S BLESSING!
THE PIGEONS BEEN POOPIN' ON THE RAFTERS AGAIN.
THE FRESH AIR OF FREEDOM!!
SNORT!
FILTERED, COOLED AND CONDITIONED.
A REFUGE FOR THE COMMON MAN...
YEP! AS USUAL, I CAN'T THINK OF ANY OF THOSE GUYS' NAMES.
UNLIMITED OPPORTUNITIES!
LOOK! THE PLAYERS' BUTLERS ARE PLAYING AN EXHIBITION INNING WITH THE PLAYERS' REHAB COUNSELORS!
CRACK!!
FOOM!!
A LAND OF SECOND CHANCES!
FOUL BALL!! 3'N'2! TRY IT AGAIN, YA BUM!!
OO! OUCH! ACK! OO!

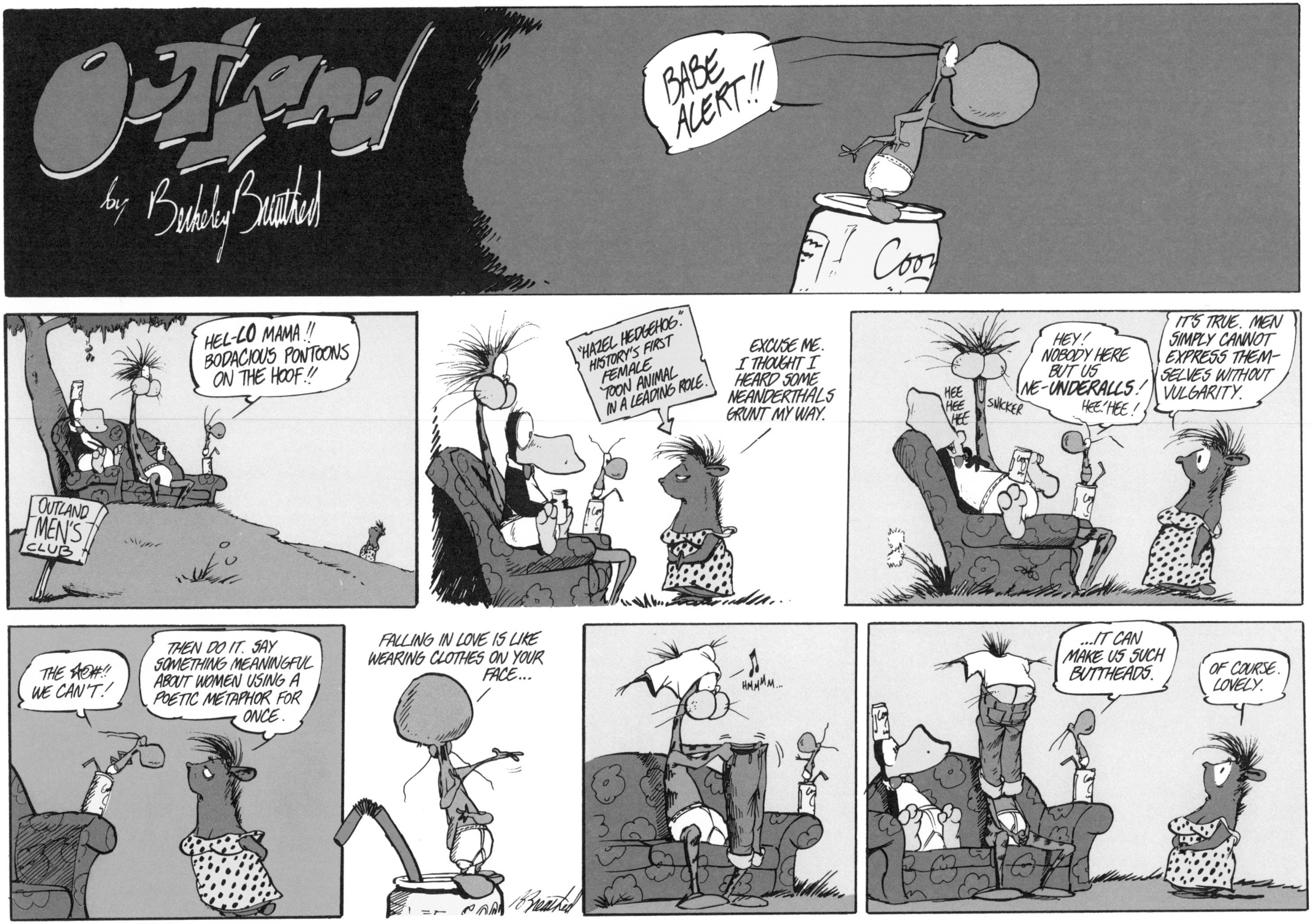
Outland
by Berkeley Breathed
BABE ALERT!!
HEL-LO MAMA!! BODACIOUS PONTOONS ON THE HOOF!!
OUTLAND MEN'S CLUB
"HAZEL HEDGEHOG." HISTORY'S FIRST FEMALE 'TOON ANIMAL IN A LEADING ROLE.
EXCUSE ME. I THOUGHT I HEARD SOME NEANDERTHALS GRUNT MY WAY.
HEE HEE HEE
SNICKER
HEY! NOBODY HERE BUT US NE-UNDERALLS! HEE! HEE!
IT'S TRUE. MEN SIMPLY CANNOT EXPRESS THEMSELVES WITHOUT VULGARITY.
THE #@#!! WE CAN'T!
THEN DO IT. SAY SOMETHING MEANINGFUL ABOUT WOMEN USING A POETIC METAPHOR FOR ONCE.
FALLING IN LOVE IS LIKE WEARING CLOTHES ON YOUR FACE...
HMMMM...
...IT CAN MAKE US SUCH BUTTHEADS.
OF COURSE. LOVELY.

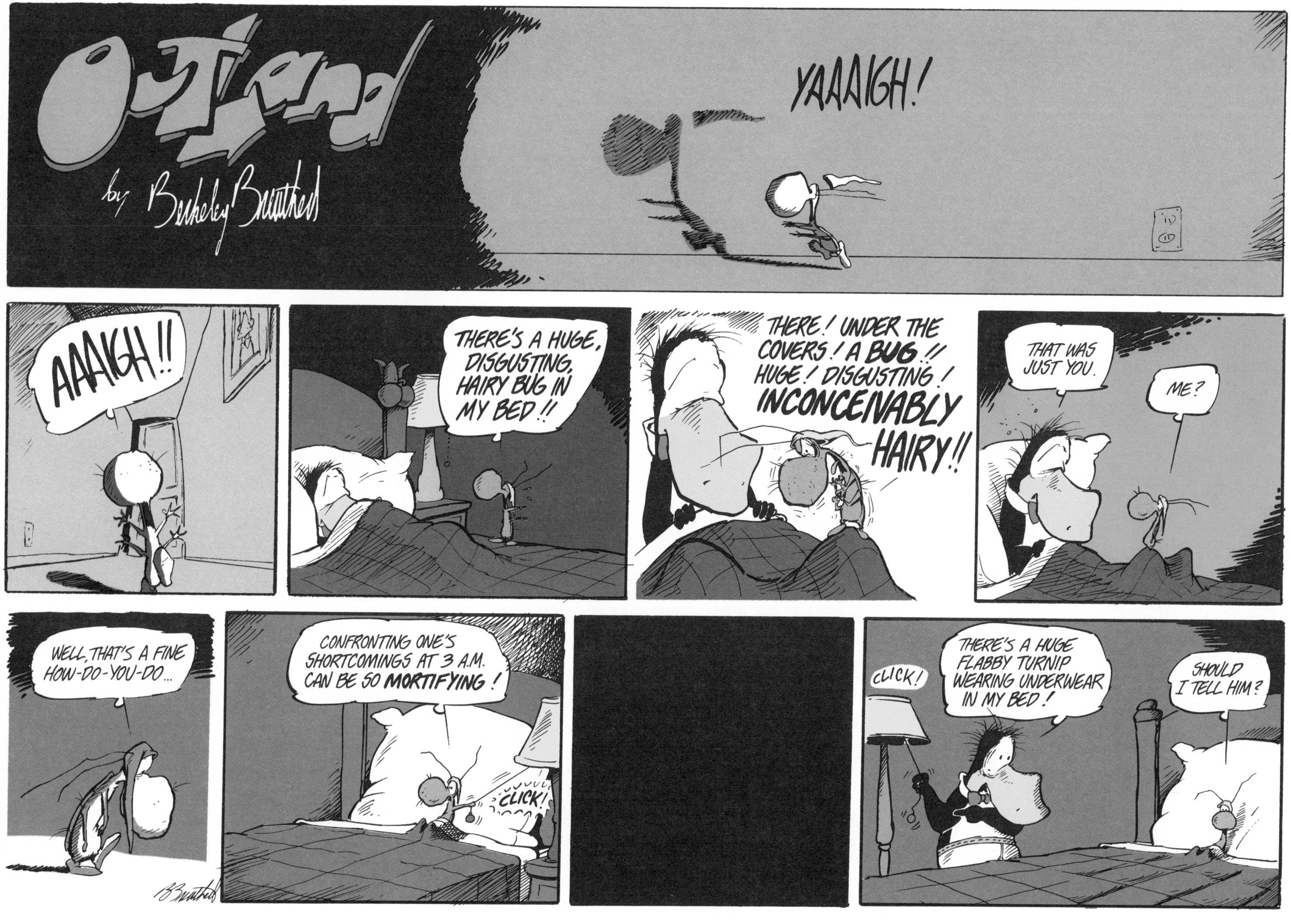
Outland
by Berkeley Breathed
YAAAIGH!
AAAGH!!
THERE'S A HUGE, DISGUSTING, HAIRY BUG IN MY BED!!
THERE! UNDER THE COVERS! A BUG!! HUGE! DISGUSTING! INCONCEIVABLY HAIRY!!
THAT WAS JUST YOU.
ME?
WELL, THAT'S A FINE HOW-DO-YOU-DO...
CONFRONTING ONE'S SHORTCOMINGS AT 3 A.M. CAN BE SO MORTIFYING!
CLICK!
CLICK!
THERE'S A HUGE FLABBY TURNIP WEARING UNDERWEAR IN MY BED!
SHOULD I TELL HIM?
B Breathed

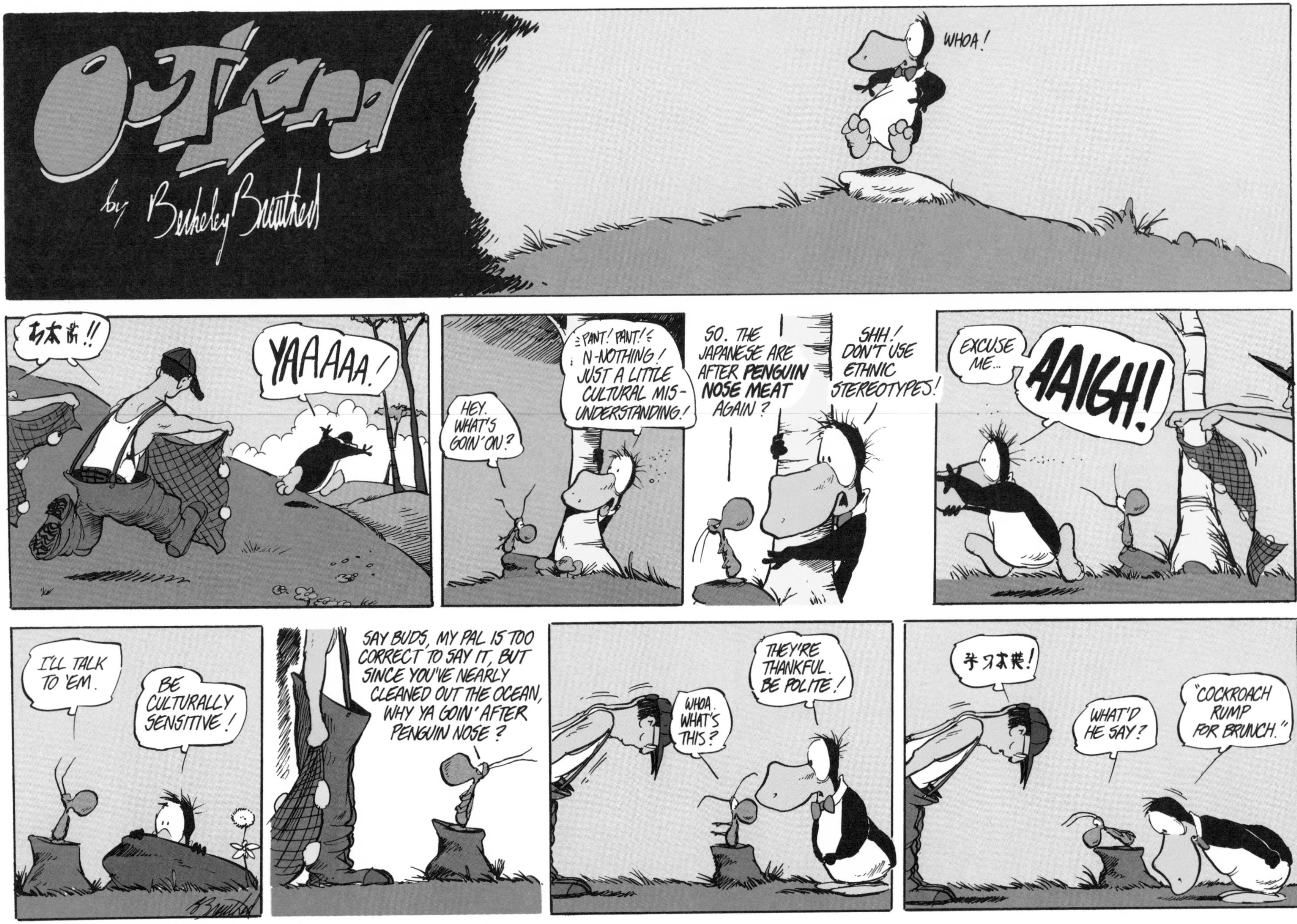
Outland
by Berkeley Breathed
WHOA!
YAAAAA!
HEY. WHAT'S GOIN' ON?
PANT! PANT! N-NOTHING! JUST A LITTLE CULTURAL MIS-UNDERSTANDING!
SO. THE JAPANESE ARE AFTER PENGUIN NOSE MEAT AGAIN?
SHH! DON'T USE ETHNIC STEREOTYPES!
EXCUSE ME...
AAIGH!
I'LL TALK TO 'EM.
BE CULTURALLY SENSITIVE!
SAY BUDS, MY PAL IS TOO CORRECT TO SAY IT, BUT SINCE YOU'VE NEARLY CLEANED OUT THE OCEAN, WHY YA GOIN' AFTER PENGUIN NOSE?
WHOA. WHAT'S THIS?
THEY'RE THANKFUL. BE POLITE!
WHAT'D HE SAY?
"COCKROACH RUMP FOR BRUNCH."

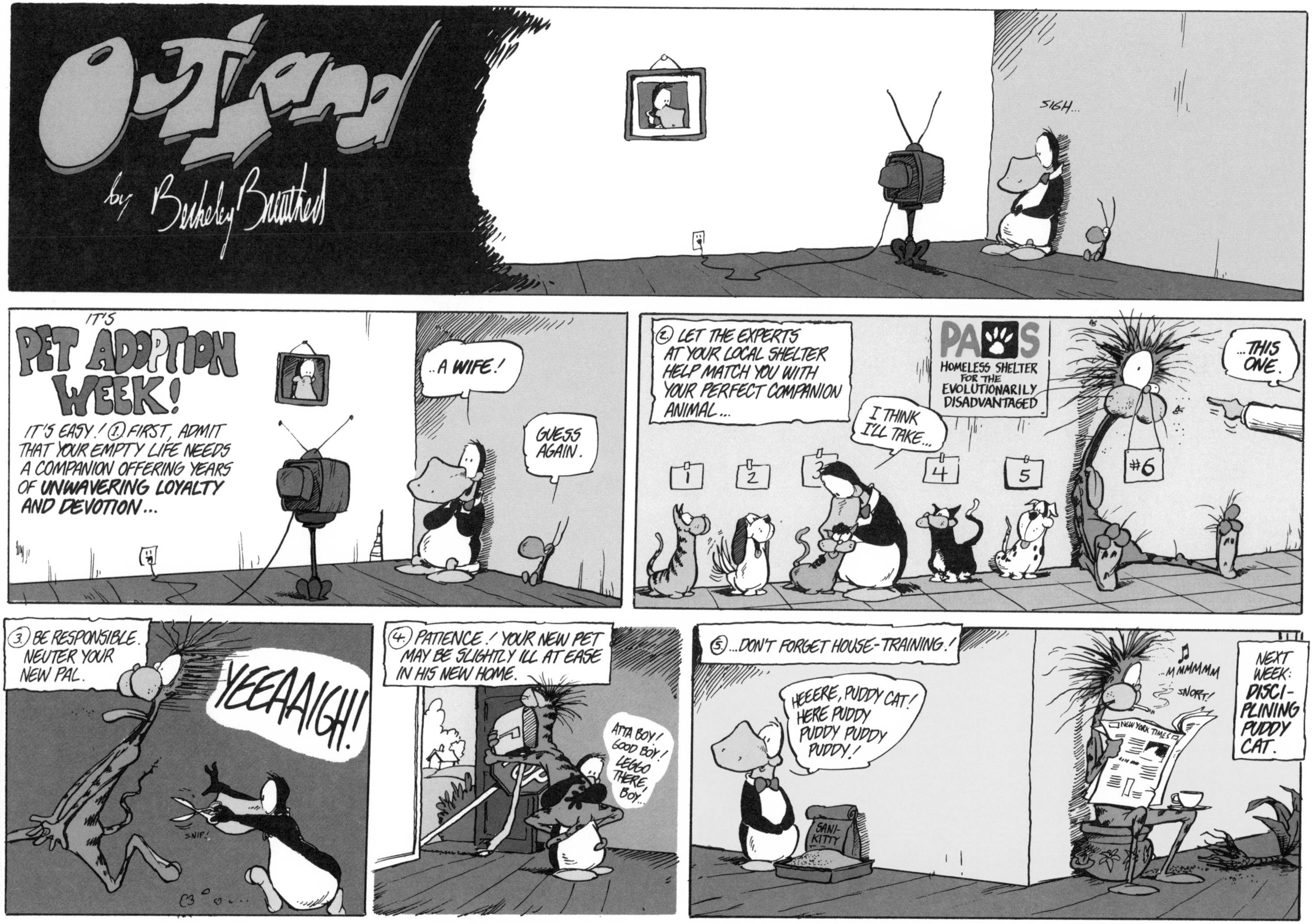
Outland
by Berkeley Breathed
SIGH...
IT'S PET ADOPTION WEEK!
IT'S EASY! 1. FIRST, ADMIT THAT YOUR EMPTY LIFE NEEDS A COMPANION OFFERING YEARS OF UNWAVERING LOYALTY AND DEVOTION...
..A WIFE!
GUESS AGAIN.
2. LET THE EXPERTS AT YOUR LOCAL SHELTER HELP MATCH YOU WITH YOUR PERFECT COMPANION ANIMAL...
PAWS HOMELESS SHELTER FOR THE EVOLUTIONARILY DISADVANTAGED
I THINK I'LL TAKE...
...THIS ONE.
1
2
3
4
5
#6
3. BE RESPONSIBLE. NEUTER YOUR NEW PAL.
YEEEAAIGH!
SNIP!
4. PATIENCE! YOUR NEW PET MAY BE SLIGHTLY ILL AT EASE IN HIS NEW HOME.
ATTA BOY! GOOD BOY! LEGGO THERE, BOY...
5. ...DON'T FORGET HOUSE-TRAINING!
HEEERE, PUDDY CAT! HERE PUDDY PUDDY PUDDY PUDDY!
SANI-KITTY
...MMMMMM
SNORT!
NEW YORK TIMES
NEXT WEEK: DISCIPLINING PUDDY CAT.

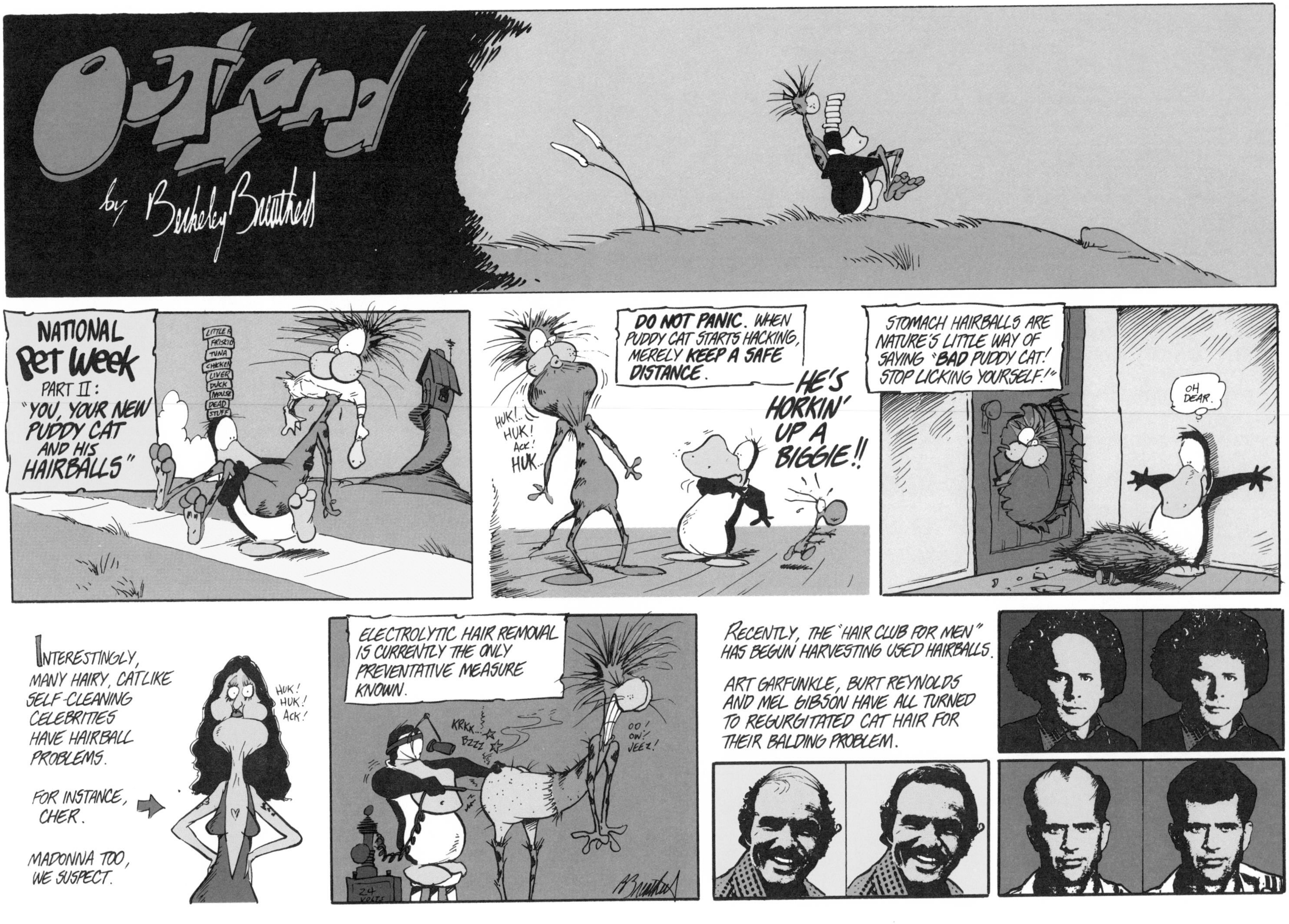

Outland
by Berkeley Breathed
NATIONAL Pet Week
PART II: "YOU, YOUR NEW PUDDY CAT AND HIS HAIRBALLS"
TUNA
CHICKEN
LIVER
DUCK
MOUSE
DEAD STUFF
DO NOT PANIC. WHEN PUDDY CAT STARTS HACKING, MERELY KEEP A SAFE DISTANCE.
HUK!.. HUK! ACK! HUK..
HE'S HORKIN' UP A BIGGIE!!
STOMACH HAIRBALLS ARE NATURE'S LITTLE WAY OF SAYING "BAD PUDDY CAT! STOP LICKING YOURSELF!"
OH DEAR.
INTERESTINGLY, MANY HAIRY, CATLIKE SELF-CLEANING CELEBRITIES HAVE HAIRBALL PROBLEMS.
FOR INSTANCE, CHER.
MADONNA TOO, WE SUSPECT.
HUK! HUK! ACK!
ELECTROLYTIC HAIR REMOVAL IS CURRENTLY THE ONLY PREVENTATIVE MEASURE KNOWN.
KRKK..
BZZZ
OO! OW! JEEZ!
24 VOLTS
B Breathed
RECENTLY, THE "HAIR CLUB FOR MEN" HAS BEGUN HARVESTING USED HAIRBALLS.
ART GARFUNKLE, BURT REYNOLDS AND MEL GIBSON HAVE ALL TURNED TO REGURGITATED CAT HAIR FOR THEIR BALDING PROBLEM.

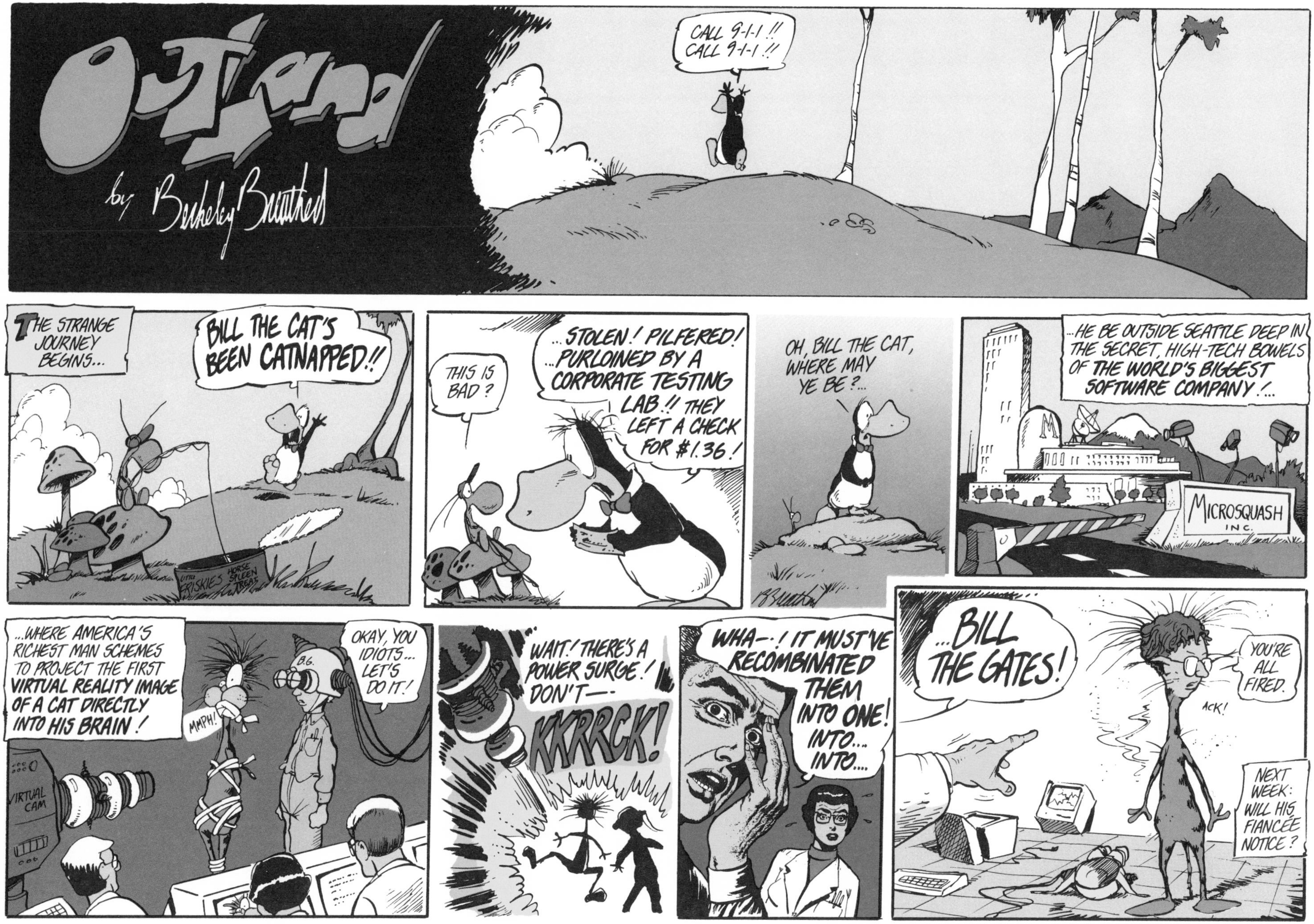
Outland
by Berkeley Breathed
CALL 9-1-1 !! CALL 9-1-1 !!
THE STRANGE JOURNEY BEGINS...
BILL THE CAT'S BEEN CATNAPPED!!
FRISKIES HORSE SPLEEN TREATS
THIS IS BAD ?
...STOLEN! PILFERED! ...PURLOINED BY A CORPORATE TESTING LAB!! THEY LEFT A CHECK FOR $1.36 !
OH, BILL THE CAT, WHERE MAY YE BE ?...
...HE BE OUTSIDE SEATTLE DEEP IN THE SECRET, HIGH-TECH BOWELS OF THE WORLD'S BIGGEST SOFTWARE COMPANY !...
MICROSQUASH INC.
...WHERE AMERICA'S RICHEST MAN SCHEMES TO PROJECT THE FIRST VIRTUAL REALITY IMAGE OF A CAT DIRECTLY INTO HIS BRAIN !
OKAY, YOU IDIOTS... LET'S DO IT!
B.G.
MMPH!
VIRTUAL CAM
WAIT! THERE'S A POWER SURGE! DON'T—
KKRRCK!
WHA—! IT MUST'VE RECOMBINATED THEM INTO ONE! INTO.... INTO....
...BILL THE GATES!
YOU'RE ALL FIRED.
ACK!
NEXT WEEK: WILL HIS FIANCÉE NOTICE ?

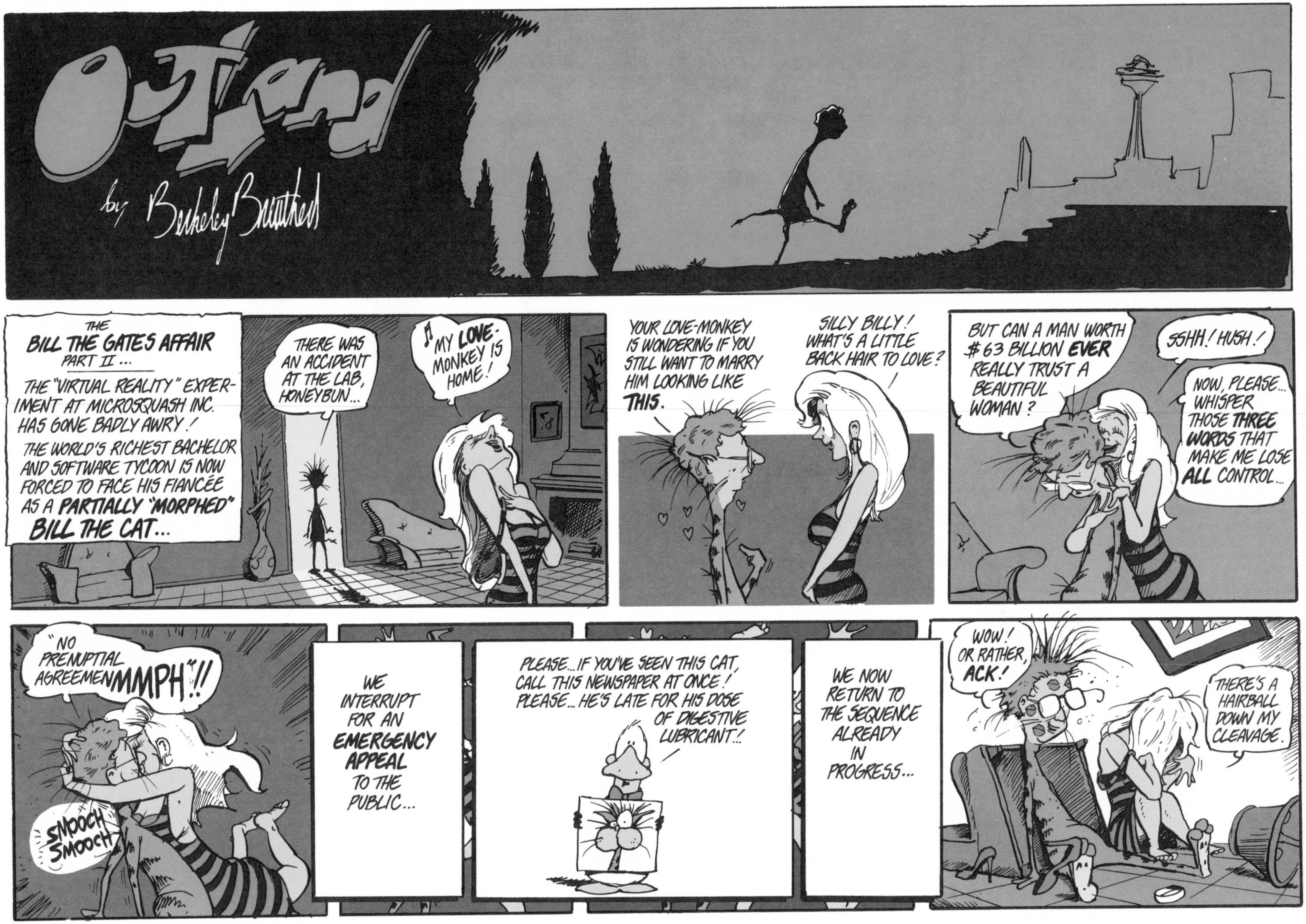
Outland
by Berkeley Breathed
THE BILL THE GATES AFFAIR PART II ...
THE "VIRTUAL REALITY" EXPERIMENT AT MICROSQUASH INC. HAS GONE BADLY AWRY!
THE WORLD'S RICHEST BACHELOR AND SOFTWARE TYCOON IS NOW FORCED TO FACE HIS FIANCÉE AS A PARTIALLY "MORPHED" BILL THE CAT...
THERE WAS AN ACCIDENT AT THE LAB, HONEYBUN...
MY LOVE-MONKEY IS HOME!
YOUR LOVE-MONKEY IS WONDERING IF YOU STILL WANT TO MARRY HIM LOOKING LIKE THIS.
SILLY BILLY! WHAT'S A LITTLE BACK HAIR TO LOVE?
BUT CAN A MAN WORTH $63 BILLION EVER REALLY TRUST A BEAUTIFUL WOMAN?
SSHH! HUSH!
NOW, PLEASE... WHISPER THOSE THREE WORDS THAT MAKE ME LOSE ALL CONTROL...
"NO PRENUPTIAL AGREEMENMMPH"!!
SMOOCH SMOOCH
WE INTERRUPT FOR AN EMERGENCY APPEAL TO THE PUBLIC...
PLEASE... IF YOU'VE SEEN THIS CAT, CALL THIS NEWSPAPER AT ONCE! PLEASE... HE'S LATE FOR HIS DOSE OF DIGESTIVE LUBRICANT!!
WE NOW RETURN TO THE SEQUENCE ALREADY IN PROGRESS...
WOW! OR RATHER, ACK!
THERE'S A HAIRBALL DOWN MY CLEAVAGE.

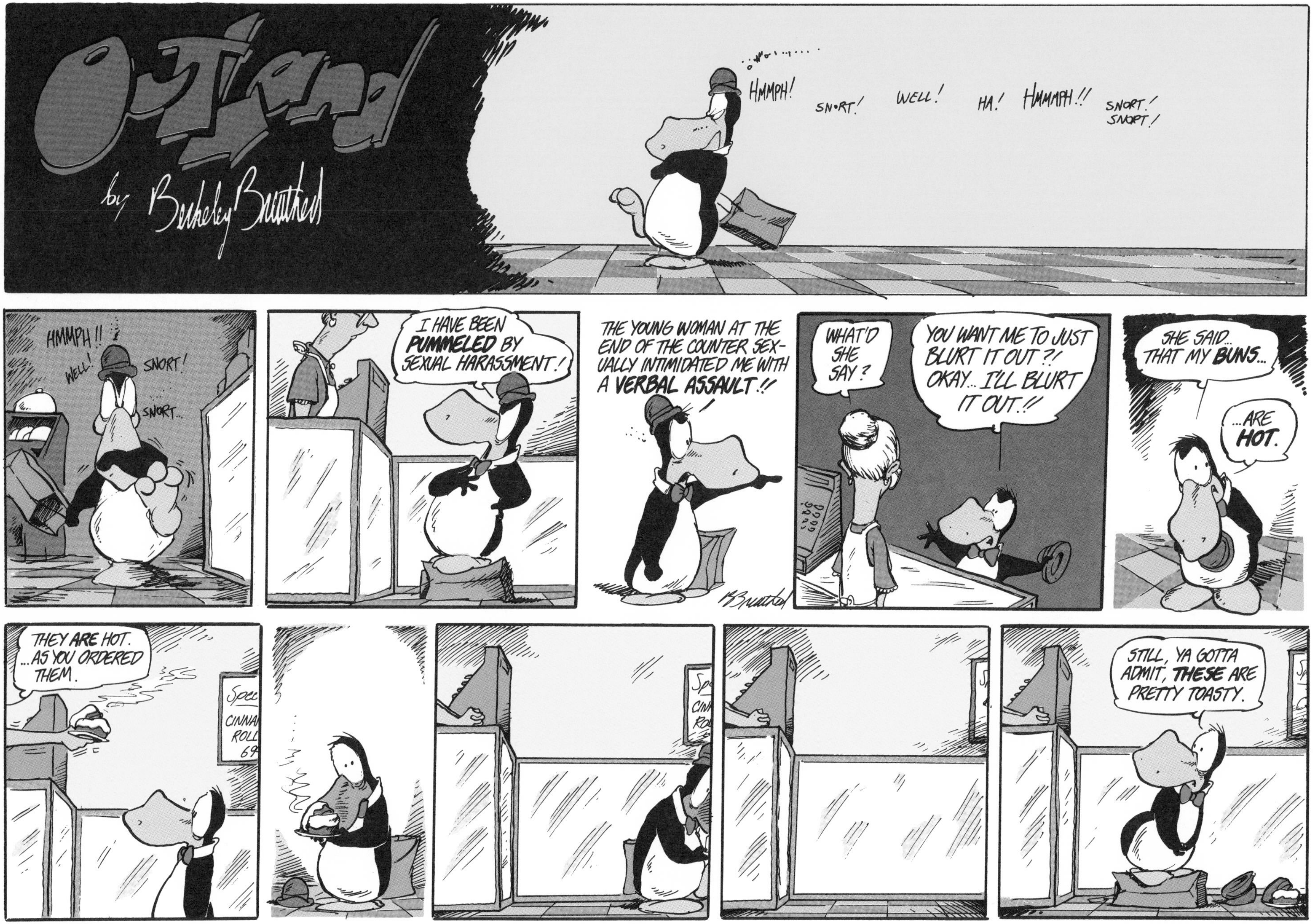

Outland
by Berkeley Breathed
HMMPH!
SNORT!
WELL!
HA!
HMMMPH!!
SNORT! SNORT!
HMMPH!!
WELL!
SNORT!
SNORT...
I HAVE BEEN PUMMELED BY SEXUAL HARASSMENT!
THE YOUNG WOMAN AT THE END OF THE COUNTER SEXUALLY INTIMIDATED ME WITH A VERBAL ASSAULT!!
WHAT'D SHE SAY?
YOU WANT ME TO JUST BLURT IT OUT?! OKAY... I'LL BLURT IT OUT!!
SHE SAID... THAT MY BUNS...
...ARE HOT.
THEY ARE HOT. ...AS YOU ORDERED THEM.
STILL, YA GOTTA ADMIT, THESE ARE PRETTY TOASTY.

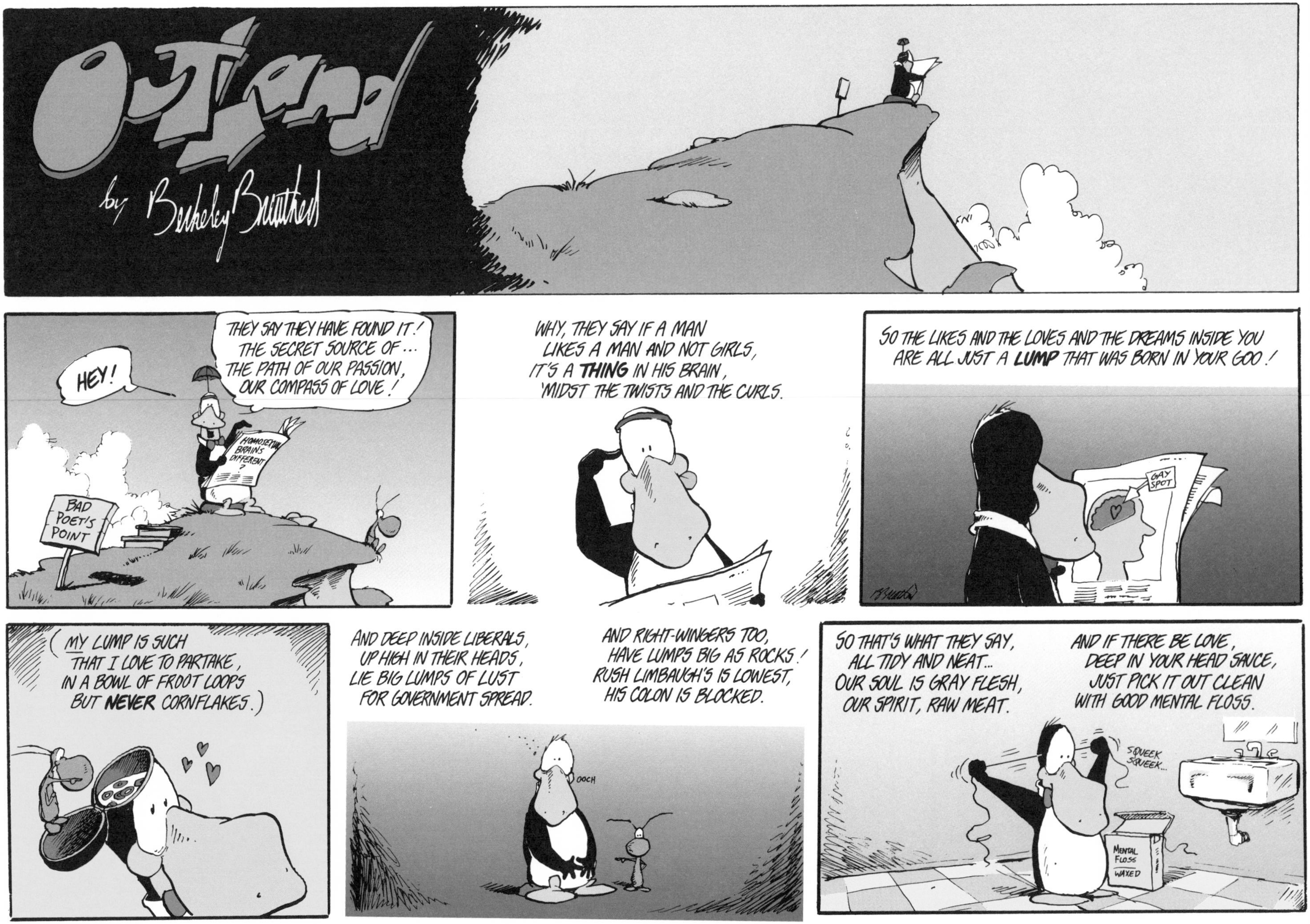
Outland
by Berkeley Breathed
HEY!
THEY SAY THEY HAVE FOUND IT! THE SECRET SOURCE OF... THE PATH OF OUR PASSION, OUR COMPASS OF LOVE!
HOMOSEXUAL BRAINS DIFFERENT?
BAD POET'S POINT
WHY, THEY SAY IF A MAN LIKES A MAN AND NOT GIRLS, IT'S A **THING** IN HIS BRAIN, 'MIDST THE TWISTS AND THE CURLS.
SO THE LIKES AND THE LOVES AND THE DREAMS INSIDE YOU ARE ALL JUST A **LUMP** THAT WAS BORN IN YOUR GOO!
GAY SPOT
(MY LUMP IS SUCH THAT I LOVE TO PARTAKE, IN A BOWL OF FROOT LOOPS BUT **NEVER** CORNFLAKES.)
AND DEEP INSIDE LIBERALS, UP HIGH IN THEIR HEADS, LIE BIG LUMPS OF LUST FOR GOVERNMENT SPREAD.
AND RIGHT-WINGERS TOO, HAVE LUMPS BIG AS ROCKS! RUSH LIMBAUGH'S IS LOWEST, HIS COLON IS BLOCKED.
OOCH
SO THAT'S WHAT THEY SAY, ALL TIDY AND NEAT... OUR SOUL IS GRAY FLESH, OUR SPIRIT, RAW MEAT.
AND IF THERE BE LOVE, DEEP IN YOUR HEAD SAUCE, JUST PICK IT OUT CLEAN WITH GOOD MENTAL FLOSS.
SQUEEK SQUEEK...
MENTAL FLOSS WAXED

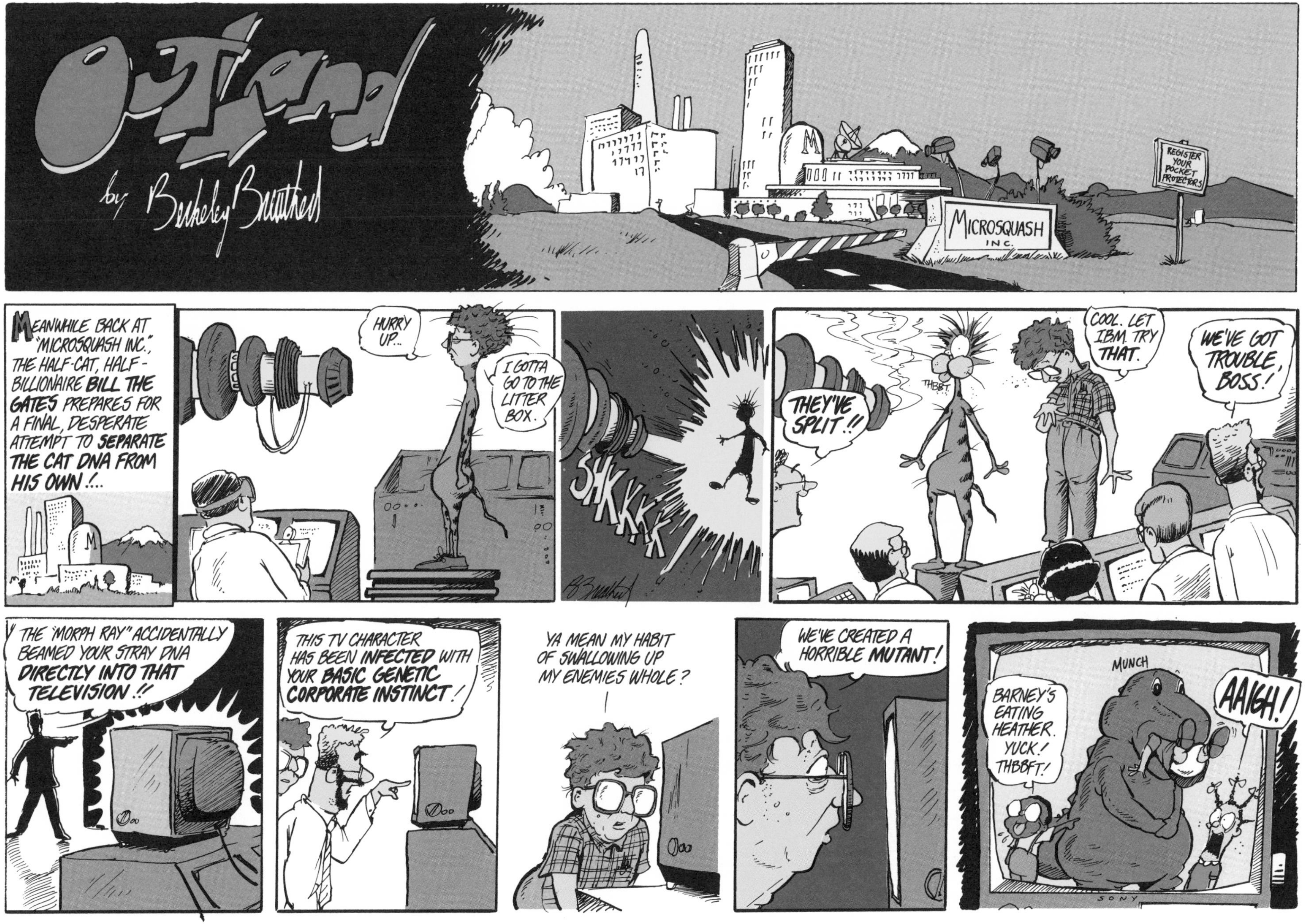
Outland
by Berkeley Breathed
REGISTER YOUR POCKET PROTECTORS
MICROSQUASH INC.
MEANWHILE BACK AT "MICROSQUASH INC.", THE HALF-CAT, HALF-BILLIONAIRE BILL THE GATES PREPARES FOR A FINAL, DESPERATE ATTEMPT TO SEPARATE THE CAT DNA FROM HIS OWN!...
HURRY UP...
I GOTTA GO TO THE LITTER BOX.
SHKKKKK!
THEY'VE SPLIT!!
THBBT.
COOL. LET IBM TRY THAT.
WE'VE GOT TROUBLE, BOSS!
THE "MORPH RAY" ACCIDENTALLY BEAMED YOUR STRAY DNA DIRECTLY INTO THAT TELEVISION!!
THIS TV CHARACTER HAS BEEN INFECTED WITH YOUR BASIC GENETIC CORPORATE INSTINCT!
YA MEAN MY HABIT OF SWALLOWING UP MY ENEMIES WHOLE?
WE'VE CREATED A HORRIBLE MUTANT!
MUNCH
BARNEY'S EATING HEATHER. YUCK! THBBFT!
AAIGH!
SONY

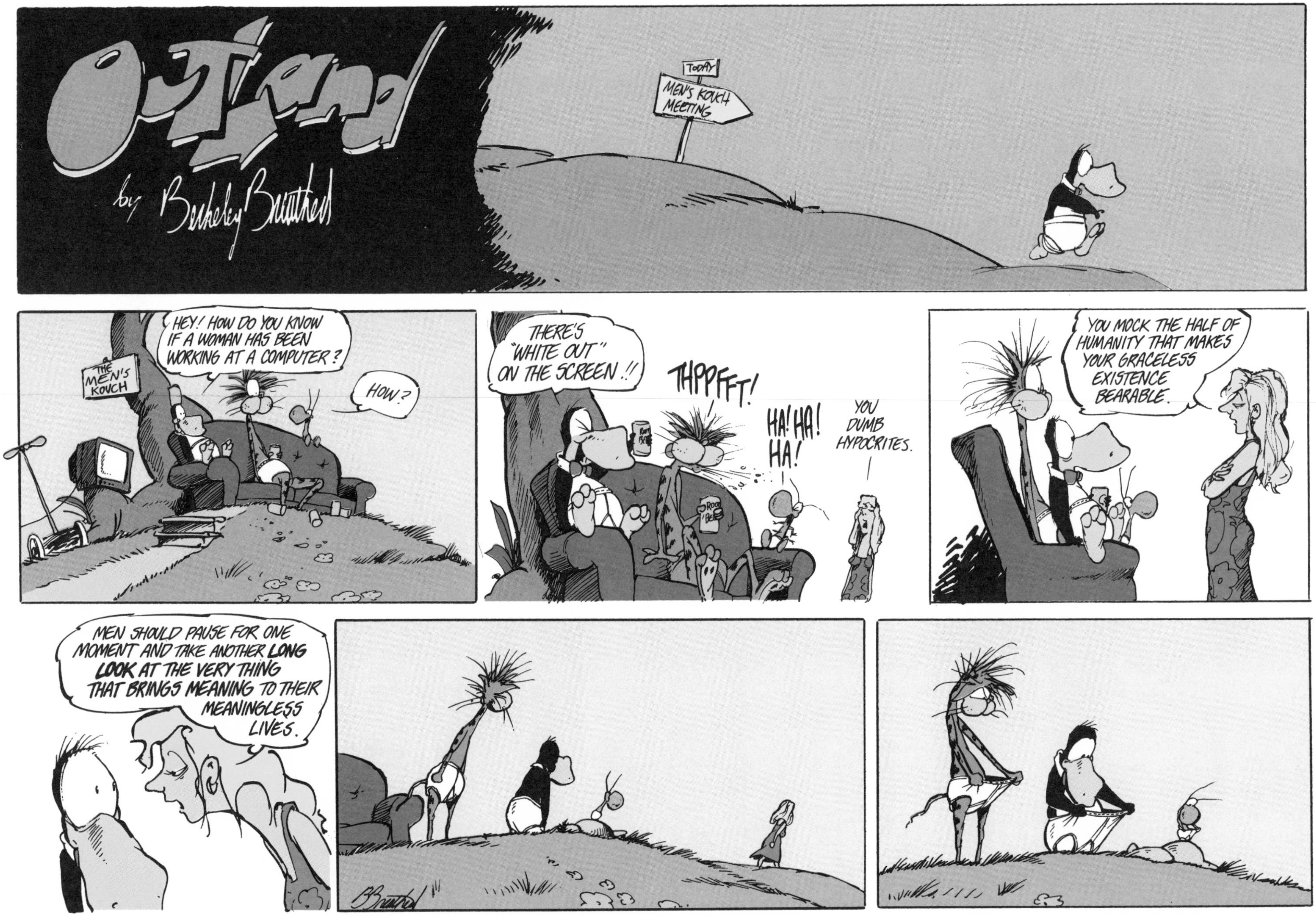
Outland
by Berkeley Breathed
TODAY
MEN'S KOUCH MEETING
THE MEN'S KOUCH
HEY! HOW DO YOU KNOW IF A WOMAN HAS BEEN WORKING AT A COMPUTER?
HOW?
THERE'S "WHITE OUT" ON THE SCREEN!!
THPPFFT!
HA! HA! HA!
YOU DUMB HYPOCRITES.
YOU MOCK THE HALF OF HUMANITY THAT MAKES YOUR GRACELESS EXISTENCE BEARABLE.
MEN SHOULD PAUSE FOR ONE MOMENT AND TAKE ANOTHER **LONG LOOK** AT THE VERY THING THAT BRINGS **MEANING** TO THEIR MEANINGLESS LIVES.
B Breathed

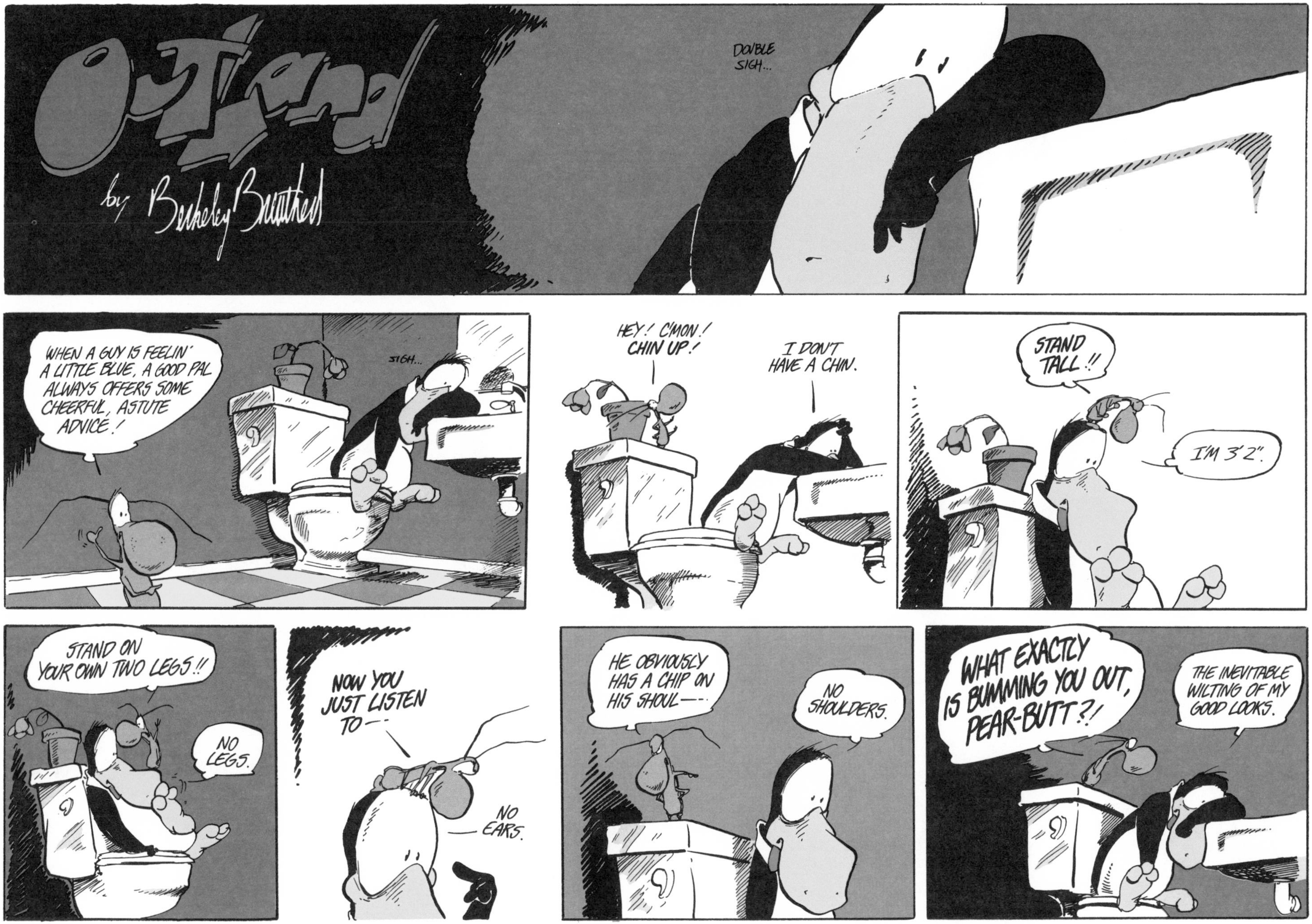
Outland
by Berkeley Breathed
DOUBLE SIGH...
WHEN A GUY IS FEELIN' A LITTLE BLUE, A GOOD PAL ALWAYS OFFERS SOME CHEERFUL, ASTUTE ADVICE!
SIGH...
HEY! C'MON! CHIN UP!
I DON'T HAVE A CHIN.
STAND TALL!!
I'M 3'2".
STAND ON YOUR OWN TWO LEGS!!
NO LEGS.
NOW YOU JUST LISTEN TO—
NO EARS.
HE OBVIOUSLY HAS A CHIP ON HIS SHOUL—
NO SHOULDERS.
WHAT EXACTLY IS BUMMING YOU OUT, PEAR-BUTT?!
THE INEVITABLE WILTING OF MY GOOD LOOKS.

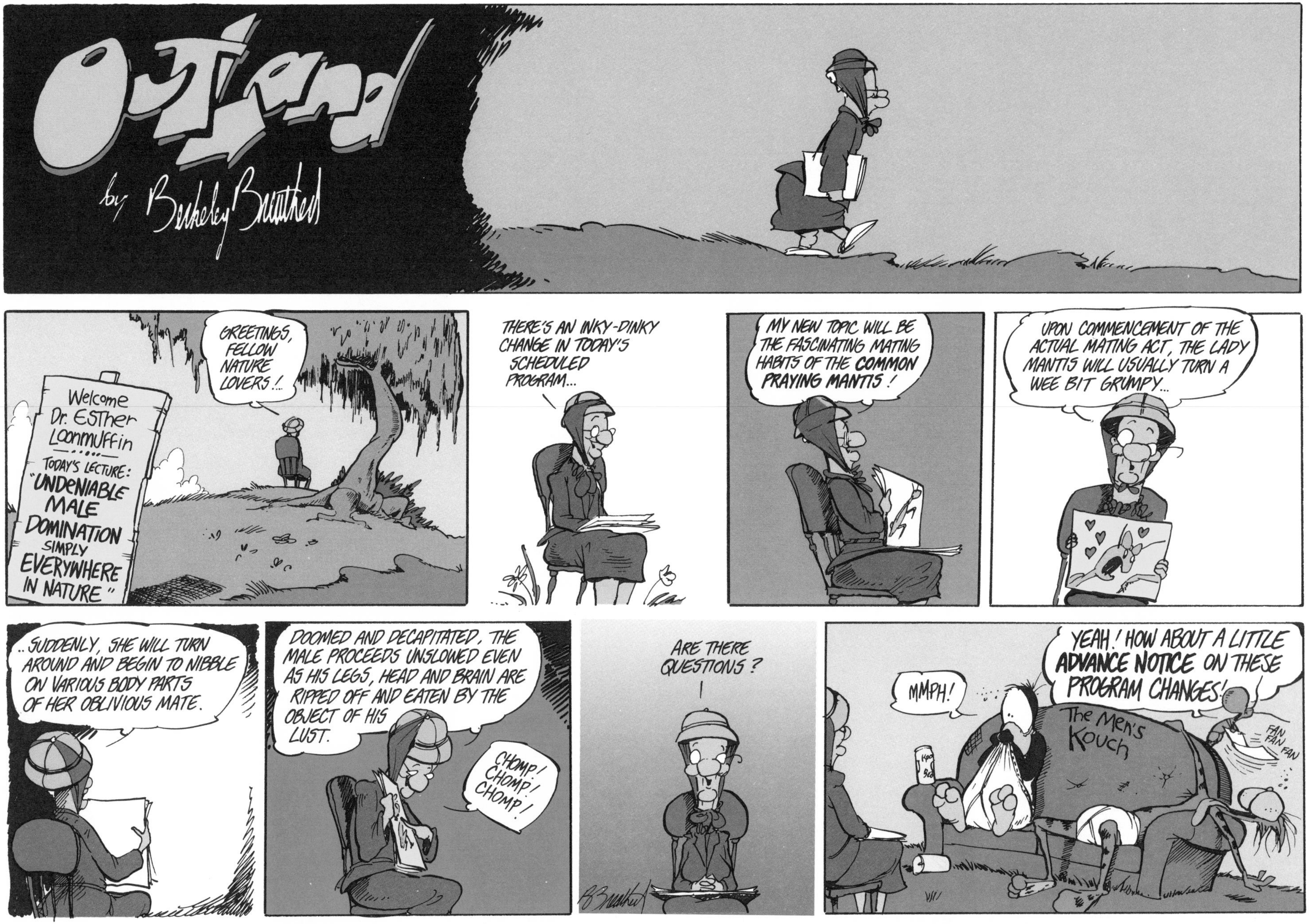
Outland
by Berkeley Breathed
Welcome Dr. Esther Loonmuffin
Today's Lecture: "Undeniable Male Domination Simply Everywhere in Nature"
GREETINGS, FELLOW NATURE LOVERS!..
THERE'S AN INKY-DINKY CHANGE IN TODAY'S SCHEDULED PROGRAM...
MY NEW TOPIC WILL BE THE FASCINATING MATING HABITS OF THE COMMON PRAYING MANTIS!
UPON COMMENCEMENT OF THE ACTUAL MATING ACT, THE LADY MANTIS WILL USUALLY TURN A WEE BIT GRUMPY...
..SUDDENLY, SHE WILL TURN AROUND AND BEGIN TO NIBBLE ON VARIOUS BODY PARTS OF HER OBLIVIOUS MATE.
DOOMED AND DECAPITATED, THE MALE PROCEEDS UNSLOWED EVEN AS HIS LEGS, HEAD AND BRAIN ARE RIPPED OFF AND EATEN BY THE OBJECT OF HIS LUST.
CHOMP! CHOMP! CHOMP!
ARE THERE QUESTIONS?
MMPH!
YEAH! HOW ABOUT A LITTLE ADVANCE NOTICE ON THESE PROGRAM CHANGES!
The Men's Kouch
FAN FAN FAN

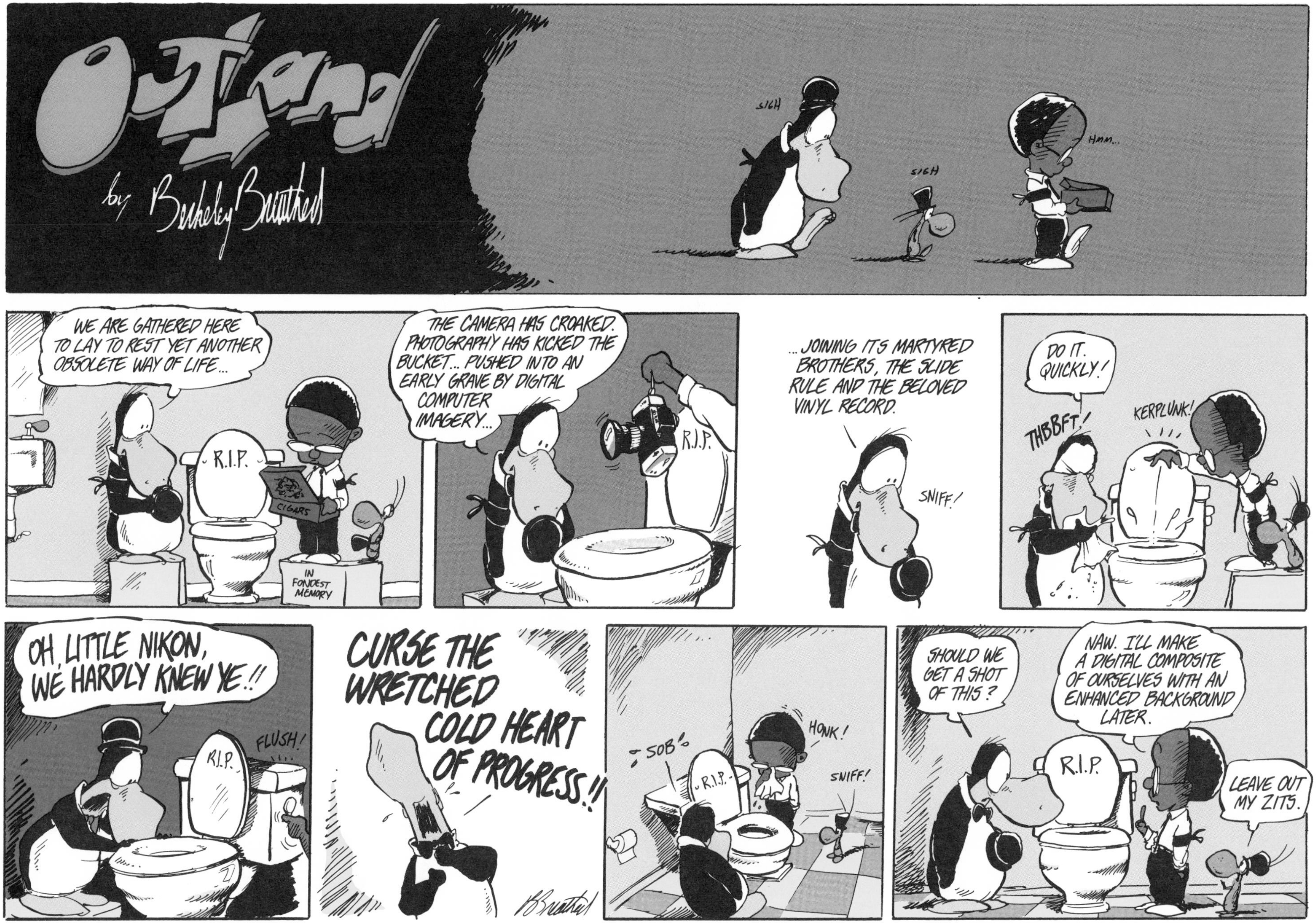
Outland
by Berkeley Breathed
SIGH
SIGH
HMM...
WE ARE GATHERED HERE TO LAY TO REST YET ANOTHER OBSOLETE WAY OF LIFE...
R.I.P.
CIGARS
IN FONDEST MEMORY
THE CAMERA HAS CROAKED. PHOTOGRAPHY HAS KICKED THE BUCKET... PUSHED INTO AN EARLY GRAVE BY DIGITAL COMPUTER IMAGERY...
R.I.P.
...JOINING ITS MARTYRED BROTHERS, THE SLIDE RULE AND THE BELOVED VINYL RECORD.
SNIFF!
DO IT. QUICKLY!
THBBFT!
KERPLUNK!
OH, LITTLE NIKON, WE HARDLY KNEW YE!!
R.I.P.
FLUSH!
CURSE THE WRETCHED COLD HEART OF PROGRESS!!
B Breathed
SOB
R.I.P.
HONK!
SNIFF!
SHOULD WE GET A SHOT OF THIS?
NAW. I'LL MAKE A DIGITAL COMPOSITE OF OURSELVES WITH AN ENHANCED BACKGROUND LATER.
R.I.P.
LEAVE OUT MY ZITS.

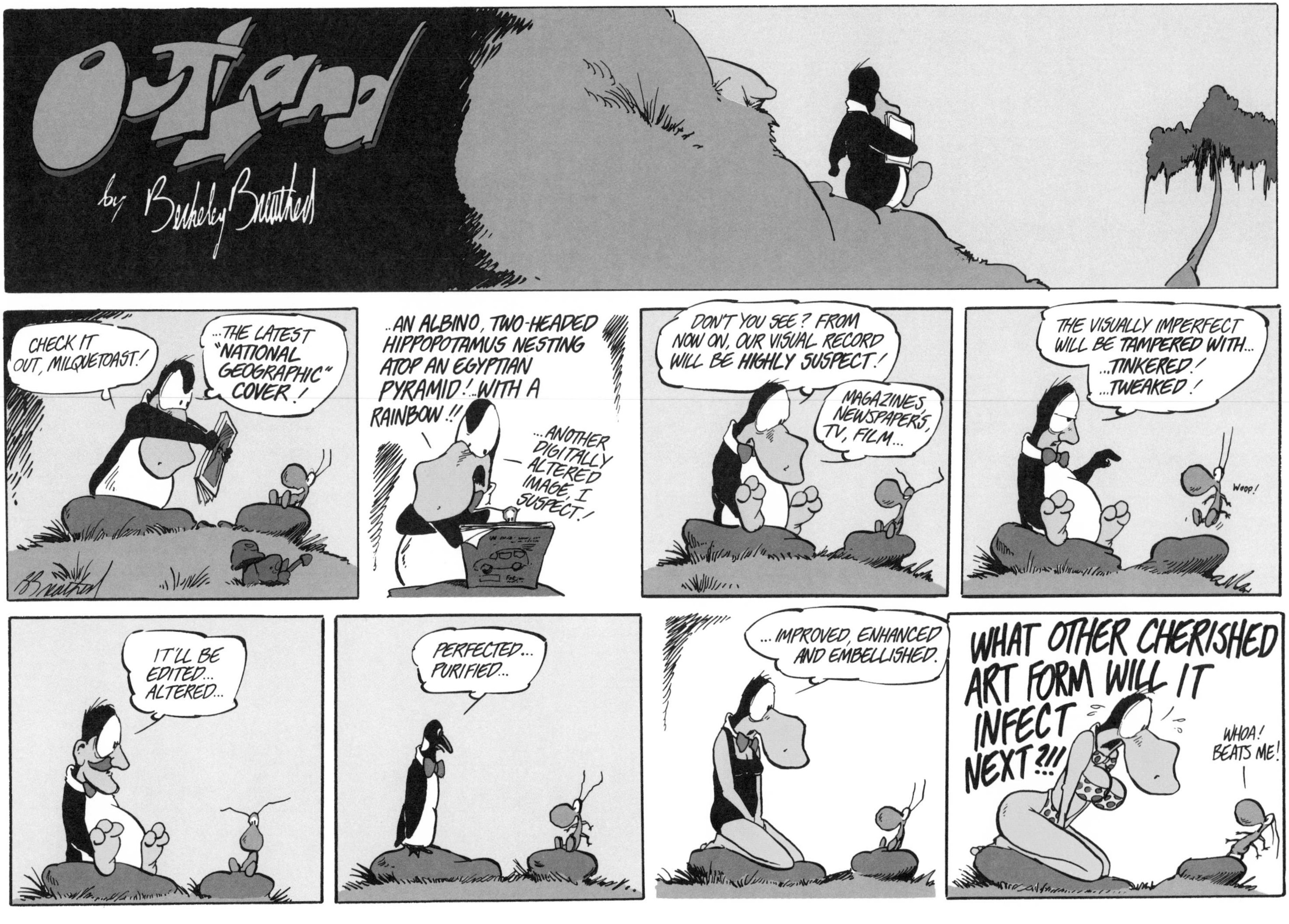
Outland
by Berkeley Breathed
CHECK IT OUT, MILQUETOAST!
...THE LATEST "NATIONAL GEOGRAPHIC" COVER!
..AN ALBINO, TWO-HEADED HIPPOPOTAMUS NESTING ATOP AN EGYPTIAN PYRAMID!..WITH A RAINBOW!!
...ANOTHER DIGITALLY ALTERED IMAGE, I SUSPECT!
DON'T YOU SEE? FROM NOW ON, OUR VISUAL RECORD WILL BE HIGHLY SUSPECT!
MAGAZINES, NEWSPAPERS, TV, FILM...
THE VISUALLY IMPERFECT WILL BE TAMPERED WITH... ...TINKERED! ...TWEAKED!
WOOP!
IT'LL BE EDITED... ALTERED...
PERFECTED... PURIFIED...
...IMPROVED, ENHANCED AND EMBELLISHED.
WHAT OTHER CHERISHED ART FORM WILL IT INFECT NEXT?!!
WHOA! BEATS ME!

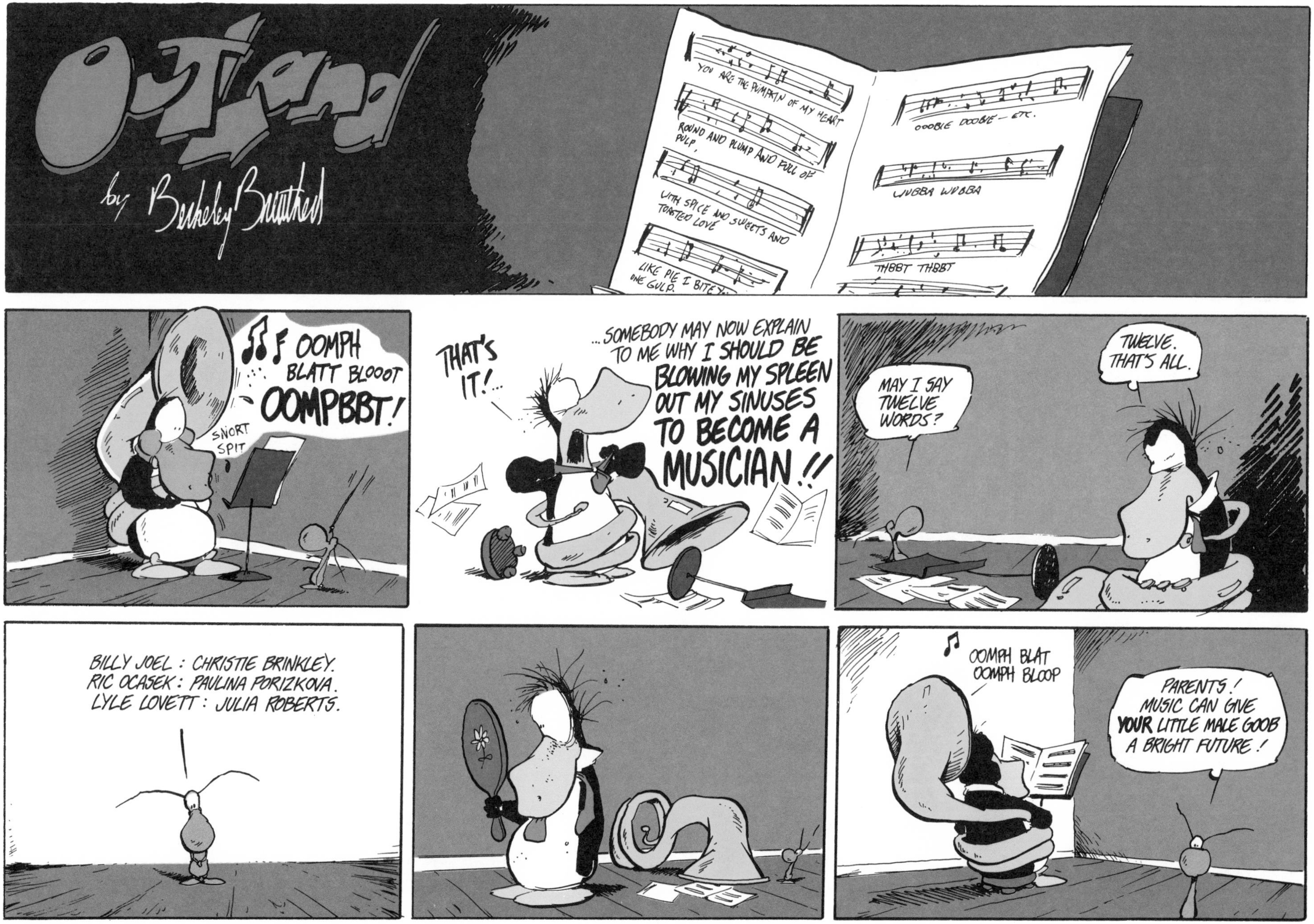
Outland
by Berkeley Breathed
YOU ARE THE PUMPKIN OF MY HEART
ROUND AND PLUMP AND FULL OF PULP,
WITH SPICE AND SWEETS AND TOASTED LOVE
LIKE PIE I BITE YOU
ONE GULP.
OOBIE DOOBIE — ETC.
WUBBA WUBBA
THBBT THBBT
OOMPH BLATT BLOOOT OOMPBBT!
SNORT SPIT
THAT'S IT!...
...SOMEBODY MAY NOW EXPLAIN TO ME WHY I SHOULD BE BLOWING MY SPLEEN OUT MY SINUSES TO BECOME A MUSICIAN!!
MAY I SAY TWELVE WORDS?
TWELVE. THAT'S ALL.
BILLY JOEL : CHRISTIE BRINKLEY.
RIC OCASEK : PAULINA PORIZKOVA.
LYLE LOVETT : JULIA ROBERTS.
OOMPH BLAT OOMPH BLOOP
PARENTS! MUSIC CAN GIVE YOUR LITTLE MALE GOOB A BRIGHT FUTURE!

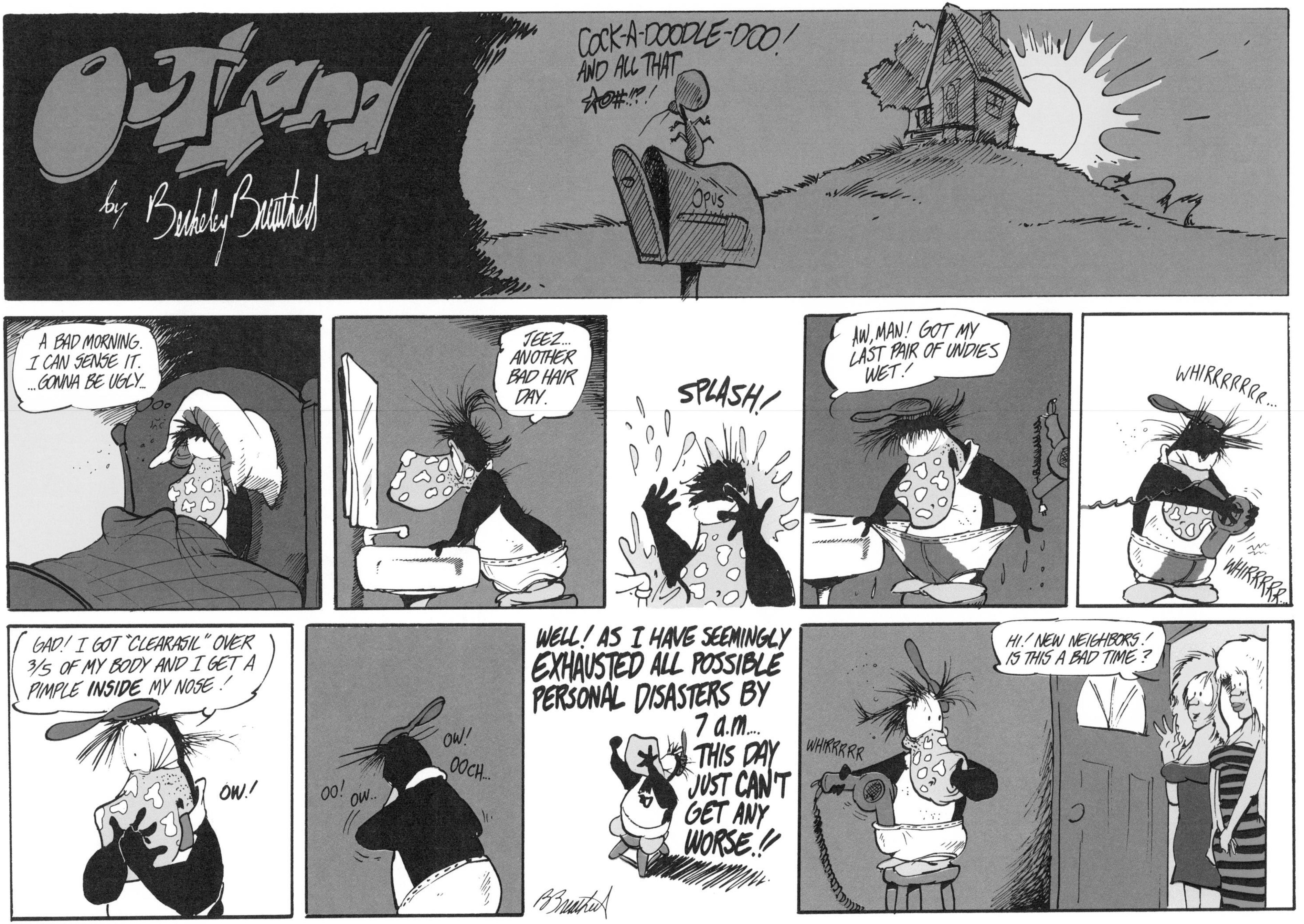
Outland
by Berkeley Breathed
COCK-A-DOODLE-DOO! AND ALL THAT *@#!!?!
OPUS
A BAD MORNING. I CAN SENSE IT. ...GONNA BE UGLY...
JEEZ... ANOTHER BAD HAIR DAY.
SPLASH!
AW, MAN! GOT MY LAST PAIR OF UNDIES WET!
WHIRRRRRRR...
WHIRRRRRR...
GAD! I GOT "CLEARASIL" OVER 3/5 OF MY BODY AND I GET A PIMPLE INSIDE MY NOSE!
OW!
OW!
OOCH...
OO! OW..
WELL! AS I HAVE SEEMINGLY EXHAUSTED ALL POSSIBLE PERSONAL DISASTERS BY 7 a.m.... THIS DAY JUST CAN'T GET ANY WORSE.!!
B Breathed
HI! NEW NEIGHBORS! IS THIS A BAD TIME?
WHIRRRRR

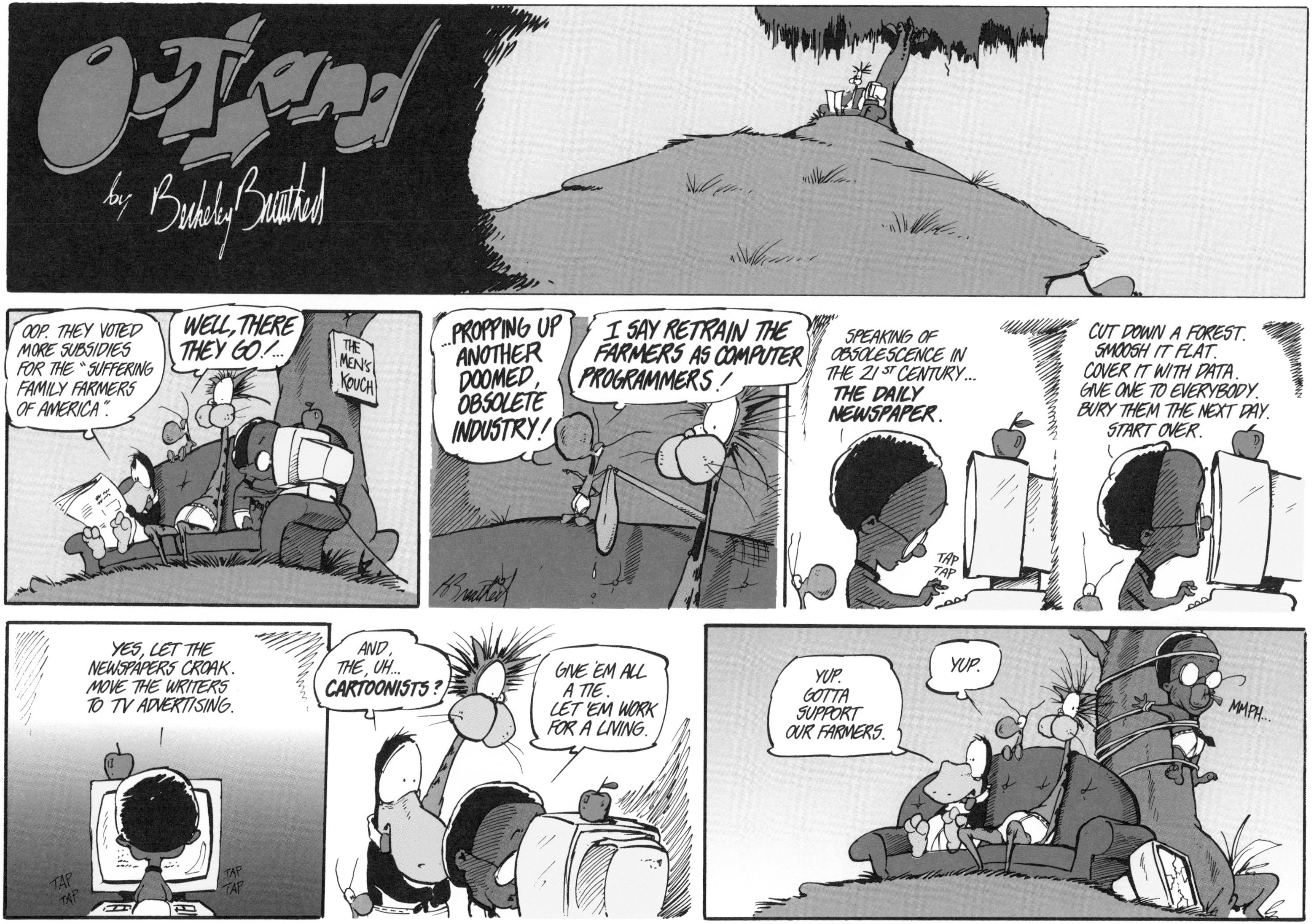

Outland
by Berkeley Breathed
OOP. THEY VOTED MORE SUBSIDIES FOR THE "SUFFERING FAMILY FARMERS OF AMERICA".
WELL, THERE THEY GO!...
THE MEN'S KOUCH
...PROPPING UP ANOTHER DOOMED, OBSOLETE INDUSTRY!
I SAY RETRAIN THE FARMERS AS COMPUTER PROGRAMMERS!
SPEAKING OF OBSOLESCENCE IN THE 21 ST CENTURY... THE DAILY NEWSPAPER.
TAP TAP
CUT DOWN A FOREST. SMOOSH IT FLAT. COVER IT WITH DATA. GIVE ONE TO EVERYBODY. BURY THEM THE NEXT DAY. START OVER.
YES, LET THE NEWSPAPERS CROAK. MOVE THE WRITERS TO TV ADVERTISING.
TAP TAP
TAP TAP
AND, THE, UH... CARTOONISTS?
GIVE 'EM ALL A TIE. LET 'EM WORK FOR A LIVING.
YUP. GOTTA SUPPORT OUR FARMERS.
YUP.
MMPH...

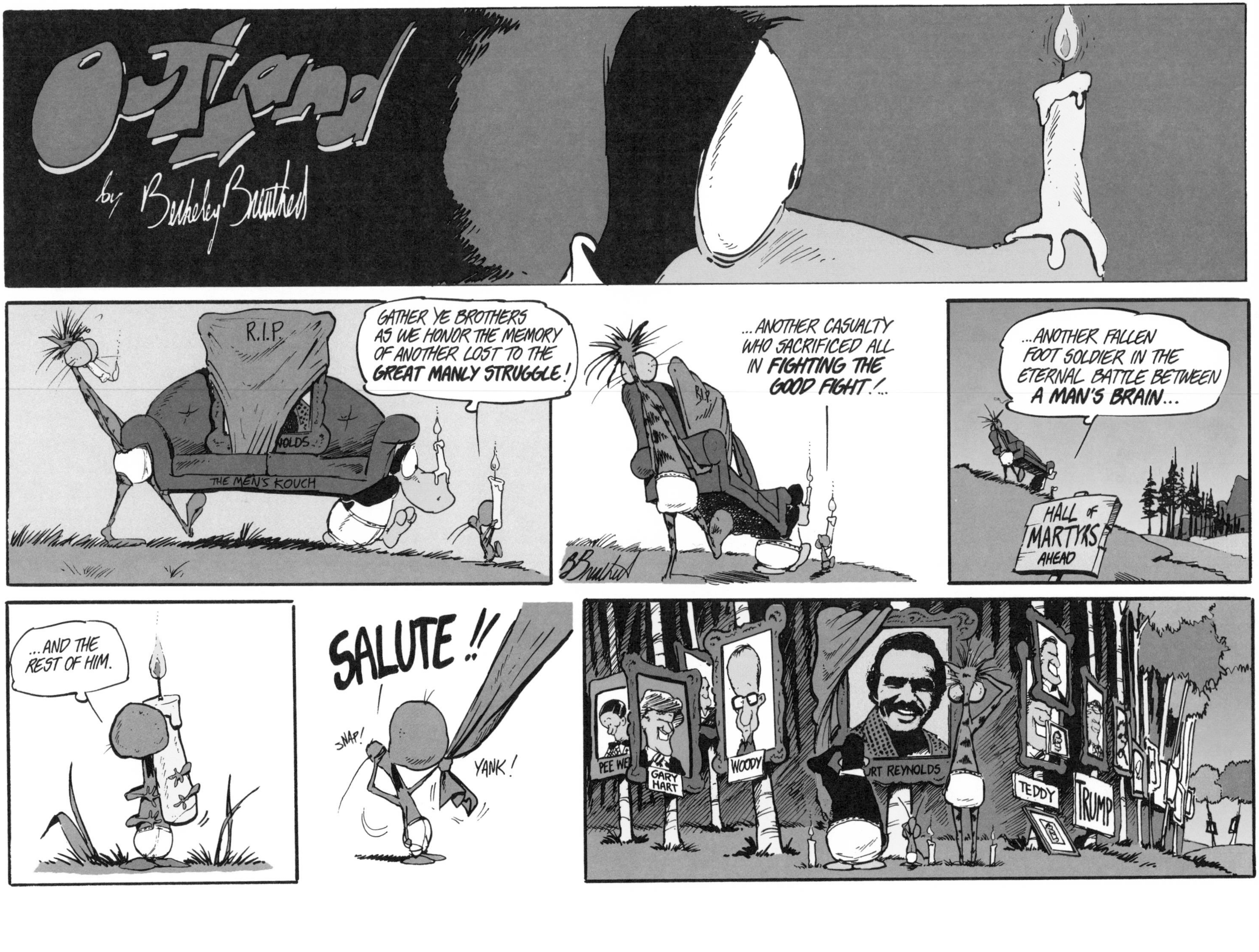

Outland
by Berkeley Breathed
R.I.P.
THE MEN'S KOUCH
GATHER YE BROTHERS AS WE HONOR THE MEMORY OF ANOTHER LOST TO THE **GREAT MANLY STRUGGLE**!
...ANOTHER CASUALTY WHO SACRIFICED ALL IN **FIGHTING THE GOOD FIGHT**!...
...ANOTHER FALLEN FOOT SOLDIER IN THE ETERNAL BATTLE BETWEEN **A MAN'S BRAIN...**
HALL OF MARTYRS AHEAD
...AND THE REST OF HIM.
SALUTE!!
SNAP!
YANK!
GARY HART
WOODY
URT REYNOLDS
TEDDY
TRUMP

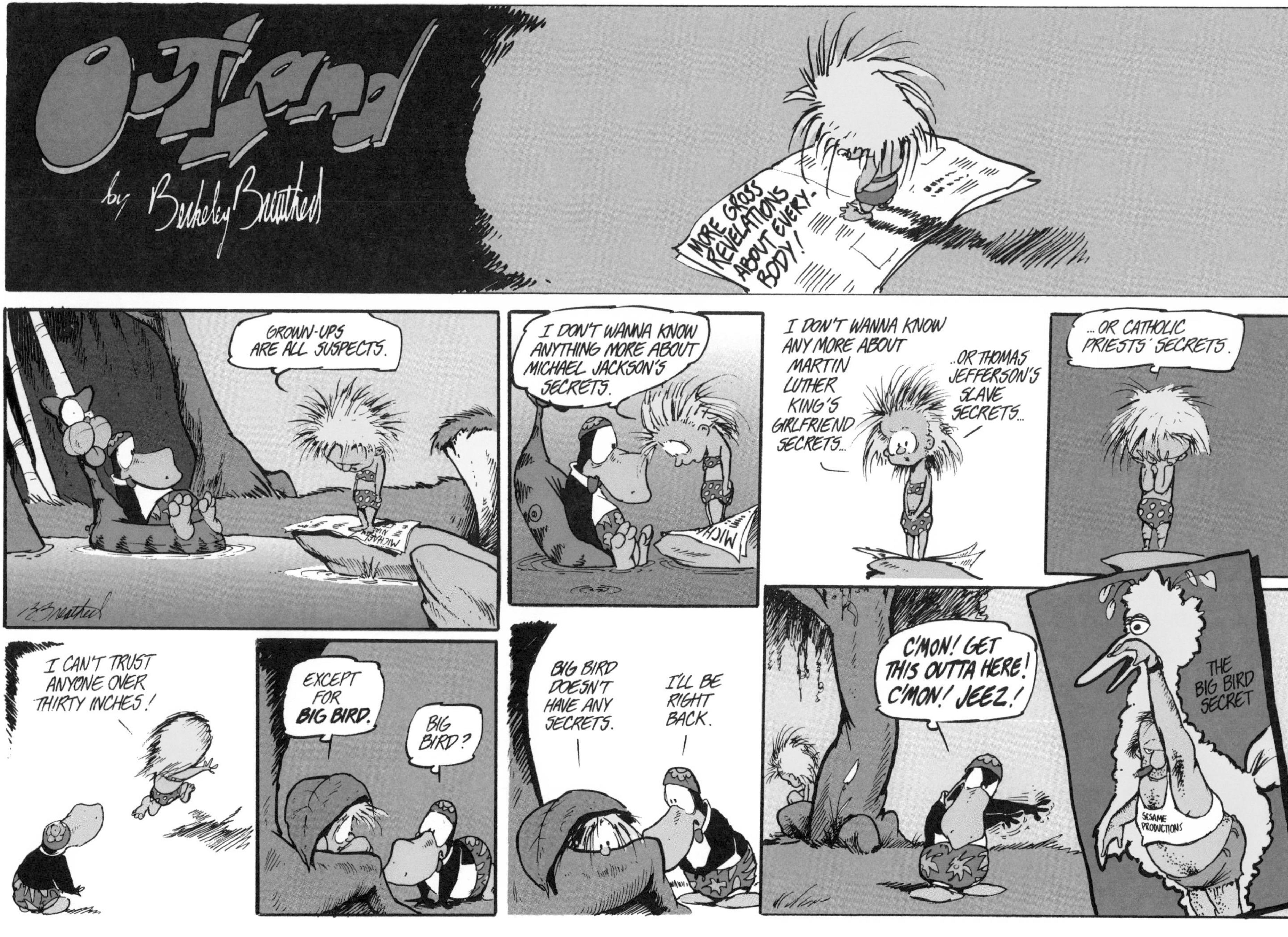

Outland
by Berkeley Breathed
MORE GROSS REVELATIONS ABOUT EVERY-BODY!
GROWN-UPS ARE ALL SUSPECTS.
I DON'T WANNA KNOW ANYTHING MORE ABOUT MICHAEL JACKSON'S SECRETS.
I DON'T WANNA KNOW ANY MORE ABOUT MARTIN LUTHER KING'S GIRLFRIEND SECRETS...
...OR THOMAS JEFFERSON'S SLAVE SECRETS...
...OR CATHOLIC PRIESTS' SECRETS.
I CAN'T TRUST ANYONE OVER THIRTY INCHES!
EXCEPT FOR BIG BIRD.
BIG BIRD?
BIG BIRD DOESN'T HAVE ANY SECRETS.
I'LL BE RIGHT BACK.
C'MON! GET THIS OUTTA HERE! C'MON! JEEZ!
THE BIG BIRD SECRET
SESAME PRODUCTIONS

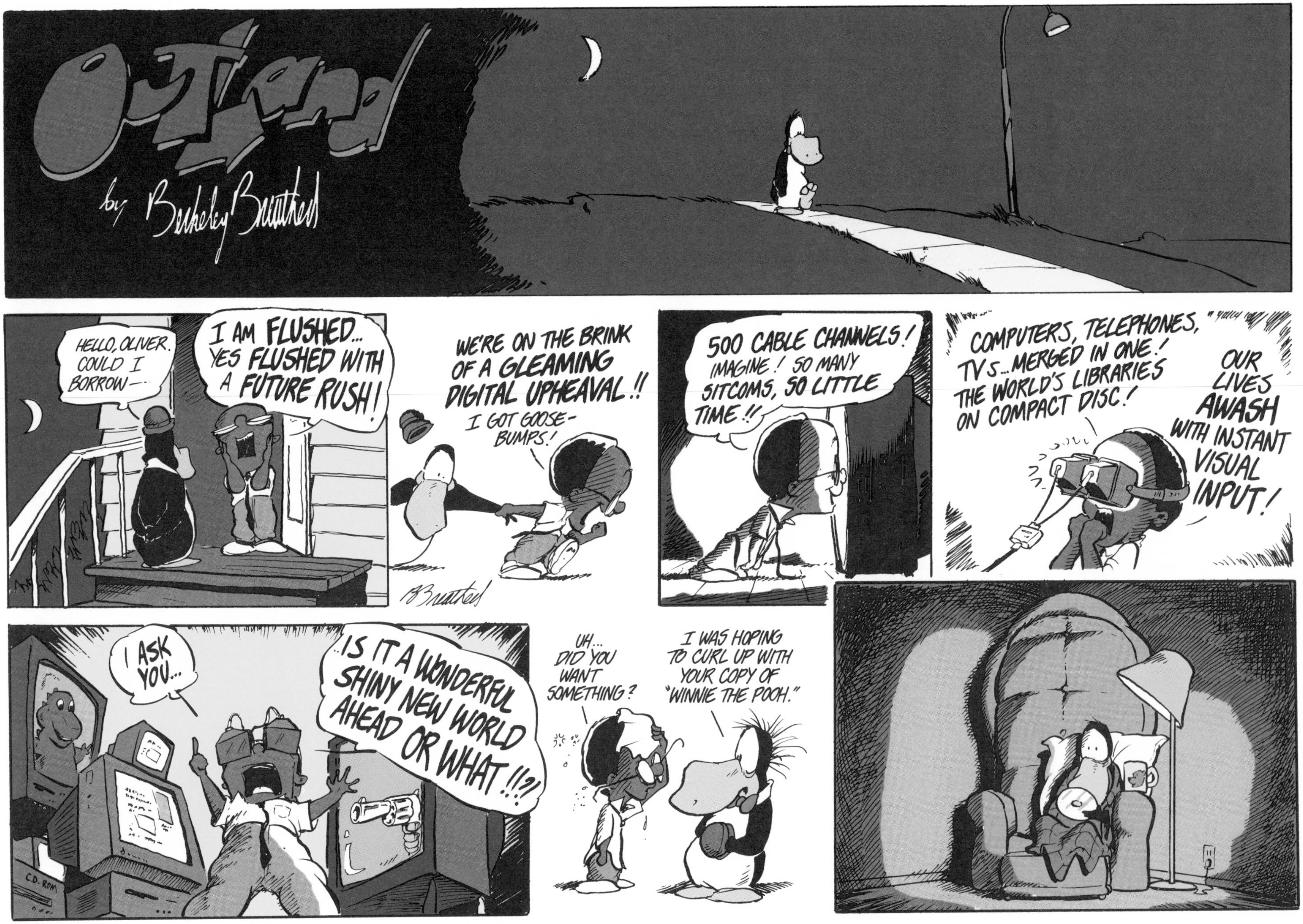
Outland
by Berkeley Breathed
HELLO, OLIVER. COULD I BORROW—
I AM FLUSHED... YES FLUSHED WITH A FUTURE RUSH!
WE'RE ON THE BRINK OF A GLEAMING DIGITAL UPHEAVAL!!
I GOT GOOSE-BUMPS!
B Breathed
500 CABLE CHANNELS! IMAGINE! SO MANY SITCOMS, SO LITTLE TIME!!
COMPUTERS, TELEPHONES, TV'S... MERGED IN ONE! THE WORLD'S LIBRARIES ON COMPACT DISC!
OUR LIVES AWASH WITH INSTANT VISUAL INPUT!
I ASK YOU...
..IS IT A WONDERFUL SHINY NEW WORLD AHEAD OR WHAT!!?!
C.D. ROM
UH... DID YOU WANT SOMETHING?
I WAS HOPING TO CURL UP WITH YOUR COPY OF "WINNIE THE POOH."

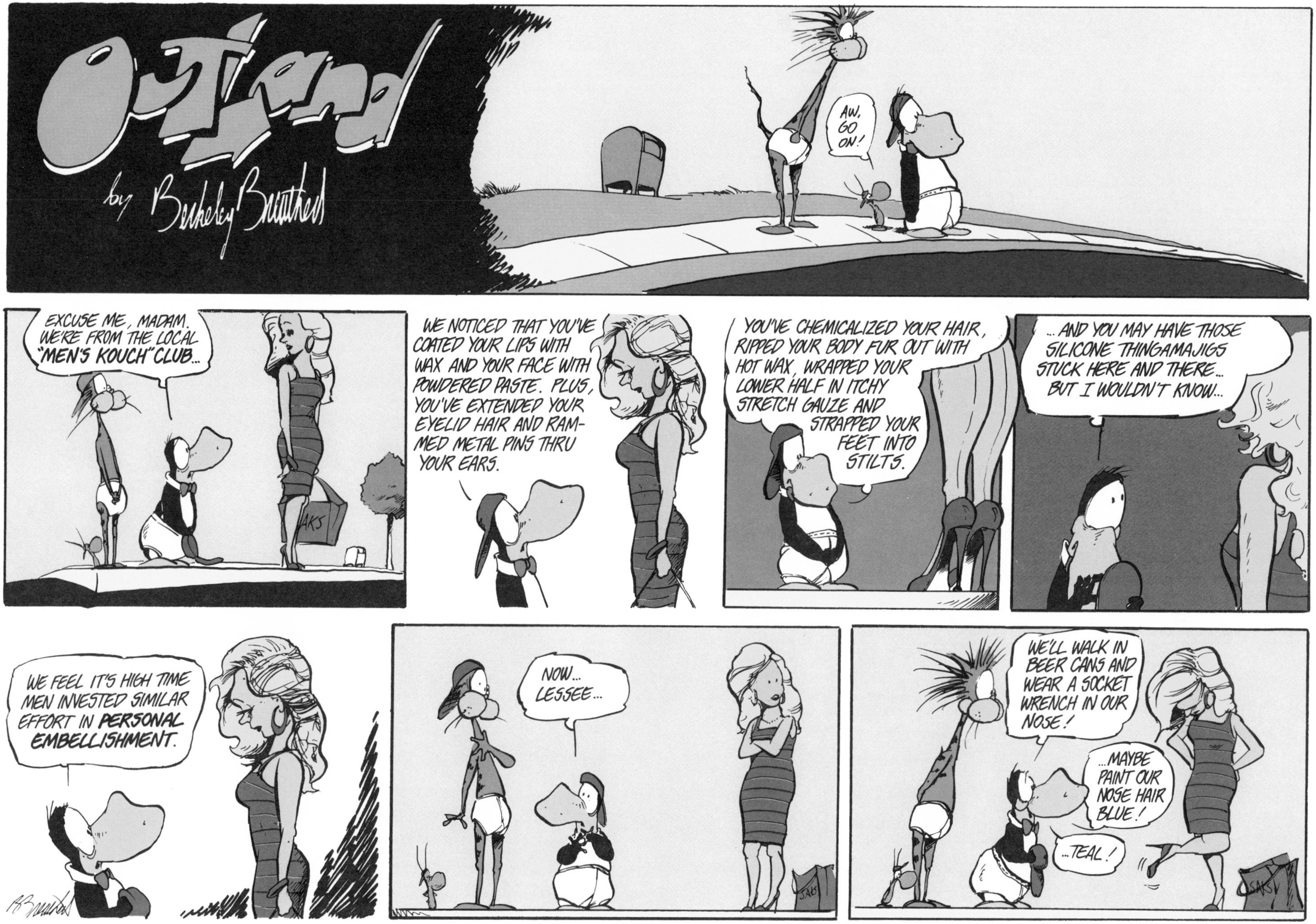
Outland
by Berkeley Breathed
AW, GO ON!
EXCUSE ME, MADAM. WE'RE FROM THE LOCAL "MEN'S KOUCH" CLUB...
WE NOTICED THAT YOU'VE COATED YOUR LIPS WITH WAX AND YOUR FACE WITH POWDERED PASTE. PLUS, YOU'VE EXTENDED YOUR EYELID HAIR AND RAMMED METAL PINS THRU YOUR EARS.
YOU'VE CHEMICALIZED YOUR HAIR, RIPPED YOUR BODY FUR OUT WITH HOT WAX, WRAPPED YOUR LOWER HALF IN ITCHY STRETCH GAUZE AND STRAPPED YOUR FEET INTO STILTS.
...AND YOU MAY HAVE THOSE SILICONE THINGAMAJIGS STUCK HERE AND THERE... BUT I WOULDN'T KNOW...
WE FEEL IT'S HIGH TIME MEN INVESTED SIMILAR EFFORT IN **PERSONAL EMBELLISHMENT**.
NOW... LESSEE...
WE'LL WALK IN BEER CANS AND WEAR A SOCKET WRENCH IN OUR NOSE!
...MAYBE PAINT OUR NOSE HAIR BLUE!
...TEAL!

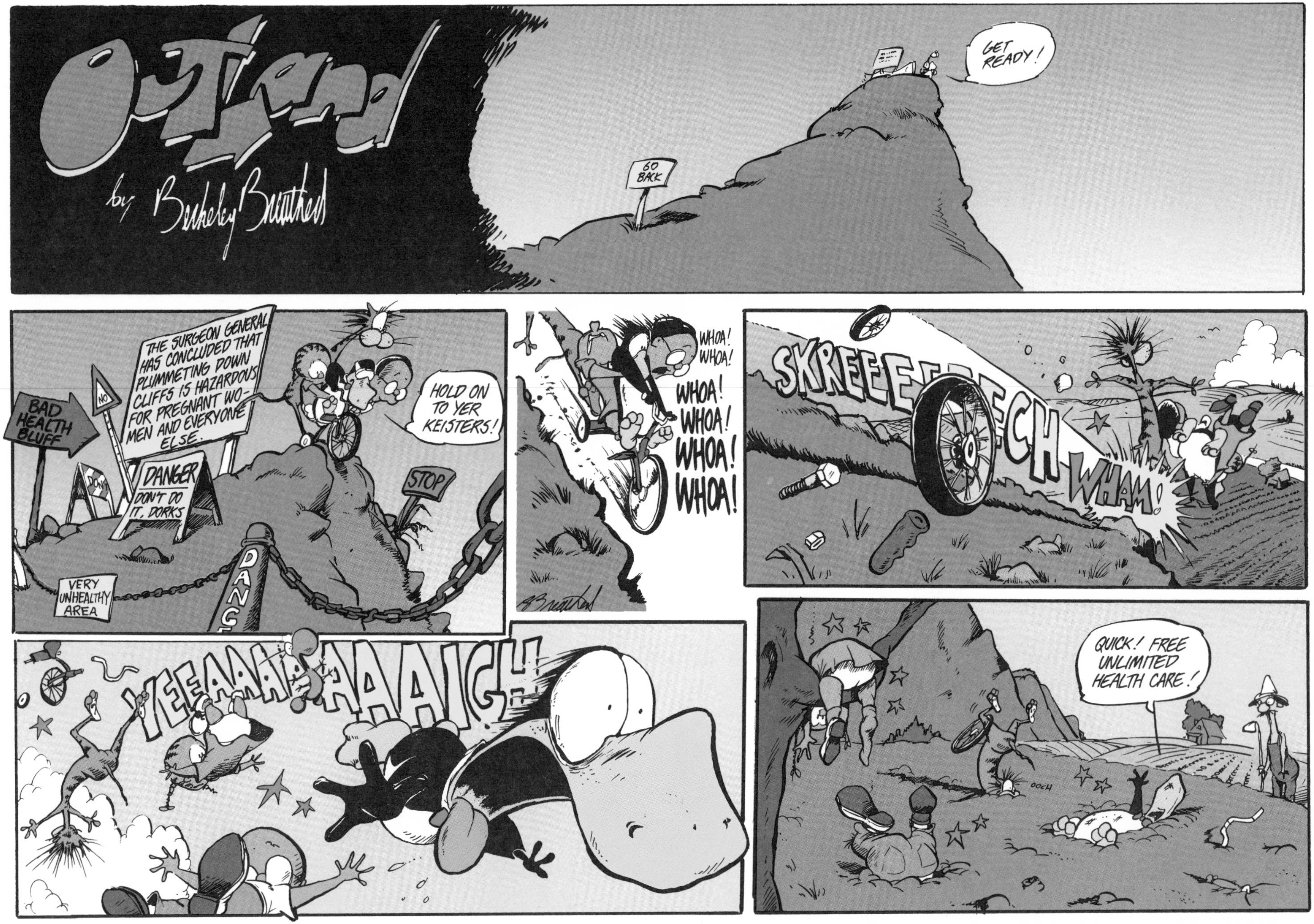
Outland
by Berkeley Breathed
GO BACK
GET READY!
BAD HEALTH BLUFF
NO
THE SURGEON GENERAL HAS CONCLUDED THAT PLUMMETING DOWN CLIFFS IS HAZARDOUS FOR PREGNANT WOMEN AND EVERYONE ELSE.
DANGER
DON'T DO IT, DORKS
STOP
VERY UNHEALTHY AREA
HOLD ON TO YER KEISTERS!
WHOA! WHOA!
WHOA! WHOA! WHOA! WHOA!
SKREEEEEEECH
WHAM!
YEEAAAAAAAAICH
QUICK! FREE UNLIMITED HEALTH CARE!
OOCH

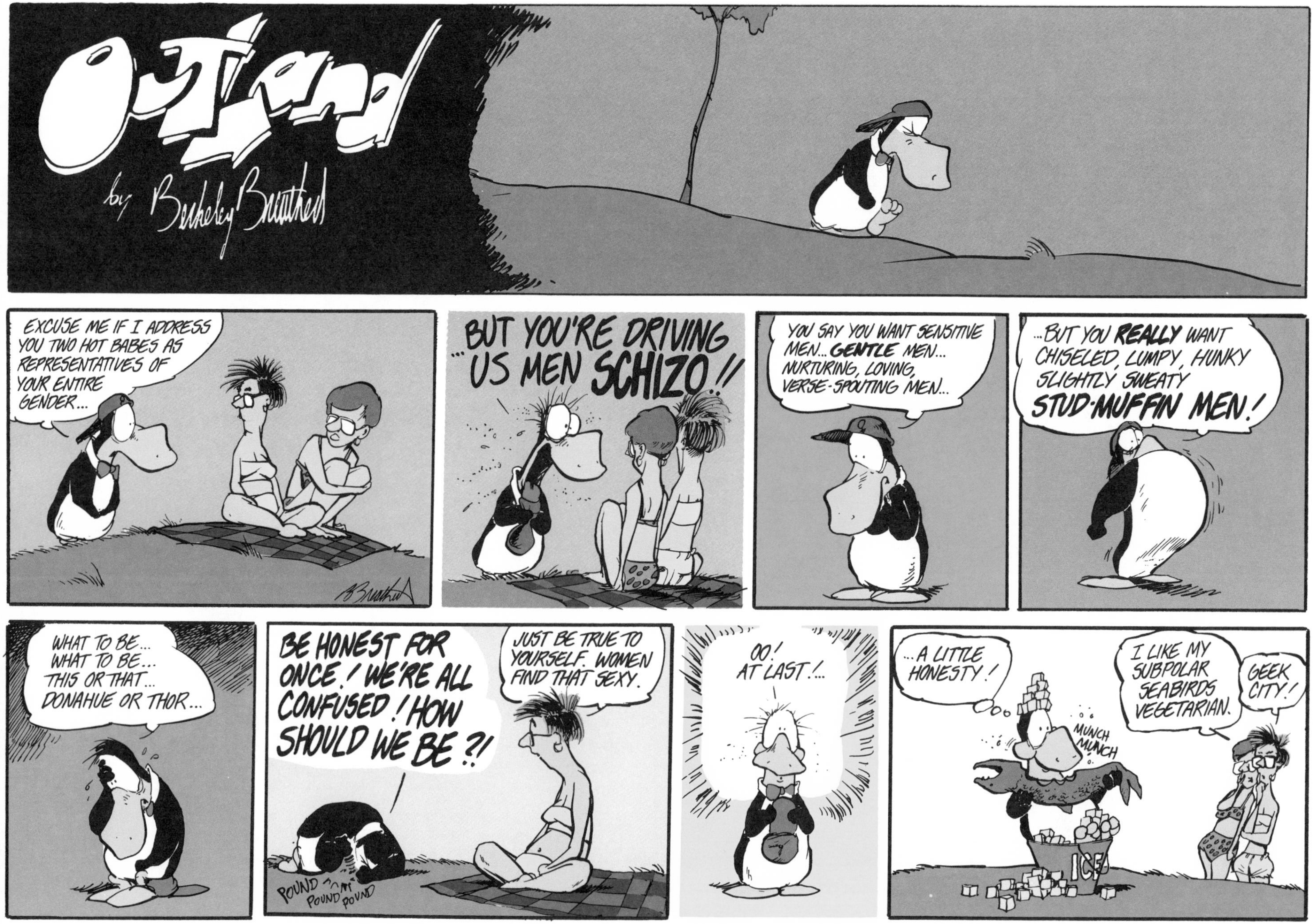

Outland
by Berkeley Breathed
EXCUSE ME IF I ADDRESS YOU TWO HOT BABES AS REPRESENTATIVES OF YOUR ENTIRE GENDER...
...BUT YOU'RE DRIVING US MEN SCHIZO!!
YOU SAY YOU WANT SENSITIVE MEN... GENTLE MEN... NURTURING, LOVING, VERSE-SPOUTING MEN...
...BUT YOU REALLY WANT CHISELED, LUMPY, HUNKY SLIGHTLY SWEATY STUD-MUFFIN MEN!
WHAT TO BE... WHAT TO BE... THIS OR THAT... DONAHUE OR THOR...
BE HONEST FOR ONCE! WE'RE ALL CONFUSED! HOW SHOULD WE BE?!
POUND POUND POUND
JUST BE TRUE TO YOURSELF. WOMEN FIND THAT SEXY.
OO! AT LAST!...
...A LITTLE HONESTY!
MUNCH MUNCH
ICE
I LIKE MY SUBPOLAR SEABIRDS VEGETARIAN.
GEEK CITY!

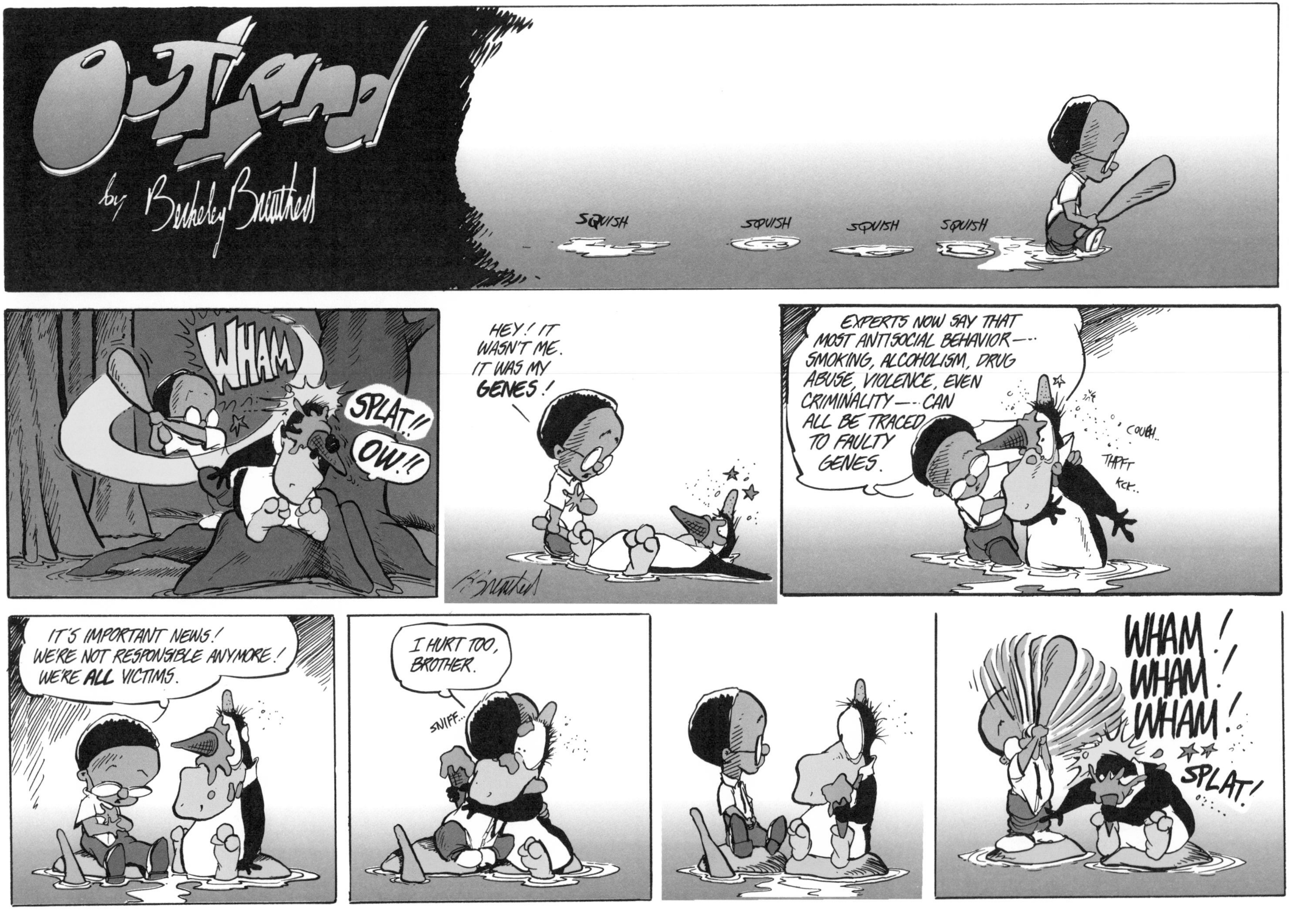
Outland
by Berkeley Breathed
SQUISH
SQUISH
SQUISH
SQUISH
WHAM
SPLAT!!
OW!!
HEY! IT WASN'T ME. IT WAS MY GENES!
EXPERTS NOW SAY THAT MOST ANTISOCIAL BEHAVIOR—SMOKING, ALCOHOLISM, DRUG ABUSE, VIOLENCE, EVEN CRIMINALITY—CAN ALL BE TRACED TO FAULTY GENES.
COUGH..
THPFT
KCK..
IT'S IMPORTANT NEWS! WE'RE NOT RESPONSIBLE ANYMORE! WE'RE ALL VICTIMS.
I HURT TOO, BROTHER.
SNIFF...
WHAM! WHAM! WHAM!
SPLAT!

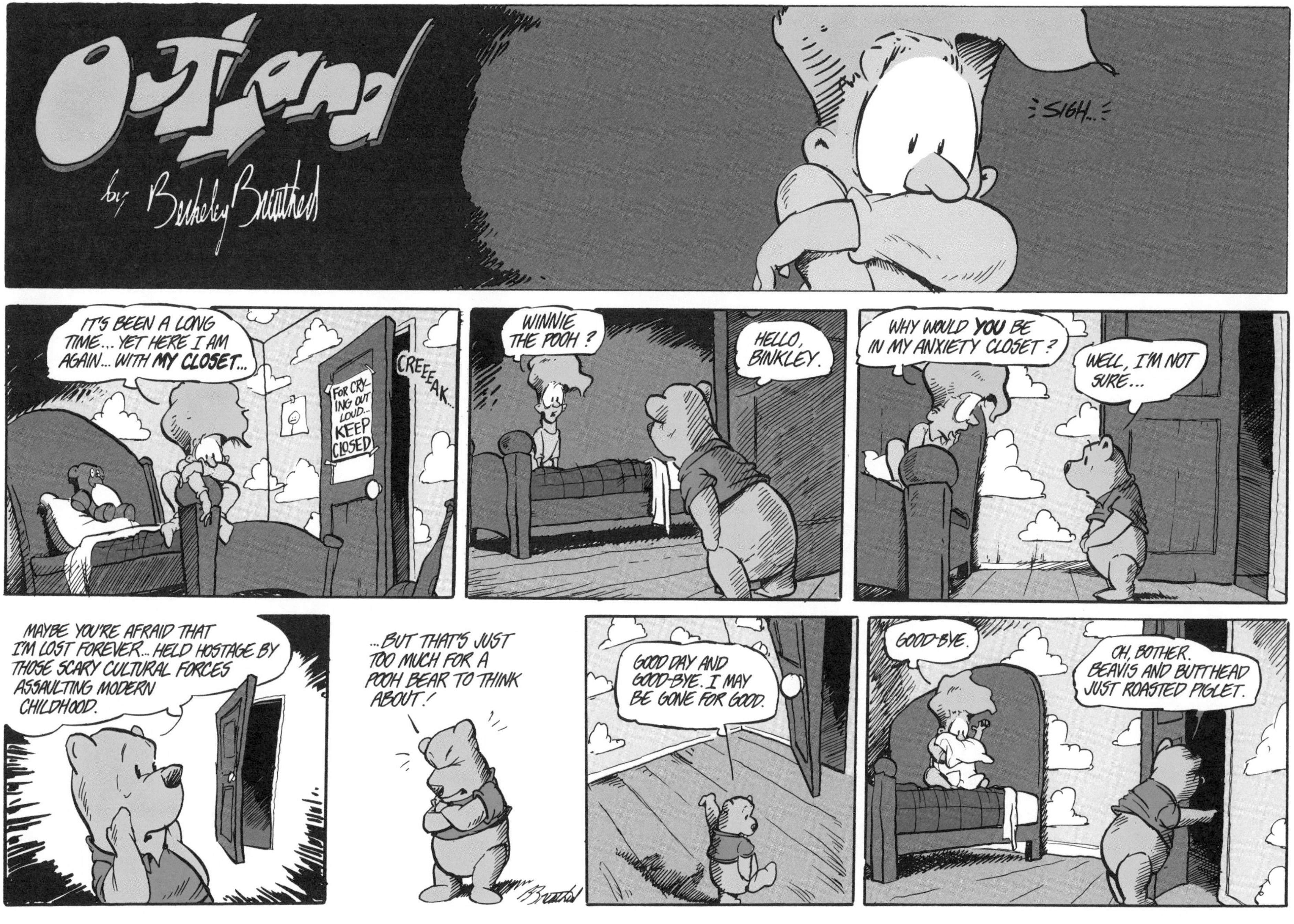
Outland
by Berkeley Breathed
SIGH..
IT'S BEEN A LONG TIME... YET HERE I AM AGAIN... WITH MY CLOSET...
FOR CRYING OUT LOUD... KEEP CLOSED
CREEEAK...
WINNIE THE POOH ?
HELLO, BINKLEY.
WHY WOULD YOU BE IN MY ANXIETY CLOSET ?
WELL, I'M NOT SURE...
MAYBE YOU'RE AFRAID THAT I'M LOST FOREVER... HELD HOSTAGE BY THOSE SCARY CULTURAL FORCES ASSAULTING MODERN CHILDHOOD.
...BUT THAT'S JUST TOO MUCH FOR A POOH BEAR TO THINK ABOUT !
GOOD DAY AND GOOD-BYE. I MAY BE GONE FOR GOOD.
GOOD-BYE.
OH, BOTHER. BEAVIS AND BUTTHEAD JUST ROASTED PIGLET.

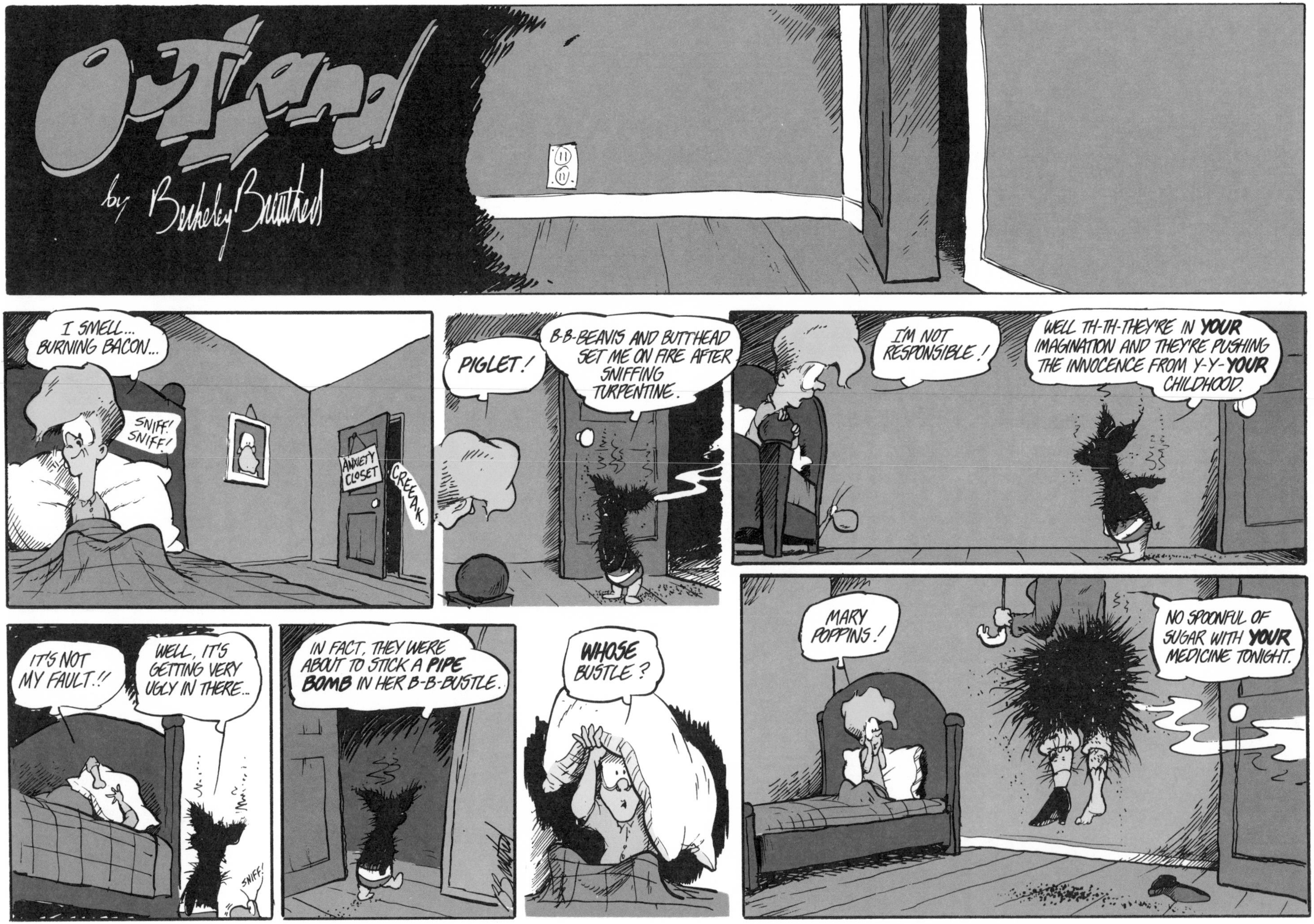
Outland
by Berkeley Breathed
I SMELL... BURNING BACON...
SNIFF! SNIFF!
ANXIETY CLOSET
CREEAK..
PIGLET!
B-B-BEAVIS AND BUTTHEAD SET ME ON FIRE AFTER SNIFFING TURPENTINE.
I'M NOT RESPONSIBLE!
WELL TH-TH-THEY'RE IN YOUR IMAGINATION AND THEY'RE PUSHING THE INNOCENCE FROM Y-Y-YOUR CHILDHOOD.
IT'S NOT MY FAULT!!
WELL, IT'S GETTING VERY UGLY IN THERE...
SNIFF!
IN FACT, THEY WERE ABOUT TO STICK A PIPE BOMB IN HER B-B-BUSTLE.
WHOSE BUSTLE?
MARY POPPINS!
NO SPOONFUL OF SUGAR WITH YOUR MEDICINE TONIGHT.

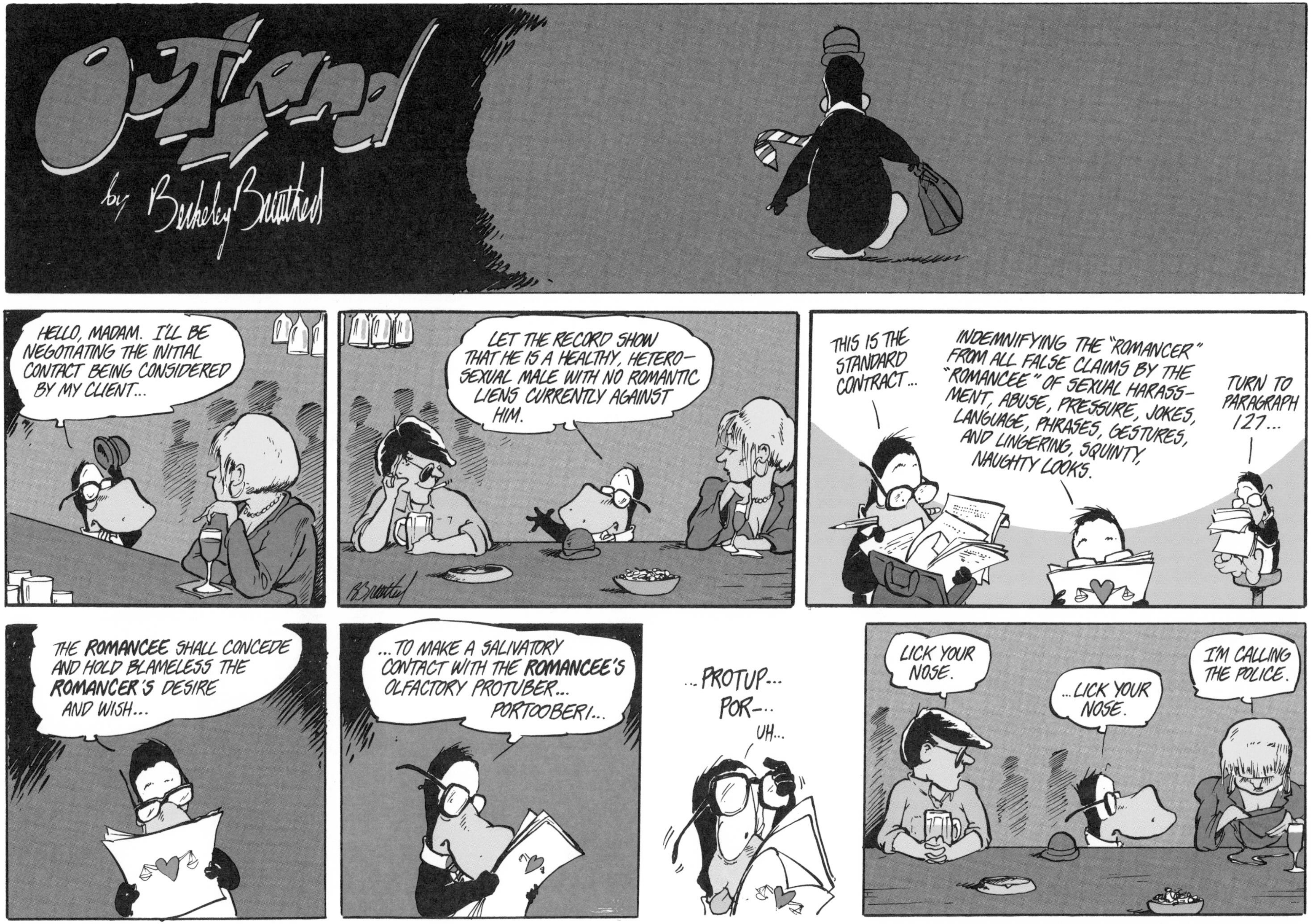
Outland
by Berkeley Breathed
HELLO, MADAM. I'LL BE NEGOTIATING THE INITIAL CONTACT BEING CONSIDERED BY MY CLIENT...
LET THE RECORD SHOW THAT HE IS A HEALTHY, HETERO-SEXUAL MALE WITH NO ROMANTIC LIENS CURRENTLY AGAINST HIM.
THIS IS THE STANDARD CONTRACT...
INDEMNIFYING THE "ROMANCER" FROM ALL FALSE CLAIMS BY THE "ROMANCEE" OF SEXUAL HARASS-MENT, ABUSE, PRESSURE, JOKES, LANGUAGE, PHRASES, GESTURES, AND LINGERING, SQUINTY, NAUGHTY LOOKS.
TURN TO PARAGRAPH 127...
THE **ROMANCEE** SHALL CONCEDE AND HOLD BLAMELESS THE **ROMANCER**'S DESIRE AND WISH...
...TO MAKE A SALIVATORY CONTACT WITH THE **ROMANCEE**'S OLFACTORY PROTUBER... PORTOOBERI...
...PROTUP... POR-...
UH...
LICK YOUR NOSE.
...LICK YOUR NOSE.
I'M CALLING THE POLICE.

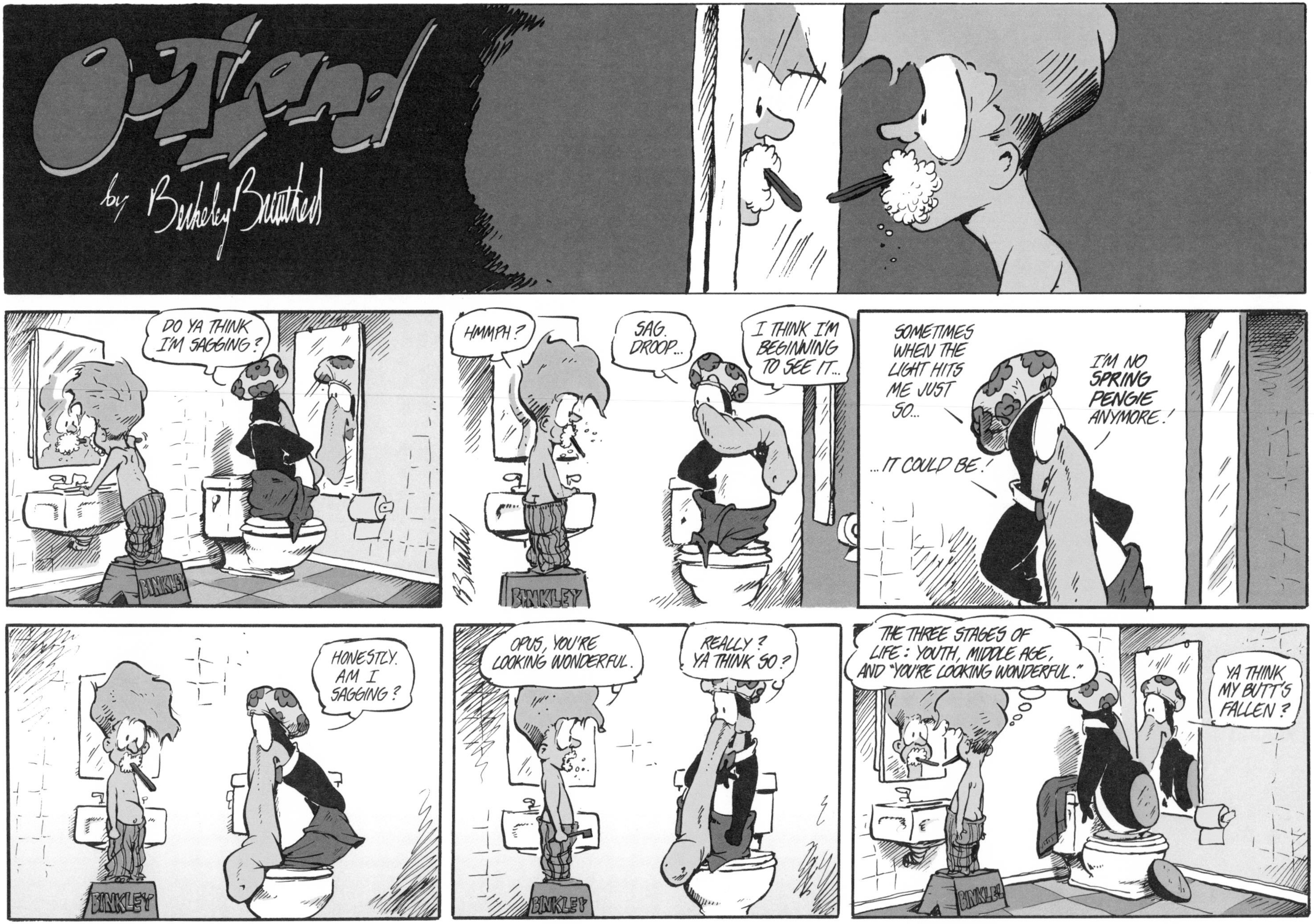
Outland
by Berkeley Breathed
DO YA THINK I'M SAGGING?
BINKLEY
HMMPH?
SAG. DROOP...
I THINK I'M BEGINNING TO SEE IT...
BINKLEY
SOMETIMES WHEN THE LIGHT HITS ME JUST SO...
...IT COULD BE.!
I'M NO SPRING PENGIE ANYMORE.!
HONESTLY. AM I SAGGING?
BINKLEY
OPUS, YOU'RE LOOKING WONDERFUL.
REALLY? YA THINK SO?
BINKLEY
THE THREE STAGES OF LIFE: YOUTH, MIDDLE AGE, AND "YOU'RE LOOKING WONDERFUL."
YA THINK MY BUTT'S FALLEN?
BINKLEY